Gender, migration and the global race for talent

Manchester University Press

Gender, migration and the global race for talent

Anna Boucher

Manchester University Press

Published by Manchester University Press
Altrincham Street, Manchester M1 7JA
www.manchesteruniversitypress.co.uk

British Library Cataloguing-in-Publication Data
A catalogue record for this book is available from the British Library

ISBN   978 0 7190 9945 8   hardback
ISBN   978 1 5261 3374 8   paperback

First published in hardback by Manchester University Press 2016
This edition first published 2019

The publisher has no responsibility for the persistence or accuracy of URLs for any external or third-party internet websites referred to in this book, and does not guarantee that any content on such websites is, or will remain, accurate or appropriate.

Typeset by Out of House Publishing
Printed in Great Britain by
TJ International Ltd, Padstow, Cornwall

This book is dedicated to Hermina Sapera

Contents

Figures

Tables

Acknowledgements

I have read works by Monica Boyd, Catherine Dauvergne, Christina Gabriel, Lesleyanne Hawthorne, Eleonore Kofman, Audrey Macklin and Parvati Raghuram in the gender and immigration policy fields. Focusing not only on the economic but also the emotional and human side of immigration policies, particularly their effect on female immigrants, these scholars have inspired me in my research on the gender dimensions of contemporary immigration selection.

Like much work on immigration, the research for this book involved a significant amount of travel. There are many people to thank, in several different countries. During my first stay in Canada in 2008, I was provided an office in the Gender Studies Department at Carleton University and was a visiting scholar in the Department of Political Science at the University of Toronto. The senior archivists at the National Archives Canada and the National Women's Archives at the University of Ottawa were extremely helpful in assisting me in accessing relevant closed files. During my second stay in Canada in 2013, I was provided with a lovely office in the School of Political Science at the University of Ottawa and the Department of Political Science at the University of Toronto. Christina Gabriel, Randall Hansen and Larry LeDuc assisted in arranging these positions. Thanks to Prue D'homme of the Standing Committee of Citizenship and Immigration who provided full access to briefs presented before the Committee in its 2009 Inquiry into Temporary Foreign Workers. Judy Bernstein and Carol English provided housing in Ottawa in 2008.

In Canberra, particular thanks to David Smith and his colleagues of the Statistics Unit within the Australian Department of Immigration and Citizenship (DIAC) who compiled and provided me with gender-disaggregated admissions data and other unpublished statistics. The librarians at the DIAC library were also extremely helpful in locating old statistical reports during my first stay in Canberra in 2009. Over this period, I was gratefully a visiting fellow at the National Europe Centre at the Australian National University in 2008 and in the Research School of Political Science in 2013. Alice and Michael Kingsland provided friendly and affordable accommodation in Canberra in 2009.

I have been fortunate to receive funding for this project from the following sources: The Commonwealth Fellowship, the London School of Economics and Political Science (LSE), the International Council of Canadian Studies, the

University of London Central Research Fund, the Zeit-Ebelin Bucerius Scholarship in Migration Studies, the National Europe Centre at the Australian National University, the Institute of Public Administration and the University of Canberra's Public Administration Trust Fund Grant, and the Faculty Support Research Scheme and Special Study Period Support from the University of Sydney's Faculty of Arts and Social Science. A particular thanks goes to the Zeit-Ebelin Bucerius Scholarship. In addition to the financial support this fund provided, it has allowed me to gain insights from both established migration scholars, as well as emerging researchers in the field, including Hamutal Bernstein, Anne Hartung and Abigail Williamson.

At the LSE where I completed my doctorate, thanks to Michael Bruter, Justin Gest, Simon Hix, Jane Lewis, Sarah McLaughlin, Edward Page, Julia Pomares, Mike Seiferling, Matt Skellern, Eiko Thielemann, Nick Vivyan, Markus Wagner and the LSE Interlibrary Loans team. Australian colleagues have offered useful insights on methodology and argument in particular: Susan Banki, Betsi Beem, Deborah Brennan, Terry Carney, Louise Chappell, Charlotte Epstein, Graeme Gill, Dimitria Groutis, Megan MacKenzie, Allan McConnell, John Mikler, Pippa Norris, Stuart Rosewarne, Simon Tormey, Di Van DenBroek, Ariadne Vromen, Chris Warhurst, Colin White and Chris Wright. Skilled migration experts Lucie Cerna and Lesleyanne Hawthorne provided useful expert feedback on several chapters. Excellent research assistance was provided by Emma Franklin, Daniel Ghezelbash, Max Grömping, Aaron Roper and Catrina Yu. The chapters of this book benefited from feedback in presentations and seminars in the Departments of Sociology and Work and Organizational Studies at the University of Sydney and from comments from colleagues at the European Conference on Politics and Gender in Belfast in 2009 and in Budapest in 2011, the American Political Science Association General Meeting in Chicago in 2013, the Australian National University Research School of Politics and International Relations Seminar Series in Canberra in 2013, the International Organization for Migration meeting on skilled immigration and gender in Geneva in 2014 and the Institute for International Migration workshop on skilled immigration at Oxford University, also in 2014.

Thanks to Tony Mason of Manchester University Press for helpful advice and guidance through the review process.

To the 128 anonymous elite interviewees in both Australia and Canada who participated in the production of this book by giving their time and knowledge, thank you. Without your help, many of the events analysed in this book would not be covered and my understanding of immigration policy in Australia and Canada would be greatly diminished.

Chapter 3 republishes some parts of Anna Boucher (2013) 'Bureaucratic Control and Policy Change: A Comparative Venue Shopping Approach to Skilled Immigration Policies in Australia and Canada', *Journal of Comparative Policy Analysis* 15 (4): 349–67.

To my husband Kåre Martens and to my parents, Robert and Tessa Boucher, for all the love and support you have given me over the years, I am very grateful.

Abbreviations

ALP	Australian Labor Party
ANESBWA	Association of Non-English Speaking Background Women of Australia (1986–97)
ANZSCO	Australia and New Zealand Standard Classification of Occupations (since July 2010)
CAAIP	Committee to Advise on Australia's Immigration Program (Australia, 1988, also known as the 'FitzGerald Report' or 'FitzGerald Inquiry')
CCR	Canadian Council for Refugees
CEC	Canadian Ethnocultural Council
CEDAW	Convention on the Elimination of Discrimination Against Women
Charter	Canadian Charter of Rights and Freedoms, 1982
CIC	Citizenship and Immigration Canada
CLC	Canadian Labour Congress
Coalition	The Liberal-National Coalition government (Australia (1996–2007)
DIAC	Department of Immigration and Citizenship (Australia) (2007–October 2013)
DILGEA	Department of Immigration, Local Government and Ethnic Affairs (Australia) (1987–93)
DIMA	Department of Immigration and Multicultural Affairs (Australia) (1996–2001)
DIMIA	Department of Immigration and Multicultural and Indigenous Affairs (Australia) (2001–6)
EIC	Employment and Immigration Canada (responsible for immigration until 1994)
EMAs	Enterprise Migration Agreements (Australia)
EOI	Expression of Interest
FECCA	Federation of Ethnic Communities' Councils of Australia
FSWP	Federation Skilled Worker Program
GBA	Gender-Based Analysis
IELTS	International English Language Testing System

ILO	International Labour Organisation
IMDB	Longitudinal Immigration Database (Canada)
IRPA	Immigration and Refugee Protection Act (2002) (Canada)
IRPR	Immigration and Refugee Protection Regulations (2002) (Canada)
JSCM	Joint Standing Committee on Migration (Australia)
LCP	Live-in Caregiver Program (Canada)
LMO	Labour Market Opinion
LSIA	Longitudinal Survey of Immigrants to Australia
Metro	Metro Toronto Chinese and Southeast Asian Legal Centre (Toronto, Canada)
MODL	Migrant Occupations in Demand List
MWAC	Migrant Workers Alliance for Change (Toronto)
NAC	National Action Committee on the Status of Women (Canada's peak feminist organization over the period of analysis)
NAWL	National Association of Women and the Law, Canada
NESB/s	Non-English-Speaking-Background(s) (Australia)
NOC	National Occupational Classification (Canada)
NOIVMWC	National Organization of Immigrant and Visible Minority Women of Canada
OCASI	Ontario Council of Agencies Serving Immigrants (Canada)
OECD	Organisation for Economic Co-operation and Development
ORE	Occupations Requiring English
RMA	Regional Migration Agreements (Australia)
SOL	Skilled Occupation List (Australia)
SWC	Status of Women Canada
TFWP	Temporary Foreign Worker Program (Canada)
TSMIT	Temporary Skilled Migration Income Threshold (Australia)
VoC	Varieties of Capitalism

Introduction

The global economy is changing as the economic power base moves from West to East. Post-industrial societies are ageing. No longer possessing a competitive advantage in manufacturing and production, governments in these states face pressure to diversify their economies, to invest in technology and to develop human capital in order to stay ahead. Future economic success depends upon having a smart and skilled economy to promote growth. Within this context, the immigration of skilled workers facilitates the buoyancy of Western economies and alleviates some of the structural challenges represented by population ageing. In fact, skilled immigration not only offsets the decline in the domestic workforce: in many countries, it is becoming the key source of labour market growth (e.g. External Reference Group 2008: 21). Some commentators go so far as to claim that '[s]killed immigration will define the landscape of the global labour market over the longer term' (Alexander *et al.* 2012: 5).

Within this changing economic context, states aggressively compete over skilled immigrants in what has been referred to alternately as the 'global race for talent' (Shachar 2006) or the search for 'the best and the brightest' (Thompson 2001). Once a discrete tool peculiar to the settler states of the United States, Canada and Australia, many countries are now adopting skilled immigration policies. Denmark, France, Germany, New Zealand, the United Kingdom and Ireland have all developed skilled immigration programmes in recent years. Meanwhile the development of the European Union (EU) Blue Card for Skilled Immigrants in 2009 has influenced the proliferation of skilled immigration policies across the European continent. Governments increasingly view skilled immigration not only as a panacea for labour shortages but also – due to the frequently high educational and employment outcomes of skilled immigrants – as a way to avoid the social and economic integration issues that have bedevilled European immigration in the past (Symons 2006). During a period where domestic population ageing contributes to ballooning welfare costs, immigration scholars have advocated the benefits of economically efficient immigration to offset these trends (Beach *et al.* 2007; Borjas 1989, 1999; Koser and Salt 1997: 294).

In addition to the purported economic benefits of skilled immigration, this approach to immigration selection is seen as fairer, more meritocratic and more transparent than previous approaches – in particular those based upon the race or ethnicity of the selected applicant (Papademetriou *et al.* 2008: 12). Leaving behind a past characterised by race-based selection, which often excluded Asians, Jews, Africans and other non-Anglo-Saxon immigrants, the adoption of skilled immigration has been declared the 'triumph of economics over discrimination' (Passaris 1984: 91). Christian Joppke (2005: ix) characterises this shift as one towards 'toward nonethnic, universalistic immigration policies'. Importantly, Joppke (2005: 2, original emphases) argues that the trend towards universalistic selection policy is particularly strong with regard to economic immigration selection where 'the state may consider the individual only for what she *does*, not for what she *is*'. Echoing these sentiments, debates in the United States over Comprehensive Immigration Reform promoted the introduction of 'merit-based' skilled immigration visas for economic immigration (Koslowski 2014, citing United States Senate 2013).

The prevailing orthodoxy emphasises the ascent of economic rationality and the decline of discrimination in skilled immigration selection. Yet, this status quo reading of skilled immigration overlooks the key ways in which discrimination can continue indirectly. This book considers this central issue of discrimination and focuses in particular upon the question of gender. Feminist scholars have long argued that equality between men and women should be considered both in formal and substantive terms. 'Formal equality' denotes equal treatment on the face of policy or law. For instance, in the case of gender equality, this would require that 'women and men are treated exactly the same in all circumstances' (ALRC 1994, cited in Graycar and Morgan 2002: 28–9). However, advocates of 'substantive equality' suggest that formal equality is insufficient when it leads to different outcomes. Substantive approaches acknowledge that there are 'important, immutable differences between women and men'. Men, for instance, cannot become pregnant, nor do they nurse young children. These 'immutable differences', according to proponents of substantive equality, have implications for the ways in which policy is designed and the differing effects of policy upon the sexes.

Once we move beyond the simple question of whether skilled immigration policies exercise formal inequality between men and women towards more complex questions of substantive inequality, the global race for talent raises a myriad of discriminatory issues that must be unravelled, examined and debated. In this book I ask: 'Do highly skilled women face obstacles to entry as skilled immigrants to a greater degree than their male counterparts?' I find this to be the case and argue that gendered obstacles come into skilled immigration policy at a variety of stages of the policy cycle. They arise in the political discussions through which immigration policies are negotiated and designed in ways that often advantage male applicants and disadvantage female applicants. They also come into the selection stage when immigrants choose to apply as skilled immigrants, based upon assessment of selection criteria. Policy design often overlooks the different life course experiences of women and men, for instance whether part-time work or career breaks are acknowledged within skilled immigration design. Skilled immigration policies frequently perpetuate a stereotypical divide between an autonomous male breadwinner and an accompanying (implicitly female) spouse. Joint worker-carer models are absent from policy design. Finally, as regards actual immigration outcomes, women disproportionately enter as accompanying family members of skilled immigrants rather than as principal skilled immigrants in their own right.

Yet, this book demonstrates that gendered immigration policies are not inevitable. Immigration ministries have the capacity to alter their immigration laws to ensure that women applicants are considered on equal terms with men. Certainly, selecting governments design their policies against a backdrop of global gender inequalities in labour market opportunities. Notwithstanding this reality, I argue that governments possess the scope to develop policies that are attentive to differences between men and women immigrants, which I refer to as 'gender awareness' in policy design. I demonstrate the importance of state intervention through a detailed comparison of Australian and Canadian skilled immigration policies over a quarter century. I argue that gender issues emerge in different ways depending upon the mechanisms of skilled immigration selection; whether governments design points test models or use salary thresholds, if the focus is on general human capital or specific sectoral skills, or instead when employers wield powers over selection through 'demand driven selection models'.

To some readers, the relevance of gender in skilled immigration policy will seem initially opaque. Yet, I demonstrate that gender is a central fulcrum that informs all aspects of skilled immigration selection. The interaction of the labour market with skilled immigration selection policy is critical here. Major life course events such as education, training, professional work, child bearing, child rearing and retirement affect women differently from men. For instance, women are more likely than men to take career breaks for child bearing and rearing, leading to less linear career trajectories and delayed realisation of key career goals. Further, the ways in which skilled immigration selection policies are designed interact with and reinforce many of these gendered life course dimensions. These life course trajectories in turn interrelate with domestic definitions of 'skill' that in some instances operate to exclude or disqualify the contributions and qualifications of women. Finally, as immigration states become more competitive in the race for talent and as selecting nations place greater emphasis on human capital credentials, language abilities, vocational skills and work experience, the importance of gender is amplified. In short, the global race for talent is gendered, with significant implications for the skill accreditation, labour market outcomes, rights of stay, gendered family dynamics, including freedom from domestic violence and financial independence, of female immigrants.

Given prevailing state sovereignty over immigration selection, some will counter that gendered immigration policies are the prerogative of selecting countries and therefore unimportant as a theoretical or empirical endeavour. As Catherine Dauvergne (2009) argues, the central point of immigration policy is to discriminate. Future immigrants stand outside the nation state and immigration ministers increasingly emphasise their government's right to select 'the best and the brightest' on their own terms. Adopting an aptly Canadian metaphor in 2008, then Immigration Minister Diane Finley compared skilled immigration selection to selection onto a hockey team. If Canada simply took 'the first 25 people in the line', she argued, this might 'seem fair because they lined up in that order', but 'you might end up without a goalie' (Finley 2008: 1605). Following this argument, it is the right of the government to select the best members for 'Team Canada'.

Yet, when states rejected discriminatory immigration policies in the 1960s and 1970s, with the removal of the White Australia policy in Australia in 1973 and similar policies in Canada in 1962, they also rejected a system of selection that differentiated on the basis of people's uncontrollable innate characteristics (Joppke 2005: 2). For instance, the Australian Department of Immigration and Citizenship's (DIAC) *Fact Sheet 1* summarises that country's multicultural immigration selection policy and states that 'Australia's Migration Program does not discriminate on the basis of race or religion. This means that anyone from any country, can apply to migrate, regardless of their ethnic origin, gender or colour, provided that they meet the criteria set out in law' (DIAC 2009a). Similarly, Canada also places emphasis on diversity in selection, including gender, as evidenced by the inclusion of a requirement for gender analysis in its immigration act (IRPA 2002, s92(f)). With respect to skilled immigration in particular, one of the key objectives of the development of the points tests in Canada in 1967 was to develop a race-blind, non-discriminatory means to select migrants (Green and Green 1999). On this basis I argue that the end of discriminatory selection in these countries in the 1960s and 1970s irrevocably restrained the exercise of state sovereignty by placing an equality check on immigration policies. The non-discriminatory principle imposes some limits upon entry onto the metaphorical hockey team. Normatively, it is not permissible for a country to select a team that comprises only Anglo-Saxon players, or overwhelmingly male hockey players, or that gives more rights to some team members than others, because this runs up against the original commitment to a diverse nation that is a founding feature of non-discriminatory immigration selection. The more complex question is how policies may operate to inadvertently select such a 'team', even if this is not the stated or even implicit aim of government. It is this more subtle issue that this book explores through its analysis of the obstacles faced by highly skilled women in skilled immigration selection.

Outline of the book

Part I: the global race for talent

This book is divided into two parts. The first part considers the big picture of skilled immigration policies globally and the particular obstacles faced by women applicants in meeting skilled immigration selection criteria. Chapter 1 draws upon research from scholars of feminist industrial relations, sociology, economics and intersectional feminist studies, to develop a new theoretical framework to assess the gendered dimensions of skilled immigration policy. These theoretical accounts have long identified the particular labour market obstacles which women face due in part to their heightened levels of engagement in reproductive labour (child bearing and rearing) but also due to gendered appreciations of worth on the labour market. Chapter 1 brings the analytical insights of these theories to bear upon the area of skilled immigration.

In Chapter 2, I present a unique international data set (the 'GenderImmi data set') that I developed to analyse skilled immigration policies across twelve key OECD countries and thirty-seven visa types. Two multi-lingual coders analysed legal regulations of thirty-seven immigration visas from twelve OECD countries with high rates of net migration.[1] Drawing upon the framework established in Chapter 1, three key areas of 'gender awareness' are considered: i) the extent to which gender mainstreaming processes are incorporated into policy-making; ii) the ways in which the different life courses of men and women are acknowledged in skilled immigration policy design; and iii) the (gendered) definitions of 'skill' within such policies. This medium-N comparative analysis demonstrates that countries such as Canada and Denmark that undertake gender audits of their immigration laws or admit applicants in female-dominated occupations such as the caring fields perform better in terms of gender awareness than countries like Austria, Australia, the United Kingdom and Ireland that do not undertake such audits or that focus narrowly on selecting immigrants from male-dominated Science, Technology, Engineering and Mathematics (STEM) professions. This finding is important for the second part of the book that explains the reasons for differences in the gender awareness of Australian and Canadian skilled immigration policies.

Part II: gendering skilled immigration policy in Australia and Canada, 1988–2013

Even if we know how countries vary in terms of their attention to gender within skilled immigration policies, this analysis does not explain why such countries differ. The second part of the book provides a detailed analysis of Australian and Canadian skilled immigration policies over a quarter century (1988–2013) in order to address this explanatory question. In this part of the book, I consider how policy processes might enable, or restrict, the realisation of gender-aware skilled immigration policies. The case selection of Australia and Canada is motivated by a most-similar design that allows key explanatory variables to be isolated (Lipset 1990: xiii, cited in Bloemraad 2006: 12). Against considerable similarities – that I outline briefly below – this second part of the book explains why Canada adopted more gender- aware skilled immigration policies than Australia over the period 1988–2013.

Case selection

Although Australia and Canada are relatively small countries with populations of approximately twenty-three and thirty-five million persons respectively, they are central players in global immigration debates. Australia attracts about 219,500 permanent immigrants per year, and Canada attracts about 248,700. They also admit 125,070 and 213,573 temporary economic immigrants respectively each year (DIAC 2013a: 5; CIC 2013g).[2] Both countries have very high net immigration rates over the period 2005–10 (11 per cent in Australia and 8 per cent in Canada), ranking them as the top states in the OECD (Chiswick 2013; UNDESA 2012).[3]

Other countries often hold up Australia and Canada as exemplars of skilled immigration policies, worthy of policy transfer. The British Government adopted an 'Australian-style points test' for skilled immigration in 2008, while Denmark in 2010 also developed a points test system for selection (Sparrow 2008; Copenhagen Post 2010), a concept which actually originated in Canada in 1965 (Hawkins 1989: 39). In addition, various versions of the points test were implemented in New Zealand in 1989, the Czech Republic in 2003, Singapore in 2004 and Hong Kong in 2006 (Papademetriou 2008: 7–9). Given their importance as sources of inspiration in the skilled immigration policy field, as well as their relatively advanced policy experience, Australia and Canada provide important cases not only in their own right but also for other countries to consider.

Australia and Canada also both draw on a British colonial history, an Indigenous population and a racialised past of immigration selection, replaced in modern times with multicultural selection policies. Migration scholars refer to them both as 'settler states' (Freeman 1995) or 'classic countries of immigration' (Cornelius *et al.* 2004: 12). Institutionally, both countries are also similar with Westminster-inspired arrangements: largely majoritarian electoral systems, a fusion of executive and legislative power and a two-party-dominated model with an increasing role played by minor parties. These two countries are also both federations and share labour market similarities, often being classified as liberal market economies (Hall and Soskice 2001).

Both Australia and Canada have accessible naturalisation, within four years of landing (Australian Citizenship Act (2007) (Cth), s21; Citizenship Act (1985) (Cdn), s5(1)(c)). Both countries have truly multiethnic communities with 24 per cent of Australians foreign born and 20 per cent of Canadians (Hawthorne 2014: 4). Both countries also have similar geographical dispersal of immigrants with the bulk of new immigrants settled in key cities – Sydney and Melbourne in the case of Australia, and Toronto, Vancouver and Montreal in the case of Canada (DIAC 2007a: 14; CIC 2009a). This has resulted in similar geographical concentrations of the costs and arguably also the benefits of immigration. Finally, in recent years, these countries demonstrate important economic similarities in terms of burgeoning resource sector growth, which has seen them weather the global financial crisis well, producing strong demand for skilled labour.

Venue shopping and diversity-seeking: the theoretical approach adopted in this book

Despite these similarities, as Part I of the book demonstrates, there are nonetheless important differences in skilled immigration policies across Australia and Canada, including from a gender perspective. In order to explain this divergence, I draw upon venue shopping theory from American public policy scholarship and historical institutionalism to explore this issue (Baumgartner and Jones 1993; Mezey 1979; Pierson 2006; Pralle 2006a, 2006b; 2007; Weaver and Rockman 1991). In particular, these scholars focus on how actor engagement in different institutional venues shapes the perception of a policy problem (the 'policy image') and in turn the efficacy of actors' claims on the state for policy change. Following the argument of these scholars, I propose that the engagement of feminist and immigrant associations ('diversity-seeking groups') in key policy venues is essential to ensure gender-aware skilled immigration policies are achieved. In their absence, policies will necessarily exhibit a more economic rationalist character as bureaucracies and immigration ministers exercise considerable control over the policy process (Boucher 2013a). I define 'diversity-seeking groups' as those individuals and organisations that pursue social justice and human rights goals, as opposed to purely economic objectives in immigration policy-making. In Canada, there has been more scope for the involvement of such groups in key institutional venues than in Australia over the last twenty-five years. Such institutions included feminist bureaucratic networks within government, parliamentary committees, federalist structures and the courts. In contrast, government in Australia exercised more 'bureaucratic control' over the immigration policy process than in Canada and there was a lack of active diversity-seeking engagement. This approach is laid out in the second part of the book and is evidenced through a mixed methods approach that combines qualitative media, archival and legal analysis with 128 elite interviews undertaken with members of diversity-seeking organisations, immigration officials, senior parliamentarians and trade union and business representatives. This methodological approach is outlined in detail in Appendix 3.

Four case studies of skilled immigration policies

The argument that the engagement of diversity-seeking groups in institutional venues matters for gender-aware immigration policies is explored through four detailed case studies of Australian and Canadian immigration policies, from 1988 through to 2013. The first case study is presented in Chapter 4 and starts in 1988, a pivotal year for the economic focusing of immigration selection policy in both countries. During this time, we observe an emerging concern within government over established immigration selection methods and a tightening of family reunification routes. Both dimensions of policy reforms have significant gender implications. In Chapter 4, I argue that the restrictions on family reunification alone did not lead to less gender-aware policies, as spouses who previously came via family reunification channels had the opportunity to enter as the partners of skilled immigrants. Instead, it was the cuts to extended family categories – assisted relatives in Canada, and the concessional class and parent immigration in Australia – that held the most substantial gender implications. This is because there was no substitution effect between family flows and increased skilled immigration intake for these extended family categories.

Chapter 5 considers the second case study – changes in skilled immigration points tests in Australia and Canada over the decade from 1993 to 2003. Points tests have a long pedigree in both countries, having been adopted in Canada in 1967 and Australia in 1978. However, the period from the early 1990s onwards was marked by a refinement and increased selectivity in points tests. In Canada in 2002, a new immigration act, the Immigration Refugee Protection Act (2002) (IRPA) was passed with a renewed points test that presented a greater focus on general human capital criteria. Australia took the opposite approach to its points test design over this period, with the adoption of a specific skill model. In Chapter 5, I argue that the points test adopted in Canada was more gender aware, an outcome informed by the engagement of diversity-seeking activists in the policy process and due to the establishment of a gender-based analysis unit within Citizenship Immigration Canada (CIC). The absence of gender considerations in Australia relates to tight administrative control by bureaucrats and the immigration ministry over the policy process and their reliance on regulatory instruments to achieve key policy goals.

From 2006 onwards in both countries there has been a shift towards more selective and occupationally focused selection methods for permanent skilled immigration. A third case study, presented in Chapter 6, demonstrates that over time, Canadian policy-makers have adopted many of the methods of bureaucratic control developed in Australia during earlier periods, leading to less gender-aware policies in the permanent skilled immigration field in Canada. There has also been a growing bifurcation of 'his' and 'her' occupational modes of entry within skilled immigration programmes in both countries. Activists are also increasingly blocked from engagement in policy processes, due to the bureaucratic nature of such reforms.

In the fourth and final case study, presented in Chapter 7, I consider the rise of temporary economic immigration in both countries. Australia and Canada have both undergone mining booms since the mid-2000s. Temporary immigration is an important source of labour for their resource sectors. Recent immigration policies in both countries respond to this changing economic and industrial context, which has been accompanied by gender stratification within temporary flows: women are underrepresented in skilled temporary flows in both countries. However, in Canada, low-skilled temporary schemes have become an important avenue for the entrance of female immigrants, albeit with fewer rights than those entering on highly skilled temporary visas. Some attempts have been made by diversity-seeking activists in Canada to secure greater labour rights for these low-skilled temporary immigrants and these are documented in Chapter 7. Australia to date has eschewed low-skilled modes of entry for economic immigrants and the gender implications of this policy position are also considered in that chapter.

Differences in the gender-awareness immigration of policies across countries and through time can be attributed not only to activities by diversity-seeking groups or the institutional forums in which they participate politically, but also to 'supply-side' features of such groups. In Chapter 8, I take an inward turn and consider the internal dynamics of diversity-seeking organisations and the implications for their engagement in skilled immigration policy processes. Undertaking an audit of all major organisations in the field in Australia and Canada, I demonstrate the importance of funding mechanisms, coalition building and a flat organisational structure for diversity-seeking group strength, which is a necessary precursor to venue shopping. The final chapter concludes by considering the practical policy and theoretical implications of the gender analysis presented in this book.

Notes

1 The codebook will be available on the author's website following publication.
2 No comparative OECD data exist for temporary workers entrants for Australia and Canada in 2011–12, so these data are compiled from domestic reports.
3 This rate measures '[t]he number of immigrants minus the number of emigrants over a period, divided by the person-years lived by the population of the receiving country over that period. It is expressed as average annual net number of migrants per 1,000 population'. By way of comparison, the USA had a net migration rate over the same period of only 3 per cent.

Part I

The global race for talent: global context

1

Skill and gender: navigating the theoretical terrain

Introduction

States are increasingly selecting immigrants according to their labour market qualifications and their broad human capital. Using points tests, wage distribution curves and sector-specific visas, governments and employers evaluate newcomers on the basis of their potential contribution to domestic economies. Academics and policy-makers have paid considerable attention to these selection mechanisms and the relative human capital of skilled immigration compared with other immigration flows (e.g. Beaverstock 1994, 1996; Boeri *et al.* 2012; Boucher and Cerna 2014; Docquier and Marfouk 2005; Docquier *et al.* 2011; Favell *et al.* 2006; Hawthorne 2007; Koser and Salt 1997; Triadafilopoulos 2013; Wright 2012).

However, within a burgeoning scholarship on skill and immigration, there is limited space given to an analysis of gender. This is despite the fact that gender is central, not tangential, to our understanding of skill, labour and immigration. Women are underrepresented in highly skilled immigration flows, although they are now equally represented in resident highly educated immigrant stock (Brücker *et al.* 2013). Given that flow data are the best measure of immigration policies, this discrepancy in the gender make-up of skilled flow versus resident stock data raises the central question of whether highly skilled women face greater obstacles to entry as skilled immigrants than men. If so, what are these obstacles? It is possible that skilled immigration selection policies are devaluing the skills of some female migrants or creating structural obstacles to women's entry through these channels. This may result in their reliance upon other migratory pathways, particularly family reunification, for entry. The gap between gendered stock and flow outcomes presents an empirical puzzle for analysing the role of gender within skilled immigration selection policy. In addition, from a normative perspective, through examining the role of policy in this regard, we can also interrogate claims of non-discrimination that underpin existing policies in liberal democracies. Given the shift towards skilled immigration under way across many OECD nations, the gender implications of such policies are highly salient. Yet, to date we lack clear theoretical measures to assess whether skilled immigration policies are gendered in their design, as well as in their operation. This is the focus of the current chapter.

In this chapter, I argue that such measures are best drawn from existing studies of women's engagement in the labour market, in particular those from within feminist industrial relations, sociology, economics and intersectional feminist theory. This chapter engages with this diverse feminist scholarship to map what 'gender awareness' means within skilled immigration policy. This mapping exercise is then utilised to develop indicators of gender awareness that form the basis of the GenderImmi data set of thirty-seven skilled immigration visas, which is presented in Chapter 2.

Developing gender-aware indicators within immigration studies

In developing new indicators of gender awareness of skill immigration policy, I draw upon and extend previous studies on the relationship between gender and skilled immigration. This book builds upon existing work that interrogates skilled immigration policies from a gender perspective (e.g. Badkar *et al.* 2006; Boucher 2007; Dauvergne 2000; Dobson and Crush 2004; Fincher 1997; Fincher *et al.* 1994; Gabriel 2008; Hawthorne 1996; Iredale 2005; Kofman 2005, 2007, 2013; Kofman et al 2009; Piper and Yamanaka 2008). Despite their contributions to the field, these studies often focus on singular countries or visas. Further, generally these studies do not develop indicators of gender awareness that can be used to assess the gender implications of skilled immigration policies across a range of countries.[1] Some studies challenge prevailing assumptions of skilled immigration as exclusively male, and family immigration as exclusively female and 'dependent', but do not provide a detailed definition of what is meant by 'gender awareness' (Arat-Koc 1999b; Kofman and Raghuram 2006). There is also a tendency to consider both immigration policies and entrance data simultaneously. Whilst useful, such analysis may overlook the role of sending state factors in informing gendered immigration patterns, or can confuse the causal mechanisms at play that interactively entrench gender inequalities (see Boyd 2006 for an overview). Alternately, studies focus on the gender awareness of settlement rather than immigration selection policy (Liversage 2009).

In other areas of gender and public policy analysis, international indicators, including those derived from the Convention on the Elimination of All Forms of Discrimination Against Women (CEDAW) have been recommended as a basis for feminist analysis (Baldez 2011). Yet, CEDAW is less useful for analysis of skilled immigration policy as it does not explicitly enumerate rights for immigrant men and women. Nor does the International Convention on the Rights of All Migrant Workers and Their Families (1990) articulate key rights for female migrant workers. Indeed, the title of the Convention would seem to establish an artificially gendered division between 'male workers' and female 'family members', a division that I interrogate in Chapter 4. The Organisation for Security and Co-operation in Europe developed a 'Guide on Gender-Sensitive Labour

Migration Policies' in 2009 (OSCE 2009). This document differentiates between 'gender-biased', 'gender-blind', 'gender-neutral' and 'gender-sensitive' policies. Yet, the Organisation (2009: 24) suggests, somewhat tautologically, that labour migration policy is 'gender sensitive' if 'gender issues are reflected in labour migration' and does not identify clear indicators for undertaking this gender assessment. Recent work by the International Organization for Migration (IOM 2013) adds to the wealth of scholarship on skilled immigration and gender, but also does not provide clear indicators to compare skilled immigration policies across countries from a gender perspective. Conversely, most international quantitative 'gender analysis tools' focus on policy outcomes rather than actual policies (see for instance the Gender-Related Development Index and the Gender Empowerment Measure that focus on women's education and employment outcomes). As such, international data sets often 'capture social trends ... that relate to policy objectives or targets' rather than assessment of 'the effectiveness of policies as such' (Breitenbach and Galligan 2006: 602). Arguably, only by considering how gender plays in at the policy design stage, as well as at the policy implementation and outcomes stage, can we adequately understand the complex gendering process that occurs within skilled immigration selection.

Domestic governments have faced impediments in the development of indicators of gender awareness within skilled immigration policy. Despite considerable attention by states to gender mainstreaming across a variety of policy areas in recent decades, analysis of skilled immigration policies from a gender perspective by individual governments is very limited. The government with the most experience is Canada. As a policy sector, immigration in Canada is unique in its statutory stipulation for an annual Gender-Based Analysis (GBA) to be conducted and published in the annual ministerial immigration report to Parliament. This has been a requirement since the Immigration Refugee Protection Act was passed in 2002 (IRPA, s94.2(f)). Despite its achievements, Citizenship Immigration Canada's gender analyses are limited as a benchmark for cross-national comparison. Government-defined approaches to 'gender awareness' are rarely self-reflective on the effects of political exigencies upon such definitions. Further, the understanding of 'gender awareness' in Canada has also been gradually narrowed over time, and in some areas, reduced to the publication of gender-disaggregated data (Boucher 2010). I explore this point further in the second part of this book that focuses on the Canadian and Australian experience, where I argue that 'gender awareness' is a far more robust and complex concept than the mere provision of gender-disaggregated data.

These limitations within existing gender analysis of skilled immigration policy reflect broader concerns for feminist analysis of public policy. As Amy Mazur and Gary Goertz (2008: 3–4) note in a recent appraisal, '[d]espite the centrality of the concept [of gender] for analysis in the gender and politics literature, there is little work that provides systematic guidelines, examples, and the methodology for the

construction and use of concepts in empirically based theory building'. Responding
to this challenge, some scholars define gender awareness according to the attention paid to 'traditional' women's interests such as those involving children and
family (Carroll 1994; Dobson and Carroll 1991; Swers 2002). Alternately, feminist
activists themselves are taken to best define what gender awareness means; as such
an inductive approach, informed by lived social practice guides this definition of
gender awareness (Bratton 2005; Dobson and Carroll 1991). Yet, while the engagement of feminist activists may facilitate the creation of gender-aware policy, it is
questionable whether engagement alone is a necessary and sufficient condition
of 'gender awareness'. Such endogenous approaches to definition create obstacles
when legitimate gender issues have not yet been contested politically due to the
typical impediments to social action. In addition, an endogenous approach is less
useful in a comparative context, where feminist activists have raised concerns in
some jurisdictions, but not in others, as in the current analysis.

Developing new indicators of 'gender awareness' in skilled immigration policy

Given the limitations of existing approaches to defining 'gender awareness'
within skilled immigration policy, new indicators are needed. These indicators
are best derived from the theoretical literature, which social scientists argue can
be employed to test the validity of concepts that define and measure political
phenomenon (Collier *et al.* 2004: 203–4; Manheim *et al.* 2006: 61). As skilled
immigration is fundamentally a product of labour market processes, the relevant scholarships here are feminist industrial relations, sociology, economics
and intersectional feminist studies. Goertz and Mazur (2008: 28, 34) counsel
that in developing gender indicators for subsequent empirical analysis, it is
important to consider several factors: i) the functional role of the indicator in
the operation of a phenomenon; ii) what effect the indicator has upon outcomes;
and iii) whether the chosen indicators expand the existing empirical coverage
of analysis. These principles are applied in the following section to select the
indicators considered in Chapter 2. Underpinning this selection is the assumption that labour market variables that influence gender outcomes on the general
labour market will also in turn influence skilled immigration selection policies,
as sketched in Figure 1.1.

Figure 1.1: Relationship between gender, labour market and skilled immigration
policy

Gender mainstreaming processes: gender audits, gender units and gender-disaggregated data

Gender audits, gender units and the collection of gender-disaggregated data are common mechanisms to uncover gendered patterns within public policy processes. In many ways, monitoring the existence or absence of such gender mainstreaming processes is the clearest and simplest measure of gender awareness as it focuses on the absence or presence of key actors and activities in the policy cycle (Acker 1992; Beckwith 2010: 160–1; Kantola and Outshoorn 2007: 7; Mazur 2002: 30; Sawer 2010: 3–6). According to the OECD (2012b: 41), gender audits are a 'key policy-making tool that provides detailed, systematic information about the potentially differential effects of laws, policies and regulations on men and women'. This analysis can occur when laws and regulations are being designed or after they have been adopted (Bacchi and Eveline 2003). Women's human rights frameworks have promoted such audits, for instance the Beijing Platform for Further Action on Women stipulates gender-based analysis of policies including immigration law and policy (UN 2002: 22). Given the primacy of gender audits to the process of feminist public policy analysis by governments, the presence or absence of such audits is a crucial indicator of gender awareness. Accompanying this, I also consider the presence or absence of women's political machinery within immigration bureaucracies.

The collection and publication of gender-disaggregated data can also be viewed as a necessary precursor to gender audits, insofar that such information is required to adequately assess the effects of policy (OECD 2011a, 2011c; Swirski 2011). A lack of sufficient sex-disaggregated data in the immigration field has been criticised as 'inhibit[ing] coherent policymaking and action in favour of women migrants' (Ndiaye 2006: 10–11). There is an important difference between the collection of gender-disaggregated data for internal government usage, data available only through Freedom of Information requests and readily available public data. The former two obscure analysis of gender concerns within immigration policy, whereas the second brings such issues to the fore (Kofman 2013, 2014). Collection of publically available gender-disaggregated data therefore provides an important indicator of gender awareness of skilled immigration policies.

Despite their importance, the occurrence of gender audits and the collection of gender-disaggregated data do not alone adequately capture the gender awareness or gender relevance of skilled immigration policies. For one, the engagement of feminist actors within feminist 'friendly' bureaucratic structures may fail to ensure gender-aware policies. Gender mainstreaming may also be downgraded to a technocratic step in the policy process rather than leading to clear policy change (Rees 2005; Teghtsoonian 2005). For this reason, it is also necessary to consider substantive features of skilled immigration policies, of which acknowledgement of life course differences between men and women and definitions of 'skill' are central.

Life course factors: gender issues over the working life

The following discussion situates my broader gender analysis of skilled immigration policy within the rich and diverse social science scholarship on the labour
market and gender. I focus first on the literature on gendered career trajectories,
or how men and women's different life course events are shaped by labour market
policy. Feminist theorists in industrial relations and sociology acknowledge the
ways in which women and men engage differently over their career trajectory, due
in part to women's disproportionate engagement both in child bearing and rearing
as well as women's higher rates of unpaid domestic labour.

These life events can have significant effects on women's labour force engagement in the child bearing and rearing years and beyond (twenty-five to forty-nine),
leading to non-continuous or interrupted patterns of labour force engagement.
Across the OECD, women in the eighteen to sixty-four age bracket have on average lower levels of labour force engagement than men, although rates of engagement have been improving since the 1980s (OECD 2012b: 150). The vast majority
of women take some form of break over the child bearing and rearing period
but then return to employment. Kathryn Hynes and Marin Clarkberg's (2005)
analysis of American women finds that in the twenty-four months after child-
birth, a minority of women enjoyed continuous paid service but at the same time,
less than 25 per cent of mothers exited the labour force entirely after this period
(2005: 230–1). On this basis, these authors conclude that 'a woman's transition
into or out of employment, particularly in the period surrounding the birth of a
child, does not necessarily represent an enduring status change, but must instead
be considered in the larger context of a women's employment history' (Hynes
and Clarkberg 2005: 224). A recent study in the United Kingdom corroborates
this finding, demonstrating that entry and exit from the workforce, followed by
re-entry, is common for women in the child rearing years (often for up to a decade
as women may have several children in close succession due to fertility considerations: Kitty 2014: 95; see also Kahn *et al.* 2014: 57–8). While highly skilled women
also follow this pattern of intermittent work, they are more likely than low-skilled
women to return to work following child rearing; suggesting the interim nature
of labour force disruption over key fertility years is particularly salient for highly
skilled women (Kitty 2014). Importantly, this is also the cohort of workers of key
interest for the purposes of skilled immigration selection policy.

Women and men differ significantly in their engagement in non-continuous
work. As Deborah O'Neil and her colleagues (2008: 731) note, 'the architecture of
women's careers is constructed uniquely and differently from men's'. In contrast
to women, men's employment patterns are fairly stable and there is far less variation across countries (Steiber and Haas 2012: 344). Further, despite some developments towards gender equality in paternity leave and shared leave opportunities,
especially in the Nordic states where sharing such tasks is legislatively mandated,
the vast majority of parental leave takers are women. When men do take leave

it is generally for much shorter periods than women; often only for one week to several months and therefore far less likely to affect continuous work patterns than women (Bruning and Plantenga 1999: 200). This suggests that policies that fail to accommodate career breaks will hold very different implications for women than they do for men.

Although less acknowledged in the scholarship, non-continuous labour force engagement may also be a product of caring responsibilities for sick, disabled or elderly persons and sometimes also older children. The distribution of this work is also gendered. Research by Ursula Henz (2006) using the British Family and Working Lives Study demonstrates that those with caring responsibilities often leave the workforce and that women are twice as likely as men to leave the workforce for this reason. Therefore, other forms of unpaid care work in addition to early child rearing can contribute to women's non-continuous service.

Part-time work is often a strategy to reconcile work and family commitments, especially when children are young (Drobnic *et al.* 1999: 134). As Jane Lewis (2012: 209) has argued, '[h]istorically, the main way in which paid work and family responsibilities have been balanced has been by the expansion of part-time work for women'. Of course, the provision of part-time work is not always seen as gender friendly, especially if such work is imposed by employers, correlates with bad quality or low paid jobs, or is limited in its availability (Bukodi *et al.* 2012: 58; Gornick and Meyers 2008a: 343–4; Smith 2009: 18–19). In light of these considerations, some feminist scholars argue that shorter working hours for both sexes are to be preferred from a gender equality perspective over the provisions of part-time work to women (e.g. Gornick and Meyers 2008a: 344, 2008b: 24). Debate also prevails over whether engagement in part-time work by women is motivated primarily by individual choice or necessity (Hakim 2002; cf. Lewis 2012: 212).

Notwithstanding these critiques of part-time work, the reality is that women in all countries for which such data are collected undertake part-time work disproportionately to men. While part-time work rates have also been increasing for men since the 1980s, women still engage at twice the rate that men do globally (UNDESA 2010: 95; see also OECD 2012b: 160). There is variation in women's engagement in part-time work across nations, with particularly high female reliance in the Netherlands, Norway, Australia and Canada (see UNDESA 2010; Drobnic *et al.* 1999; ILO 2012; Lewis 2012: 209). Women's part-time engagement is stronger in the developed than the developing world (UNDESA 2010: 75) and most heavily utilised in liberal economies with more costly child care provision (Lohkamp-Himmighofen and Dienel 2000: 62). Part-time work has also been increasing for mothers of millennium-era babies (Bukodi *et al.* 2012: 62; Kalleberg *et al.* 2000: 344). Finally, adding further evidence to this picture of the importance of part-time work as a labour market engagement strategy for women, many countries have introduced laws that give parents the right to request part-time work upon return from periods of parental leave (Purcell *et al.* 2006).

Aside from reflecting the gendered reliance upon part-time work, longitudinal research also indicates that such work is utilised most when children are young and that its usage diminishes over the latter parts of the employment life course. Part-time work thus represents a 'stop-gap solution to women's employment, rather than a systematic strategy to combine family responsibilities and career' (Blank 1989: 298–9; see also Drobnic *et al.* 1999: 144).[2] The intermittent rather than ongoing nature of part-time patterns reveals the importance of adopting a dynamic life course approach in labour market policies, including skilled immigration selection policy.

Age and career milestones

As a result of non-continuous or interrupted work and engagement in part-time work, women often reach career goals later in life than men. Carmen Sirianni and Cynthia Negrey (2000: 66–7) note that speedy career trajectories are generally a product of 'continuous and uninterrupted progress along a linear time line'. However, differences in attainment of career milestones also result from the traditional breadwinner model 'where the wife provides support to the husband [in his career]' (Sabelis and Schilling 2013: 127–8). In the case of mothers, the conditions for fast career advancement are often not available and despite a shift towards more egalitarian dual-worker-carer models within working families, there are still gender differentials in this regard. Sirianni and Negrey (2000: 67) argue that '[w]ives ... are still more likely to be absent from work due to child care than husbands, interrupt their careers, work part-time, follow their spouses' geographical moves, and suffer wage and rate advancement penalties as a result'.

Women also take longer than men to reach the upper echelon of their professions, but can do well once children have matured into adulthood. United Kingdom Labour Force Survey data for instance, highlight that while men's representation in the top 3 per cent of industry decreases with age, it increases for women; particularly once women leave the 'child rearing' period (Loretto and Vickerstaff 2011: 99). In fact, compensating women for the earlier years of reduced productivity in light of likely later acceleration may make good policy sense. Catherine Weinberger's (2011) analysis of college graduates in the United States demonstrates that women who return to the labour force after the end of their child rearing stage of life (ages forty-three to fifty-two) actually experience a growth in wages proportionately greater than men of the same age.[3] Weinberger (2011: 465) attributes this relative increase in female wages to the reduced parental responsibilities enjoyed by older women, noting that '[d]ecreasing levels of parenting responsibility seem to contribute to the strong earnings growth among older women'. Joan Kahn and collaborators (2014: 57, 64–5, 67) reinforce this finding arguing that the 'motherhood penalty' upon women's careers extenuates with age as children become more independent, leading to a convergence over forty between childless women and mothers and a general 'trajectory of improvement in mother's occupational attainment over the life course'.[4] The years of highest career penalty for mothers are in their thirties, while career rewards to women accrue from the forties through to the fifties (Kahn *et al.* 2014: 65, 68). This would again support the argument that women take longer to reach high-skilled positions than men. This is not to minimise the enduring intersecting effects of age and gender discrimination faced by many older women (Duncan and Loretto 2004: 128; Loretto and Vickerstaff 2011) but rather, to acknowledge that if women's life course is to be accommodated within policy design, assumptions of linear career trajectories and equal age milestones for men and women must be challenged.

Defining 'skill'

Aside from assessing gendered life course differences, feminist industrial relations and sociological scholars have also considered the gendered ways in which the concept of 'skill' is defined. In investigating this issue, it is necessary to examine the broad and contested debates that prevail within the social sciences around this topic, not only from feminist scholars but also from the field of human capital studies within neoclassical economics. Irena Grugulis and contributors (2004: 5) identify three different approaches to defining skills. First, from a neoclassical economic perspective, skills may be seen to reside in the worker, in the sense that skills are a product of the human capital of the individual acquired over the life course (Becker 1964). Alternately, the job at hand may determine the skill level. This approach considers the type of job and the degree of control in the employment relationship (Littler 1982). Finally, social construction approaches assess 'skill' that is a product of political negotiations between different actors with different levels of power. Feminist scholarship generally fits within this third approach to the definition of skill and ensuing critiques take several forms. In the following section of this chapter, I set out first the human capital scholarship, which predominates within skilled immigration policy debates before presenting the feminist critiques of this approach.[5] Given the elusive nature of skill and the difficulty in its quantification, a variety of proxies have been developed to represent the concept (Grugulis *et al.* 2004: 5). As such, these theories are discussed in the context of their most frequently employed proxies, which are also sometimes adopted within skilled immigration policy design.

Human capital theory

Situated within neoclassical economic approaches to labour economics, human capital theory shares with that discipline key assumptions about individual decision-making, market mechanisms and personal choice. The human capital model is arguably the approach most often adopted within current government and academic analysis of skilled immigration. Generally, the focus is on the educational attainment of immigrants (e.g. Boeri *et al.* 2012; Brücker *et al.* 2013; Chaloff and Lemaitre 2009; Docquier and Marfouk 2005: 7; Docquier *et al.* 2011), although language acquisition is increasingly also viewed as human capital (e.g. Chiswick and Miller 1992, 1995, cited in Beiser and Hou 2000: 313). Governments frequently invoke the concept of human capital rhetorically in support of skilled immigration policy adoption (e.g. Evans 2010; Thompson 2001; UK Home Office 2002: para 2.18). As I discuss in Chapter 5, the Canadian points test from 2002 was dubbed a 'human capital' model due to its focus on language abilities and educational attainment.

Moving beyond the specific debates within skilled immigration over human capital to the broader field of neoclassical economics, Jean Gardiner (2000: 62) distinguishes between two definitions of human capital. The first sees human capital as the 'knowledge, skills and other attributes relevant to working capabilities'. A more focused definition, developed by the New Household economist, Gary Becker (1964), describes human capital as 'the outcome of deliberate investment [in education and work experience] on the part of individuals deciding to incur present costs for the sake of future benefits'. Both definitions of human capital are important as together they identify not only what qualities equate to 'human capital' but also the means by which human capital endowment is achieved.

These definitions suggest that human capital can be acquired either generally or specifically. It can be acquired on the job through general training in firms or educational institutions (with skills transferable across firms and sometimes even employment sectors) or through specific training (that benefits the productivity of the particular firm in which that training occurs) (Becker 1964: 8–29). Workplace training and educational training also interact in important ways. The relative emphasis placed upon these factors relates both to the extent of formalised knowledge required for a job, or alternately the importance of new technological advancements which may be more important at the workplace level (Becker 1964: 29).

I return to the salience of general and specific human capital for gender awareness later in this chapter. First, it is important to acknowledge that human capital theory makes certain key assumptions about productivity. Centrally, higher levels of knowledge and skills acquired primarily through education and workplace training are seen to translate into greater productivity and therefore higher wages (Becker 1993; McBride 2000: 161). Investment in training is viewed as an economic trade-off; short-term increases in earnings are foregone in pursuit of long-term investment in future earnings potential (Becker 1964). Further, wage levels are sometimes taken as a proxy for skill under the human capital approach. Under neoclassical economics, wages are reflective of workers' skills, which as another human capital theorist, George Borjas argues, 'are perfectly transferable between different labour markets' because 'profit-maximising employers are likely to value the same factor in any market economy' (Borjas 1987: 534). As Dan Hiebert (1999: 340) notes, a central assumption here is that workers are assigned positions in the labour market due to their 'economic worth'. This 'worth' is measured according to 'education, skill, age, experience, and past performance' and it finds expression in the wage distribution curve. As a corollary, variation in wages is attributable to different skill sets of workers.

Yet, human capital theory runs up against a global reality of deeply entrenched gender and racial inequalities in the labour market. Are these inequalities entirely attributable to differences in productivity between individuals? Faced with this empirical reality, human capital theorists have been motivated to develop theoretical accounts for such inequalities that are reconcilable with their existing assumptions. According to these theoretical extensions, women's underrepresentation in skilled professions is linked to the decision to have children, while racial clustering on the labour market is related to a lack of human capital in language and other cultural skills among ethnic minorities (Beach and Worswick 1993; Chiswick 1978; Mincer and Olec 1982). Theories of statistical discrimination add to the explanation that employers – expecting higher rates of attrition among women than men for instance – will be less likely to invest in specific skill training of women (Aigner and Can 1977; Phelps 1972). The theory of statistical discrimination operates from the assumption that as most members of a class (women) are viewed to behave in a certain way (bear children) employers will rationally discriminate against whole classes based upon their perceptions of likely future productivity (Moss and Tilly 1996: 254).[6]

Statistical discrimination does provide one explanation for the horizontal clustering of women within the service and educational sectors, and their under-representation in more firm-specific engineering and managerial occupations. Extending the statistical discrimination argument further in her analysis of the gender consequences of firm-specific human capital, Margarita Estevez-Abe (2012: 260ff.) argues that the latter have detrimental effects for women because of the interaction between specific skill training and career breaks. Under human capital models, career breaks for child caring and rearing are seen to contribute to lower wages and skill atrophy (citing Polachek 1981).[7] In short, these detrimental effects are greater for firm-specific training, where career breaks may require new skills accumulation in a new workplace, rather than allowing for portability across employers or industries. As such, Estevez-Abe argues that professions that focus on general human capital may be more adaptive to the life course vagaries experienced by many women than those focusing on firm-specific training. For the same reason, apprentice-based occupations, such as those in the trade areas, often require individuals to remain contractually bound to the same employer for a large number of years. Employer benefits accrue with apprenticeship years, again creating a statistical discrimination against employment of women who have higher rates of attrition (Estevez-Abe 2012: 262). Broadly speaking, these theorists suggest that general skill recognition may be more beneficial to women than specific skills approaches.

*Feminist industrial relations, sociological and economics critiques of
human capital theory*

Despite the contributions of statistical discrimination as an explanation for understanding gender inequalities on the labour market, human capital approaches still
overlook the political dimensions of skills definition and skill appraisal by employers. This brings me to the feminist critiques of human capital theory. Feminist
studies in industrial relations, sociology and economics challenge human capital
explanations in a number of ways. First, commentators argue that human capital
approaches are mechanistic in their account of how human capital accumulation
occurs; they fail to recognise the structural impediments to such skills accrual.
Second, critics demonstrate that attempts to equate earnings with actual skill levels fail to consider the gendered processes by which wages are negotiated; based
in part upon women's historical underrepresentation within collective bargaining
mechanisms and potentially also upon gendered socialised patterns of bargaining behaviour. Third, scholars argue that those jobs most closely associated with
women's private sphere caring and reproductive duties are commonly devalued
in wage bargaining processes. This is particularly true of care work. Each of these
critiques is examined in turn.

Structural impediments to skill accrual

Human capital theory provides individual-centred explanations for inequality
through its account of statistical discrimination. As Jamie Peck (1996: 3) criti-
cally summarises '[a]ccording to [the human capital] model, success in the labour
market is secured investments in education and training … while failure follows
from the individual inadequacies of workers'. As such, the decision to invest in
training is seen as intrinsic to the worker and largely unaffected by non-economic
externalities (Borjas 1996: 225).[8] Differences in earnings, even for those with similar human capital endowments, are explained on the basis of differences in productivity, which is itself a result of different skill levels inherent in the individual
(Borjas 1996: 233). As we saw above with the explanation of statistical gender
discrimination, following this logic, women expect discontinuous labour market participation and hence choose to under-invest in human capital, which in
turn lowers their productivity and wages (Mincer and Polachek 1974). Feminist
scholars counter that statistical discrimination converts structural impediments
to women's workforce engagement into questions of biologically informed choice
(Barker and Feiner 2004: 2). In addition, such explanations of discrimination fail
to appreciate variation across countries in labour market design and the consequences of such differences for gendered engagement in the labour market.

Theories of statistical discrimination, focusing as they do on rational employer
assumptions, provide insufficient explanations for variation in horizontal (occupational) gender segregation globally. Heidi Gottfried (2012: 43, citing Charles

2003: 269) defines horizontal segregation as the concentration of 'men in male-type occupations and women in female-type occupations', while vertical gender segregation is a form of 'hierarchical inequality, specifically men's domination of the highest status occupations'. Globally there are important differences in horizontal occupational clustering of men and women. In Eastern Africa, South-East Asia and Southern Asia and the Commonwealth of Independent States, both men and women are concentrated in skilled agriculture and fishery work. Outside of these regions, women are more likely to work in 'mid-level' occupations such as service workers in shops and market sales, while for men, agriculture, crafts and trades predominate (ILO 2012: 26; UNDESA 2010: 90). In fact, the International Labour Organisation (ILO) makes clear that horizontal concentration of women within the service sector has increased over the last two decades and that generally, women enjoy less occupational variation than men (ILO 2012: viii–ix, 2, 26). Across the OECD, there is strong female concentration within health and social work, education and community occupations (OECD 2012b: 153). There is also vertical segregation as women persist in the lower levels of occupations, and are unable to reach the apex of many professional sectors (UNDESA 2010: 91–2; see also ILO 2012: 25). These trends continue despite advancement in women's education globally, which in many countries now eclipses men's (OECD 2012b: Part IV). Such patterns challenge theories of statistical discrimination: if employer assumptions about likely fertility behaviour of women were the central reason for gender differentials on the labour market, why is there variation in occupational segregation across countries? Presumably, were this the case, employers would reach similar conclusions about women's propensity to exit the labour force for child bearing and rearing in a variety of countries.

Horizontal and vertical gender segregation in turn contributes to a significant pay gap between men and women. A 16 per cent pay gap exists globally between the sexes and this is in fact larger both in high-income countries and at higher professional levels. There is no OECD country where median wages of men and women are equal (Kofman and Raghuram 2009: 5; OECD 2012b: 166, 167). In addition, the wage gap interacts with age in important ways, leading to an average 9 per cent pay gap between men and women aged twenty-five to twenty-nine, but increasing to 24 per cent by the age bracket fifty-five to fifty-nine (OECD 2012b: 166). The OECD (2012b: 171) notes that 'gender differences in measured human capital, age (as a proxy for experience) and other demographic characteristics (such as marital status) do not account for much of the gender wage gap', challenging the assumptions of a simple equation between human capital, productivity and salary levels. In fact, the single biggest factor behind the wage gap appears to be hourly rates in various occupations (OECD 2012b: 171, citing Blau and Kahn 1997; Flabbi and Tejada 2012).

In short, feminist scholars and critical sociologists generally are not satisfied with human capital accounts of gender inequality on the labour market. They argue that such approaches focus on supply-side factors of individual employees and overlook central issues of discrimination and power (demand-side factors). Instead, these scholars suggest that both the political process by which wages are negotiated and the very definitions of what is considered 'skilled' is both socially constructed and deeply gendered.

Political negotiation and skills definition

Many of the critical approaches to skills definition focus upon the industrial context in which work is negotiated and where salaries are determined. This 'segmented' approach to labour market theory posits that there is an institutional basis for labour market outcomes determined by labour relations, labour law, workplace design, the role of trade unions, and by employer discrimination (Peck 1996: 11). The political process by which the meaning of 'skill' is essentially constructed can advantage key organisations, such as strongly organised professional bodies and trade-based unions, and disadvantage others, including women who may be underrepresented within these groups or lack other forms of collective representation (Grugulis *et al.* 2004: 5). As such, a distortion can occur through the wage negotiation process whereby the social perception of skill level does not match the actual skill level (Green 2011: 10). Drawing upon such political understandings of wage determination, Nancy Folbre (2012: 282) suggests that 'the individual and collective bargaining power of a worker is a primary determinant of earnings'. Extending this argument from a gender perspective, Folbre argues that men negotiate more aggressively than women and are more fulsomely rewarded when they do, which is likely to result in higher salaries in male-dominated professions (Folbre 2012: 282). Others have also noted that a failure on the part of women to negotiate pay is a significant determinant of gendered wage differentials that are compounded over the life course. Gendered differences in negotiation behaviour are in part informed by socialised norms of appropriate male and female demeanour and, for this reason, women can suffer a disadvantage when they negotiate in an aggressive 'male' style (Babcock and Laschever 2008). Some feminist theorists have also traced inequalities in pay across occupations to the historical dominance of men within the trade union movement and have argued that this has contributed to a higher valuation of occupations in which men predominate, as well as historical opposition to women's inclusion in some professions (i.e. Fincher 1997; Phillips and Taylor 1980; Steinberg 1990). These social constructivist approaches again challenge a simple causal link between productivity, wages and definitions of skill.

   Industrial relations scholars emphasise that employers constitute an important part of any wage negotiation process. Contrary to human capital approaches that suggest that employers select mechanistically on the basis of human capital attributes of applicants, critical approaches emphasise the role of 'soft skills' (emotional attributes) and employer bias in skills selection and wage negotiation. As Ewart Keep and Susan James (2010: 5) note, several factors vitiate against the classic human capital explanation for wage determination. First, employers are heterogeneous and may have different preferences. Second, with the rise of tertiary qualifications across many populations, the use of such achievements as the central basis for selection is devalued. 'Soft skills', in turn, become increasingly important. This argument is corroborated by recent research by the Confederation of British Industry (CBI 2007: 13) which indicates that employers place only 20 per cent weighting upon hard skills that are 'amendable to certification' with 80 per cent weighting placed upon so-called 'generic' and 'soft skills'. Soft skills include 'positive attitudes and dispositions ... leadership, industriousness perseverance, and a positive attitude towards authority' (Bowles and Ginitis 2002: 10–11). Physical appearance and social capital are also forms of soft skills that can equate to 'upper classness' (Brown and Hesketh 2004; Nickson and Warhurst 2001). This increasing focus on soft skills raises the spectre of bias in employer selection, as these factors are less clearly codified and, therefore, more prone to homophily (Fevre 1989; Jewson and Mason 1986). A substantial body of scholarship emphasises the role of racial and gender discrimination in informing perceptions of soft skills by employers (e.g. Blackburn *et al.* 2002; Moss and Tilly 1996), and this scholarship has also been applied in the immigration field, where immigrant nationality is sometimes viewed as a proxy for race (Ruhs and Anderson 2010: 14).

Aside from this emphasis on soft skills, employers may rely upon informal networks in selecting future workers. Informal networks tend to advantage men as they, again, often work from a basis of homophily, and men already dominate in positions of power (Durbin 2011: 95–6). In her analysis of the knowledge economy, Sylvia Walby (2011: 9) argues that 'networked forms of organization' can contribute to less gender equality. A key reason for this is that networks are often not subject to bureaucratic rules around gender equality, and thereby more discretionary than rule-bound modes of selection. She continues that '[n]etworks can act as forms of gendered social closure in a variety of ways. Male subcultures in employment can act as old boy's networks that create barriers in technical areas of work.' Focusing in on the role of networks within economic immigration policy, Christina Gabriel (2008: 170) similarly notes that 'women are given far less opportunities to undertake intercompany transfers, although they have an equal interest in doing so'. As Gabriel (2008: 170) adds, this observation 'takes on greater salience with the rise of mobility provisions within trade agreements and the shift in responsibility from state to private sector employers regarding temporary worker permits'. I consider this trend away from general human capital towards employer-focused skilled immigration selection models in Chapters 6 and 7.

Soft skills, care and defining skill

An additional debate within the skills literature revolves around the ways in which care work and emotional labour are valued or devalued on the labour market. This is in some ways the most radical of the critiques of the human capital model because it suggests that the occupations considered 'skilled' or 'unskilled' may be themselves identified as such on gender-biased grounds. This debate over the gendered definition of 'skill' is important in the immigration arena where the provision of overseas workers is seen as one central means of meeting care gaps in the economies of ageing societies (Cangiano *et al.* 2009; Moriarty 2010). Indeed, within migration studies, there is a rich body of work that considers the importance of care migration to feminised channels of movement (e.g. Kofman and Raghuram 2012) as well as the growing importance of immigrant care work to support the re-entry of domestic female workers into the labour market following periods of parental leave (Ehrenreich and Russell 2002; Kreimer and Schiffbänker 2005; Kilkey *et al.* 2010).

Within the feminist industrial relations and sociological scholarship, the term 'emotional labour' has emerged to define work involving a 'complex combination of facial expression, body language, spoken words, and tone of voice' (Rafaeli and Sutton 1987: 30, 33). Human interrelations, communication skills and emotional effort are central to this type of work (Steinberg and Figart 1999: 10). Stephen Appelbaum and Mary Gatta (2005: 2) place child care workers, nursery assistants, hotel housekeepers and retail clerks within the category of 'emotional labour'. A variety of feminist scholars argue that emotional labour has long been undervalued as skilled labour and that the very notion of 'skill' is in itself gendered. Anne Phillips and Barbara Taylor (1980: 79) proposed famously that '[s]kill definitions are saturated with sexual bias'. For these authors, and other feminist scholars (e.g. Sturdy *et al.* 1992; Tancred 1995: 16) skill is not an objective economic term, but rather the product of class-based and patriarchal contestations. These theorists also argue that seemingly ' "objective criteria" (e.g. knowledge and skills, mental demands, accountability and working conditions) are in themselves profoundly subjective' (Tong 1989: 59–60). Repeatedly, feminist economists and sociologists have demonstrated that care work and other forms of emotional labour are undervalued economically, even when education, experience, occupation and industry are controlled for statistically (England *et al.* 2002; Steinberg and Figart 1999). Occupations requiring 'nurturant' skills and those that provide a 'face-to-face-service' are often associated with women. Paula England and her collaborators (1994: 85) for instance, find that nurturant occupations suffer a negative wage impact, controlling for other explanatory variables such as cognitive ability, amenities, disamenities and organisational characteristics.[9]

A variety of explanations have emerged for the undervaluation of care and emotional work within skills appraisal. Makiko Nishikawa (2011: 115–16) argues that as caring skills are acquired implicitly through organisational mechanisms and relational experiences, rather than explicitly through formal educational institutions, these qualities are often not viewed as 'skilled' (see also Palmer and Eveline 2012: 265). Nishikawa's critique suggests an educational bias within existing definitions of 'skill'. Caring skills are also difficult to quantify and define, in part because they are relational and rely more upon non-credentialised 'soft skills' (Ruhs and Anderson 2010: 6) or what Eleonore Kofman (2013: 584) refers to as 'embodied knowledge' that 'results from experience gained from physical presence, practical thinking, material objects, sensory information and learning-by-doing'. As such, the mode of accrual for caring skills may be less acknowledged within existing practices that focus on formal educational and vocational training. Part of the devaluation of care and emotional labour also relates to its association with women's unpaid work in the private sphere, meaning that its contribution as paid work is often undervalued. The stereotype that caring work comes 'naturally' to women and that women give care altruistically in the private sphere (while men perform rationally and selfishly in the public sphere), may permit the undervaluation of care work within the paid economy (Folbre 2009; Gabriel and Pellerin 2008: 164–5).

Putting aside the need to challenge such gendered assumptions around bio-logically determined skill and altruism, one practical way in which to overcome this gendered delineation is to consider a larger number of professions as 'skilled'. Such an approach has been adopted in comparable worth claims, where activ-ists have argued, successfully, that certain occupations in which women predom-inate, such as nursing, should be reclassified as skilled (Steinberg 1990: 454). This approach also resonates with a preference for the general human capital approach discussed above.

Language, skill and gender: intersectional considerations

Thus far, I have focused my analysis upon gender and have excluded analysis of ethnicity and race. The question of whether and to what extent gender policy anal-ysis should simultaneously focus on a range of diversity issues is hotly debated within gender studies (Squires 2007: 156–7; Thorvaldsdóttir and Einarsdóttir 2006), in part because the importance of gender may be diminished through this process (Lewis *et al.* 2007). Due to these concerns but also because of the enormity of conducting meaningful intersectional analysis, this book does not consider this issue in detail. However, to overlook entirely the ways in which gender and diver-sity reinforce one another is impossible in the immigration field. It is on this basis that I consider language testing as a potential form of ethnic-language specific bias within skilled immigration selection criteria (Anthias and Yuval-Davis 1992; OSCE 2009: 8).[10]

The focus on language testing is rationalised by its importance both within human capital theory and also skilled immigration selection policy. Language is increasingly viewed as a form of human capital (Bellante and Kogut 1998; Boyd and Cao 2009; Chiswick and Miller 2002). According to this approach, language skills are accumulated on the basis of individual desire to invest in language training in pursuit of long-term economic returns (Chiswick and Miller 1992, 1995, cited in Beiser and Hou 2000: 313). However, human capital theorists rarely acknowl-edge possible obstacles to language learning and proficiency. The ability to learn a language is explained on intrinsic grounds; exposure to other language speakers

is the prime factor behind language learning and economic returns are viewed as
the key motivation (Chiswick and Miller 1992). A gender-aware analysis must also
consider the obstacles that women of non-English Speaking Background face in
developing second language skills. Jennifer Hyndman (1999: 7) argues that harder
language tests create greater burdens for women who due to their 'family responsibilities, societal norms, and economic circumstance' have less access to language
training than men. Similarly, Sedef Arat-Koc (1999a) argues that global gender
inequalities mean that women have fewer opportunities to gain education in foreign languages than men. As such, we must consider whether language proficiency
requirements operate as a structural obstacle within skilled immigration selection.
Language testing requirements may raise discriminatory effects for some ethnic
groups over others when some applicants already speak the native language,
whereas for others, significant new investment in skills is sought. Indeed, research
by Barry Chiswick and Paul Miller (2007) finds that the greater the difference
between the selecting country language and the country of origin language, the
less the language proficiency of an immigrant in the host society. Further, while
both women and men suffer this disadvantage, the presence of children has a far
greater impact upon the language acquisition of women then it does for men, controlling for other variables (Chiswick and Miller 2007: 32–6). Considering language is also important because it acknowledges that the disadvantages created
through skilled immigration selection may be intersectional, operating on both
gender and ethno-linguistic grounds, rather than simply on gender grounds alone.

Conclusion

This chapter has provided an overview of prevalent approaches towards labour
market engagement and skills definition, as well as gender critiques of such
approaches. The human capital approach that predominates within academic
studies of skilled immigration focuses on educational and language attainment.
Yet, the human capital approach is ill equipped to explain prevailing gendered
segregation, persistent gender wage gaps and enduring undervaluation of emotional labour globally – approaches that are refracted in the design of skilled
immigration policies. These approaches also fail to consider the differing life
courses of men and women, in particular, women's far greater preponderance
in part-time than full-time work and the heightened role of career breaks and
delayed career trajectories for women than men, related to differences in child
bearing and rearing. These critiques from feminist industrial relations and sociology are vital in broadening our understanding of the gendered nature of the
global labour market, including, I argue, the regulation of skilled immigration.
In the following chapter, I employ this theoretical discussion to develop indicators of gender awareness, which are then used to assess an array of current
skilled immigration policies.

Notes

1 An important exception here is Kofman (2013) who develops a typology of different types of knowledge that can be used to critique the focus on technical knowledge within European skilled immigration systems. Her critique is employed in the analysis of the undervaluation of care work in this chapter.

2 Cf. Eichhorst and Leschke (2012) who also find high reliance on part-time work by women in order to care for older children.

3 Note however that in real terms, the gendered wage gap remains for older women as well as women in the child rearing stages (Weinberger 2011).

4 In most countries, a gendered wage gap between men and women nonetheless remains. This is informed by a variety of factors and not only women's absence from the labour market during the child rearing years.

5 The second control-orientated approach to skill has not been given as much attention either in policy debates around skilled immigration or academic analysis for some time (Keep 2013). For this reason, it is not considered here.

6 Philip Moss and Chris Tilly (1996) also develop the theory of statistical discrimination with regard to African-American men.

7 For a critique of the assumptions of choice underpinning Polachek's approach, see England (1982).

8 George Borjas (1996: 229) does identify non-economic factors that might affect the assessment of 'r' or the rate of return on deferred earnings. However, this is not central to his analysis.

9 Jonathan Payne (2009: 361–2) has contested the idea that emotional labour is skilled given the limited level of control and task variation within such work. Feminist scholars are yet to deal with this particular counter-argument against the calls to reappraise emotional labour as skilled work.

10 For some, this treatment of ethnic and racial bias will be insufficient. I acknowledge that ethnic and racial bias play into immigration selection in a wide variety of ways and language testing is but one of these.

2

Gender awareness of skilled immigration policies across the OECD: presenting the GenderImmi data set

Introduction

When assessing the gender awareness of actual skilled immigration policies, it is necessary to consider gendered differences in life course events and different policy measures of 'skill'. On a process level, it is also essential to evaluate whether policy-makers incorporate gender assessment into policy design through gender mainstreaming audits and the collection of gender-disaggregated skilled immigration data. In this chapter, I apply the theoretical insights from Chapter 1 to develop indicators of gender awareness, which I then use to assess a variety of skilled immigration visa policies across twelve OECD countries and thirty-seven visa classes. This chapter presents the key findings of this empirical analysis based on a unique data set on skilled immigration and gender (the GenderImmi data set).

While the gender outcomes of skilled immigration is no doubt in part determined by individual agency and global gender inequalities, I argue that policy-makers in selecting countries also possess considerable scope in designing gender-aware selection policies. No one leader in the field emerges, although Canada does rank highly due to its use of gender audits and collection of gender-disaggregated immigration data, as well as attention to women's and men's differing life course trajectories. Yet, settler states, including Canada, are also more likely to emphasise youth, work experience and language testing, which can disadvantage female immigration applicants. Conversely, many continental European countries focus on wage thresholds to select immigrants, which reinforces global gendered wage gaps. At the same time, these states are also less likely to emphasise specific occupational sectors, an approach which generally targets key male-dominated professions. These findings are important not only to map the dependent variable of analysis in future chapters of the book (the extent of gender awareness of policies) but also more broadly for policy-makers and intergovernmental organisations interested in understanding how gender awareness of skilled immigration policies vary across countries. The next section of this chapter provides an overview of the indicators of gender-awareness indicators developed from the theoretical scholarship set out in Chapter 1. This is followed by explanation of the method and case selection, and then by the application of the indicators to the GenderImmi data set. In the final section of the chapter, I synthesise the findings of the analysis.

Development indicators of gender awareness within skilled immigration policies

The feminist scholarship set out in Chapter 1 provides a rich theoretical basis upon which to develop indicators of gender awareness within skilled immigration policy. As I argued in Chapter 1, such an exercise is necessary given the absence of an existing method to compare such policies cross-nationally. Aside from general information on the title of the visa and whether it is classed as temporary or permanent, the following indicators were considered:

Related to policy process issues and the availability of gender-disaggregated data, I considered the following:

- whether a gender audit of the visa was undertaken by a relevant government body;
- whether a gender auditing unit exists within immigration departments; and
- whether gender-disaggregated data are publically available for the visa.

With regards to life course career issues and their potential importance for gender awareness of labour market policies I considered:

- acknowledgement of career breaks in selection criteria;
- acknowledgement of part-time work in selection criteria;
- age limits; and
- entry dispensations for younger applicants.

Acknowledgement of career breaks in skilled immigration selection criteria reflects women's higher propensity for entrance and exit from the workforce, especially over the key child bearing and rearing years. At the same time, acknowledgement of part-time work is an important indicator that captures women's propensity to engage in part-time work in order to accommodate child bearing and, particularly, rearing. This is separate from the requirement that immigrants be employed on a full-time basis to ensure maintenance of visa conditions. The potentially gendered nature of settlement policy and rights to remain was not considered in the data set.

Age limits imposed for skilled immigration selection are important to consider from a gender perspective because they intersect with the key child bearing and rearing years for women – the late twenties and early thirties. The motherhood penalty on wages is also greatest for women in their thirties. Age limits overlook the fact that women's highest earning capacity occurs later than men's. Entry or selection dispensations for younger applicants exacerbate these forms of discrimination on gender grounds.

Finally, I consider a series of indicators that capture the ways in which skill is defined within skilled immigration selection criteria, and the possible obstacles to skills accrual that men and women face, namely whether:

- a wage threshold is used to select applicants and whether higher earning applicants received dispensations in meeting selection criteria;
- selection is largely determined by government or by employers;
- certain sectors are preferenced, or a general human capital model is adopted;
- care and emotional labour are recognised under skilled selection mechanisms; and
- language proficiency is treated as an assessable skill.

I consider the use of wage thresholds as this captures the ways in which skilled immigration selection reinforces existing gendered pay gaps. Also, as Eleonore Kofman (2013) argues, wage thresholds are increasingly employed as a key selection criterion across Western European skilled immigration selection regimes. I differentiate between government- and employer-determined selection to address the central issue of whether opportunities for employer discrimination arise in the selection process. Given the increased focus on 'soft skills' within recruitment, a growing role for employers within skilled immigration selection is highly relevant from a gender perspective. The focus on sectoral preference goes to the issue of general versus specific human capital models. As discussed in Chapter 1, general human capital models are seen to more adequately accommodate female career trajectories than specific human capital approaches. The recognition of care work and other forms of emotional labour captures the extent to which emotional labour is acknowledged as 'skilled work' within skilled immigration selection policy. Finally, considering language proficiency as an assessable skill is important given the possible challenges that language testing poses for female applicants, including women's lower rates of access to second language training. This indicator also captures the intersection of gender and ethno-linguistic disadvantage.

Case selection and method for the skilled immigration data set

These theoretically derived indicators were utilised in the creation of the GenderImmi data set of thirty-seven skilled immigration visa classes across twelve OECD countries. Case selection was based upon countries with high current patterns of skilled immigration as reflected in recent OECD *International Migration Outlook* reports (OECD 2011b, 2012a). I focus on the OECD because it is in those countries that the most available data and laws on immigration policy are available. This is not to discount the importance of skilled immigration to non-OECD countries, in particular Singapore, Hong Kong and South Africa, rather to focus on countries for which the most reliable legal and policy data are available. The analysis does not consider all relevant visa categories for the selected countries, rather the largest categories and those most obviously related to skilled immigration. To this end, flow data within each country were referred to in order to select the most relevant countries and visas. Ultimately, the country selection was: Austria, Australia, Belgium, Canada, Finland, France, Germany, Ireland, New Zealand, Norway, the United Kingdom (UK) and the United States (US). This selection represents an array of nations with variation in welfare states, labour markets, immigration histories (Cornelius *et al.* 2004; Freeman 1995) and policy attention to gender equality. Finally, in most cases, the analysis only covers visa categories that governments themselves identify as 'skilled'. However, for Canada, I include the Live-in Caregiver Program (LCP), a visa that allows entry of domestic helpers into Canada. While officially categorised as a low-skilled visa, some scholars have argued that this visa effectively brings highly skilled care workers into Canada (e.g. Macklin 1992). For this reason, I include the LCP within the current analysis. For the purposes of comparative historical analysis in future chapters of this book, the coding also encapsulates earlier consolidations of permanent skilled immigration points tests from Australia and Canada from 1999 and 2002 respectively, in addition to 2013 consolidations. For all other countries, the analysis only covers the immigration rules at 2 July 2013.[1] The various visas are organised into categories of selection approaches in Table 2.1.

Method

The thirty-seven visa categories were assessed according to the relevant indicators identified above. Binary, continuous and qualitative responses were recorded, depending upon the indicator of interest. The coding relied upon national laws, regulations and policy manuals from the relevant countries. These were assessed in English and, where not available, through translation by bilingual coders. The codebook is available online.[2] It is important to note that the focus was on the legal provision in actual policy documents. As such, the policy did not consider the implementation or interpretation of these laws by bureaucrats, which could contribute to further gendering effects beyond the laws themselves. For instance, discretion exercised by street level bureaucrats (Lipsky 1980) can be wielded in gendered and racially biased ways, but can also be mitigated through various administrative processes (Christensen *et al.* 2012; Wilkins 2007). Analysis of issues of implementation is beyond the scope of the current chapter, although it is considered in part in the focused case studies of Australia and Canada.

Table 2.1: Variation in skilled immigration selection methods across twelve OECD countries

Selection method	Description	Countries and relevant visas
Temporary, employer-sponsored work permit system	Temporary visa that requires employer to sponsor the individual through a job offer. Sometimes includes a labour market test to ensure no domestic worker is qualified for the position. Sometimes does not require employer to petition the application, but there must be a job offer in place.	Australia: Temporary Worker (457) visa Austria: 'Red-White-Red Subcategory Shortage occupations' and EU Blue Card Canada: Work Permit system; Live-in Caregiver Program; High and Low Skilled Temporary Immigration Denmark: Positive List Scheme; Pay Limit Scheme United States: L1, HB1 and 2 Finland: EU Blue Card; Residence Permit for an Employed Person; Specialist France: EU Blue Card Germany: Employee-Visa (Fachkräfte) Ireland: Green Card Permit; Work Permit New Zealand: Essential Skills Work Category Norway: Skilled Worker Residence Permits UK: Tier 2 (points-based – general); Tier 2 (points-based – intercompany transfer)
Temporary work permit system	Temporary visa that is untied to an employer. Sometimes on the basis of the immigrant's entrepreneurial or managerial skill. Generally offered to the elite or 'most skilled' immigration categories.	Austria: "Red-White-Red Subcategory Very Highly Skilled" and "other Key Workers Subcategory" Belgium: Highly skilled employees, Managers Danish: 'Greencard scheme' Germany: Blue Card System; Sole contractor New Zealand: Silver Fern
Permanent employer-based system	Permanent residency visa that allows an immigrant to settle in the country after having worked for an employer for a number of years.	Australia: Employer-Nomination Scheme Canada: Canadian Experience Class; Provincial Nominee Class United States: Employment third preference

Selection method	Description	Countries and relevant visas
Permanent general human capital model	Visa relies upon an enumerated sum of points or requirements for different factors. While a skills level threshold is set, beyond that, key occupations are not preferenced. Generally, more attention is paid to language ability and educational achievements than occupational factors.	Canada: Federal Skilled Worker points test (2002–8) United States: Employment second preference
Point-based system based on current sectoral demand	Visa relies upon an enumerated sum of points for different factors. Relevant skills vary according to current sectoral demand, which is usually set out on a skills list.	Australia: Skilled Independent visa Canada: Federal Skilled Worker Visa (since 2008); Federal Skilled Trades Class (since 2013) New Zealand: Skill Migration Category

Source: GenderImmi data set (created by author).

To ensure coder reliability, two coders both trained in immigration law coded all relevant visa regulations. The original intercoder reliability rating was 97.2 per cent and, following a coder meeting, all discrepancies were reconciled. This coding approach is similar to existing undertakings to typologise skilled immigration regimes in so far that they consult and then code relevant policies according to a variety of indicators (e.g. Cerna 2008, 2014; Chaloff and Lemaitre 2009; Gest *et al.* 2014; Kahanec and Zimmermann 2010; Lowell 2005; OECD 1998, 1999; Papademetriou *et al.* 2008). Yet, several factors differentiate this study from existing approaches. First, none of these existing undertakings explicitly considers gender relevant indicators. Second, many existing typologies focus on the nature of labour market controls and protections for domestic workers but do not necessarily focus on other more detailed aspects of skilled immigration admission, including the definition of skill, the differentiation between human capital and specific skill approaches, or reliance upon employer sponsorship (see only Papademetriou *et al.* 2008: 4). Finally, as Eleonore Kofman (2014: 2) argues, there is reason to believe that Western European skilled immigration selection methods differ substantially from those of more traditional settler states, necessitating evaluation of both from a gender perspective. In the following section of this chapter, I consider each of the relevant indicators according to both visa class and country.

Empirical findings and analysis

Gender mainstreaming processes: gender audits, gender units and gender-disaggregated data

Gender audits of public policy are an important means to draw policy attention to gender issues. In some countries, researchers external to government undertake gender audits of skilled immigration policies (e.g. Pillinger 2007 in Ireland and Badkar *et al.* 2006, 2007 in New Zealand). Generally, however, gender analysis of actual policies is sparse, and not undertaken by government. Even the Scandinavian countries of Norway, Denmark and Finland, that otherwise pride themselves on their general equality policies and are pioneers in areas of gender mainstreaming, do not undertake gender audits of their immigration selection policies (see OECD 2012b: section 3.1). This fact alone is surprising, given the proliferation of gender mainstreaming tools across industrialised economies into a variety of other policy domains. An important exception here is Canada, which has undertaken Gender-Based Analyses within its yearly Annual Reports to Parliaments since 2002. This practice, protected through provisions in the Immigration Refugee Protection Act, was a product of contestation by feminist actors (see Boucher 2010 for a history). Gender analysis is also a common feature within regulatory impact assessment statements of new immigration laws in Canada and, more recently, Treasury and Cabinet submissions (e.g. CIC 2012a). As such, Canada is currently the only country of the twelve that maintains a consistent practice of undertaking gender audits of its skilled immigration policies and programmes, and the only country with a gender auditing capacity within its immigration department. In the UK, Equality Impact Assessments were undertaken by the Home Office and the UK Border Agency in the development of its Points Based System, although Eleonore Kofman and collaborators (2009: viii, 23) argue that there is inadequate attention to gender issues within these audits, with simple notation of male and female skilled immigrant application outcomes. Further, despite calls in 2003 for the gender mainstreaming of immigration policies across Europe, in 2010, the European Women's Lobby (EWL) explicitly criticised the European Union for failing to 'integrate a gender perspective in immigration policies' (EWLA 2003; EWL 2010).

The GenderImmi data set similarly reveals a lack of available gender-disaggregated data on immigrant admissions. Only Canada publishes some gender-disaggregated data distinguishing between primary and secondary applicants (CIC 2011b).[3] Norway publishes detailed gender-disaggregated data for settlement outcomes, but not for entry (UDI 2013). Australia, New Zealand and the UK make gender-disaggregated immigration data available upon request, or via Freedom of Information inquiries, although these are time consuming to undertake (Badkar *et al.* 2007; Kofman 2013). Further, this lack of readily publically available data has been criticised by feminist scholars who argue that it in turn impedes detailed analysis of the role of gender within skilled immigration policies (Boucher 2007: 394–5; Kofman *et al.* 2005: 11).

Gendered career trajectories and life course events

Age

Age limits are a common feature of skilled immigration selection. They reflect a prevailing concern among policy-makers to limit the fiscal burden on host societies of retiring immigrant workers. Age has also been shown to be a central factor informing the economic outcomes of new immigrants, with youthful immigrants often performing better on the labour market (Schaafsma and Sweetman 2001). The economic rationale for the inclusion of age as a key skilled immigration selection criterion is therefore clear. As argued in Chapter 1, age can have different effects for women compared with men, given prevailing gendered life course trajectories. In Canada, New Zealand and Australia, the older are penalised in permanent skilled immigration schemes through fewer points. Regulations for the Federal Skilled Worker Program in Canada designate zero points for those forty-nine years or older, while the Canadian Federal Skilled Trades Class designates zero points for those fifty-four or older.[4] Increasingly, governments are favouring the very young, with both Australia and Canada allocating top points to those under thirty-five in their recent permanent skilled immigration reforms,[5] while Austria preferences those under thirty years in all of its visa classes.[6] In several countries, there is a maximum age beyond which applicants may no longer apply – forty years in Austria,[7] fifty years if employer sponsored in Australia,[8] fifty-six years in New Zealand for the standard skilled immigration visa and thirty-five years for the boutique temporary 'Silver Fern' visa.[9] In Germany, sole contractors over forty-five years cannot apply if they do not have a means to support themselves in old age.[10] In contrast, for other visas in other countries, such as the UK's Tier-2 system, there is no age threshold,[11] nor for visas in Belgium,[12] Finland,[13] France,[14] Ireland[15] or the United States.[16] Arguably, equal treatment of applicants irrespective of age has less negative gender impacts as it acknowledges the slower career trajectory many women face in light of child bearing and rearing breaks, as well as a continued glass ceiling in many occupations.

Work breaks and gendered life courses

Allowance for previous part-time work and the acknowledgement of non-continuous work experience are additional important indicators of gender awareness. Provision for these elements in policy design is particularly relevant given that work experience has taken on increased weighting within skilled immigration selection in many countries in recent years (Papademetriou *et al.* 2008: 22). The GenderImmi data set reveals considerable variation in attention to both these life course issues.

In many countries, for many highly skilled visas, full-time work experience is a condition of entry. Legal stipulation occurs in a variety of ways. For instance in Austria,[17] in the US for all three visas, the EB-3, the H1B and the L1 visas[18] and Australia for the Skilled Independent visa[19] full-time work experience is an explicit visa requirement. Under New Zealand's permanent skilled immigration visas, points are allocated for part-time work experience but are calculated pro rata.[20] In some countries, dispensations are given for the accumulation of work experience over a number of years, situated within a longer period (i.e. non-continuous work experience is permitted). For instance, in the United States, applicants for the L1 Intracompany Transfer Visa have three years to gain the necessary one year of full-time work experience.[21] This option for 'interrupted' or 'non-continuous' work experience is available in seventeen of the visas considered. It is more common in the settler state countries (Australia, Canada, New Zealand) and in the United Kingdom than in the continental European countries.

Yet, even when part-time or non-continuous work experience is not explicitly excluded as a condition of admission or visa maintenance, such experience can be excluded implicitly through wage thresholds that render part-time work, in practice, unachievable. This is the case for the transposition of the EU Blue Card from 2009 into the domestic laws of many member states. The minimum gross salary for a skilled immigrant ranges from 1.2 to 1.5 times the national domestic mean salaries and in many cases is significantly higher (Cerna 2010: 26; Kofman 2014: 119; see also Table 2.2 below). While the effect of salary thresholds upon the possible recognition of part-time work is not always clearly articulated in policy documents, with some visas, such as the UK's Tier 2 (points based – general) employer sponsored visa, it is clear that part-time work cannot be pro-rated to equate to full-time salaries.[22] Conversely, in several countries, educational attainments, rather than work experience are the key selection criterion (for instance France for the Highly Skilled Immigrant Visa).[23] This requirement would seem to reduce the gendered pressures of continuous or full-time work experience that is placed upon female applicants and thereby offers a more gender-aware approach.

Definitions of 'skill' and their implications for gender awareness

As discussed in Chapter 1, 'skill' can be defined in a number of ways and is measured through different policy proxies. These different proxies carry with them different gender implications. I consider these different proxies in turn and explore how these approaches play out in skilled immigration regulation.

Table 2.2: Wage distribution amounts in different countries in Euros

Country	Visa	Amount
Australia	Temporary Worked Long-Stay 457 visa	54,409.50
Austria	Key workers subcategory (sectoral demand)	25,200–30,456 per year for those > 30
	EU Blue Card	50,113
	Red-White-Red Card (very qualified persons)	12,000
	Red-White-Red (other key workers)	12,000
Belgium	Highly skilled employees	37,721
	Managers	62,934
	EU Blue Card	49, 995
Denmark	Pay Limit Scheme	50,250
Finland	EU Blue Card	56,004
	Specialist	48,000
France	EU Blue Card	52,752
Germany	EU Blue Card (standard professions)	46,400
	EU Blue Card (in-demand professions)	36,192
Ireland	Green Card	60,000
	Work Permit	30,000
Norway	Skilled Worker Residence Permit (with bachelor degree)	48,212
	Skilled Worker Residence Permit (with masters degree)	50,107
UK	Tier 2 (points-based – general, on shortage list)	23,741
	Tier 2 (Intercompany transfer,)	28,398

Notes: Most of these amounts are indexed for 2012. Amount standardised into Euros, based on exchange rate on 2 July 2013. The salary range for each visa class is given where appropriate: www.oanda.com.
Source: GenderImmi data set (created by author).

Human capital methods of selection – the choice between general and specific human capital

Chapter 1 identified the crucial distinction in human capital theory between general and specific skill. This distinction is critical not only from a gender perspective but also because these theoretical approaches are increasingly translated into skilled immigration selection models that focus on 'sectors in demand' – key economic sectors that face labour market gaps. Some analysts have argued that the general human capital approach to immigration selection, insofar that it accepts a broad range of occupations, is more gender aware than other methods of skilled immigration selection. Citizenship Immigration Canada in its first Gender-Based Analysis of the Federal Skilled Worker points test in 2002, for instance, proposed that in expanding the range of relevant occupations, the newly adopted points test would have a gender positive effect (CIC 2001a). This view has been corroborated by Eleonore Kofman and Parvati Raghuram (2009: 4–5) who argue that general human capital approaches may be 'more equal' than other selection methods. Christina Gabriel (2005: 172) in contrast has been more sanguine about the possible gender awareness of human capital models for highly skilled immigration selection. She argues that skilled immigration is gendered, irrespective of which mode of selection is adopted. She argues that the focus on high levels of education and language training required within both general and specific understandings of human capital renders both problematic from a gender perspective. Nonetheless, insofar that the general human capital model accepts a broader range of occupations and insofar that general human capital skills are more portable, such an approach would appear to be more gender aware than a specific focus. Indeed, a study by Citizenship Immigration Canada reveals that during the period that Canada adopted a general human capital model (2002–2008), gender distributions in its Federal Skilled Worker Program improved significantly (CIC 2011b). I return to this crucial issue of specific versus general human capital models in Chapters 5 and 6.

Looking at the broader GenderImmi data set, it is clear that most countries are eschewing a general human capital model in favour of more targeted, sector specific approaches. As Table 2.1 above reveals, as of July 2013, no country, other than the United States under its Employment Second Preference, adopts a pure 'human capital' model, with Canada discarding this approach in 2008 and Australia in 1999.

Since the global financial crisis in 2008–9, specific human capital approaches are increasingly common in skilled immigration selection. As Jonathon Chaloff and Georges Lemaitre (2009: 35–6) argue, concerns over the protection of domestic workers motivated the development by governments of targeted occupational shortage lists (also known as 'occupation in demand lists'). These lists enumerate the professions under which immigrants can apply and are changed frequently in response to labour market fluctuations. Australia, Canada, New Zealand, Ireland and the UK all have some form of occupational list within their skilled immigration programmes.[24] Sectoral focus takes on a heightened importance in New Zealand and Australia where an Expression of Interest (EOI) system now supplements traditional points test methods for permanent skilled immigration. Applicants do not have a right to immigrant entry. Rather, they may express an interest in admission, which is then assessed by the relevant immigration department. In essence, the EOI system means those occupations identified as being in demand have a higher chance of success and are quickly prioritised for visa processing.[25]

The gender implications of specific skills lists depend greatly upon the ways in which these lists are created, and the occupations that are on the list. In several countries, narrowing of occupational lists in recent years has seen the removal of key professions in which women predominate. For instance, in Ireland, female immigrants are underrepresented in the highly paid occupations included on the list, and overrepresented in the feminised sectors of catering, domestic work and care, all of which have been removed in recent years (Pillinger 2006, 2007: 20–1). Given global horizontal gender segregation, women are generally underrepresented within the natural sciences and information communication technology (ICT) – both areas that now predominate on relevant skill lists (Kofman and Raghuram 2009: 4; Truss *et al.* 2012: 739). In addition to this sectoral narrowing under way in skilled occupational lists, some countries also undertake vertical segregation, in the sense that only the upper ranks of occupational hierarchies are considered. For instance, the list for Australia's temporary long-stay visa (457s) includes child care centre managers but not child care workers.[26] Given prevailing vertical gender segregation across industries, a movement towards 'top tier' sectoral occupations could inform differential opportunities for male and female applicants.

Horizontal concentration of women in key occupations may nonetheless also benefit female applicants if the areas in which they are located are on the shortage list (Badkar *et al.* 2006: 8). The most obvious occupation here is nursing, which is frequently included on skills lists. For instance, in New Zealand, the bulk of skilled female applicants enter through one subcategory – Life Science and Health Professionals – mostly as nurses and midwives (Badkar *et al.* 2006: 24, 2007: 130–1). In Australia nurses make up a large section of women's entry into General Skilled Migration (Hawthorne 2011: xvi). Generally, however, analysis suggests that specific-skills approaches tend to focus on male-dominated professions and exclude those where women predominate – a point explored further below.

Wage threshold methods of selection

The wage threshold is a key proxy for 'skill' within skilled immigration selection policies, especially in many European Countries since the transposition of the EU Blue Card in 2009 (Cerna 2010: 26).[27] Wage thresholds hold clear gender implications given global gendered pay gaps. Under the wage threshold approach, a minimum wage is set as the threshold criterion for entry (see Cerna 2014). Wage thresholds are intended in part to protect immigrant workers against exploitation by ensuring that they receive a decent wage commensurate to skill sets. Such thresholds may also play an important domestic labour market protection role. Yet, wage thresholds also hold deeply gendered implications. Insofar that wage distribution selection methods rely principally upon wages, existing global gendered wages gaps are reinforced. Wage thresholds can present a limited method for defining skill when the political realities of wage negotiations are factored into the equation.

Australia, Canada and the US do not use wage limits for their permanent skill migration visas, which is beneficial from a gender perspective. That said, both Australia and Canada employ national skill classification systems to define skill, which can in turn lead to the exclusion of low-paid and female-dominated occupations from admission, an issue I return to below in the discussion of emotional labour and work.

Employer-determined methods of selection

The global financial crisis has also contributed to an increased focus upon employer-determined models of selection (Chaloff and Lemaitre 2009: 21). Also known as the 'demand driven models', employer-determined approaches exist for both temporary and permanent skilled immigration visas, and can be combined with sectoral demand, or wage distribution requirements. These approaches give power to employers as the central arbiters of selection either because a job offer is a condition of entry, or because employers must petition immigration departments to seek a visa on behalf of the applicant (OECD 2006: 113–14).

When choosing immigrants, employers rely not only upon relevant qualifications but also 'soft skills' and existing networks. The potential discriminatory effects of employer-determined approaches are reflected in recent studies of skilled immigration. Lesleyanne Hawthorne (2011: 157) highlights that the top ten countries for selection under the employer-sponsored visa into Australia differ greatly from the permanent skilled independent immigration visa. Within the employer-sponsored visa categories, there is a much stronger preference for applicants from English-Speaking Background countries than for the permanent points-tested visas. A survey conducted of Australian employers in the fields of accounting, information technology, medicine, nursing and trades, found that when employing former international students, employers considered human capital qualifications such as grades and enrolment achievements but also 'soft' qualities such as 'cultural fit' and 'perceived overall employability' (Arkoudis *et al.* 2009: Chapter 5; Hawthorne 2011: xiii). Employer preference for applicants with university qualifications from Western countries has been long recognised in the immigration scholarship (Dobrowolsky and Tastsoglou 2006: 21; Kofman 2004: 654; Perrenas 2000). Gender discrimination in employer sponsorship has been less explored, although preference for male over female applicants is observable in the employer-sponsored green-card permit system in Germany (Badkar *et al.* 2006: 8). In general, a focus on employer selection heightens the capacity for employers to undertake these subtle forms of ethnic- or gender-based adjudication that are precluded from more transparent forms of state-based immigration selection, such as points tests. As Hawthorne (2011: 157) argues, employer-determined selection methods 'allow employers to filter the characteristics of future [applicants], a trend likely to significantly affect future diversity'. These issues are not without significance: employer-determined selection predominates as a form of skilled immigration selection across the OECD, making up twenty-three of the thirty-seven visas.

Emotional labour and care work as skilled work

Irrespective of whether skilled immigration selection models are government- or employer-initiated, there is an enduring and growing demand for care and health service workers in most post-industrial societies. Structural ageing and a gradual inversion of the dependency pyramid exacerbate the need for such workers (OECD 2012a: 74–5; Spencer *et al.* 2010: 15). Personal and service sectors are both heavily feminised and immigrant-dominated occupations (Kofman and Raghuram 2009: 1–2). A central question therefore is whether immigration policies recognise care work and other forms of emotional labour as skilled work. As Christina Gabriel and Hélène Pellerin (2008: 162–3) argue, different rights and privileges flow to immigrants depending on whether they are classified as 'skilled' or 'unskilled'. These rights and privileges range from easier entry requirements, to different incentives to locate, to different rights to (or exclusions from) permanent settlement, to varying levels of regulatory scrutiny following entry. Assuming that structural economic demand exists for such work, the exclusion of care workers from skilled immigration channels may lead some workers to enter via other immigration routes, such as through family reunification, asylum or, when it exists, through low-skilled, temporary routes, such as the Live-in-Caregiver Program in Canada. Irregular migration is also a common mode of entry for care workers (Piper and Yamanaka 2008; Spencer *et al.* 2010: 25–6). Entrants on low-skilled temporary visas generally have fewer portability rights to permanent residency than those coming through highly skilled temporary channels and significantly fewer social, political and civic rights after entry (Gabriel 2005: 173–4). As such, the labelling of an occupation as either 'skilled' or 'unskilled' can have fundamental implications for the future residency, rights and status of an immigrant. I explore these issues in detail in Chapter 7.

Given this relevance of the 'skilled/unskilled' divide, it is necessary to consider whether states classify key forms of emotional labour as skilled occupations. I adopt Appelbaum and Gatta's (2005: 2) definition of 'emotional labour' as comprising child care workers, retirement home workers, nursery assistants, hotel housekeepers and retail clerks. The GenderImmi data set indicates that in most skilled immigration schemes, there are limited avenues for care workers, or other forms of emotional labourers, to enter. Some visa classes explicitly exclude these occupations, through their sectoral lists or occupational definitions of skill on which such jobs are not listed. For instance, some skilled visas, such as the Red-White-Red Card (Shortage Occupations) in Austria[28] or the EU Blue Card in Germany[29] or the Federal Skilled Worker and Federal Skilled Trades Class in Canada[30] only list male-dominated science and technology professions and trade occupations. In other skilled immigration schemes, this gendering effect occurs implicitly, given that care work does not meet national occupational classification thresholds. For instance, given that permanent skilled immigration to Australia and Canada is limited to top-level occupational classifications, care workers, who are classed in lower 'lesser-skilled' ranks, are necessarily excluded.[31] In other OECD countries, although care work is not explicitly excluded from skilled immigration admission criteria, salary thresholds bar care workers as they generally garner low wages.

A practical example arose in negotiations over the new skilled immigration points system in the UK during the mid-2000s. After changes in 2007, care work was no longer classified as 'skilled' as such workers did not meet formal qualification requirements nor were such workers paid over £7.02 pounds per hour – both central requirements for the newly created 'Tier 2' admission (Cangiano *et al.* 2009: 39–40). As a result of these restrictions, by 2007 only 1,005 care workers entered the UK, compared with 22,000 between 2001 and 2006. In 2008, this situation worsened when the shortage list salary threshold for Tier 2 was raised to £8.80 per hour (MAC 2008). Following contestation by care sector workers and trade unions, the level was reduced to £7.80. Yet, in 2011, all forms of care workers were removed from the skilled list, meaning that there is now effectively no longer a mechanism to bring care workers into the UK via skilled immigration channels (UKBA 2011).[32]

The GenderImmi data set identified a few limited exceptions to the general rule that skilled immigration regulation does not include entry mechanisms for emotional labourers. The Greencard Scheme and the Positive List Visa in Denmark both provide entry for child care workers (Spencer *et al.* (2010: 25–6). The LCP (Live-In Caregiver Program) in Canada also creates a special temporary visa exclusively, as the title suggests, for caregivers who live in the home of the person to whom they provide care. However, this visa is generally viewed in Canada as a 'low-skilled' visa and does not confer the same rights and privileges as permanent highly skilled visas.[33] A small number of visas also provide entry points for other forms of emotional labour. For instance, the Australian permanent Employer Nomination Scheme visa and the temporary 457 visa both provide entry for forms of community workers and child care managers.[34] Yet overwhelmingly, the occupational areas where women predominate do not fit within skilled immigration selection criteria.

The obstacles of language proficiency

Language testing has increased as a key method of selection within skilled immigration selection as well as within citizenship tests globally (McNamara and Shohamy 2008). As discussed in Chapter 1, language testing can pose greater challenges for women then men given the impediments of child rearing to the accrual of competency in a second language (Chiswick and Miller 2007). The GenderImmi data set demonstrates considerable variation in attention to language proficiency across skilled immigration visas. Fifteen of the thirty-seven visa classes include language proficiency in the native language of the host society as a selection requirement. Language proficiency is more often a criterion for permanent entry and for government-based modes of selection, such as the Greencard Scheme in Denmark[35] or the Skilled Independent class in Australia,[36] than for temporary employer-sponsored visas, where the employer theoretically vets the potential immigrant for language skill through the application process. In some countries, such as the UK, citizens of former British colonies are excluded from language testing requirements,[37] although in other countries such as Canada, these dispensations have been removed. While it is impossible to benchmark countries against language requirements – as many adopt tests specific to their country's language – it is clear that formalised language testing is most often a requirement in the Anglo-Saxon countries (Australia, Canada, New Zealand, Ireland and the United Kingdom). Of these countries, Australia enforces the highest levels of language testing under the International English Language Testing System (IELTS), requiring Level 6 (component English) in all four categories of assessment, for its Skilled Independent (permanent) visa.[38] In several countries, including Denmark for its EU Blue Card, higher levels of language proficiency attract more points under the selection grid.[39] The implication of increased language testing not only for female applicants but also those of linguistically diverse backgrounds is clearly an issue that demands further attention. Yet, at present, none of the countries examined undertakes ethnic or linguistic analysis of its immigration policies.[40]

Concluding analysis

Around the world, women work less than men in paid work and more than men in unpaid work. When paid and unpaid work are combined, women work more than men overall, although enjoy fewer economic returns for their labour. Women in paid work are employed disproportionately in lower ranked and paid jobs, and are clustered in the service and care sectors. There is strong horizontal and vertical gender segregation in the world of work, particularly within the post-industrial nations that select the bulk of the world's skilled immigrants. Women work more in part-time positions than men and take far longer periods of leave for child bearing and rearing purposes (UNDESA 2010: Chapter 4). The United Nations, in its World Women's Survey of Work, depicts a fairly depressing and highly gendered global labour market, particularly at the higher skilled echelons and particularly within advanced industrial economies. On this basis, some might contend that any form of skilled immigration selection will necessarily mimic these patterns.

Certainly, this chapter makes clear that key features of skilled immigration policy are gendered cross-nationally. The first relates to the definitions and proxies for 'skill' within skilled immigration policies. As Martin Ruhs and Bridget Anderson (2010: 26–7) note, '[t]here is a tension between the notion of "skills" as technical and formally measureable and the more conceptually equivocal use of the term that has come to characterize not just employers' expressions of demand for labour, but debates and policies in employment, education, and training more generally'. The slipperiness of the term 'skill' may in part have motivated governments to adopt definitions that evade these hard questions or that pass decision-making onto others (such as through employer-determined models). As this chapter has discussed, there is considerable variation in the ways in which 'skill' is measured within immigration selection from education levels (general human capital), to workplace-specific qualifications, to wage thresholds, to sectoral demand, to language proficiency. One shared commonality is that most countries and visas fail to recognise care work and other forms of emotional labour as skilled labour. In some countries, such as Ireland and the UK, care work has been removed from skill shortage lists.

How do the data presented in this chapter fit together to map a picture of gender patterns in skilled immigration policies across the OECD? Does the analysis reveal exemplars and laggards in terms of attention gender issues in skilled immigration policy? Table 2.3 provides a summarised index of gender awareness, which aggregates all binary variables considered in this chapter. As such, it excludes both wages and age limits. Weighting all indicators equally, it is apparent that visa classes vary in the extent of their awareness. Interestingly, aside from Canada which scores highly across all of its visas due to its collection of gender-disaggregated data, gender analysis of immigration laws and the presence of an institutionalised gender unit within its immigration bureaucracy, no one country ranks consistently on the index. Generally, permanent visas tend to rank more highly than temporary ones and visas requiring general human capital such as education or language rank higher than those with specific sectoral demands. For instance, the Canadian Federal Skilled Worker visa from 2002 is the highest ranked on the index, and Denmark's Pay Limit Scheme also ranks highly as it does not target particular sectors and allows for career breaks. Short-term, employer-sponsored work permits with sectoral focus, and those accompanied with wage thresholds (such as in Norway and Ireland) rank lower. Australia and Canada have both dropped in their rankings over time, an issue that I return to in the qualitative case studies in the second part of this book. At present there are no clear exemplars for gender-aware skilled immigration policies, with all states demonstrating possible areas for improvement. Indeed, while Canada is a leader in the publication of gender-disaggregated data and gender auditing of immigration policy, other policy developments in Canada have been mixed from a gender perspective.

Attempts to categorise the data set into groups or categories of gender awareness have been unsuccessful, with neither Factor Analysis nor Qualitative Comparative Analysis eliciting clear 'types'. This suggests that there are different pathways to gender awareness (or unawareness) within skilled immigration selection, rather than one 'ideal' category or typology. This analysis also highlights that classic gender-awareness regimes such as the welfare state typologies (e.g. Gottfried 2012: Chapter 7; Lewis 1992) do not explain gender awareness within skilled immigration policies.

The variation across countries in gender awareness raises an important explanatory question: why do skilled immigration policies differ with regard to their

Table 2.3: Gender-awareness index of skilled immigration policies

Visa	Gender ranking
Canada Federal Skilled Worker (2002)	7
Canada Federal Skilled Worker (2013)	6
Canada Live-in Caregiver	6
Canada Federal Skilled Trades (2013)	5
Denmark Pay Limit Scheme	5
Canada Temporary Foreign Worker Permit	4
Denmark Positive List Scheme	4
New Zealand Essential Skills Work Category (Temporary)	4
UK Tier 2 Intercompany Transfer	4
Belgium EU Blue Card	4
Denmark Greencard Scheme	4
New Zealand Skilled Migrant Category (Permanent)	4
Austria EU Blue Card	3
Australia Temporary Skilled 457 Visa	3
Belgium Highly Skilled Employees	3
Belgium Manager	3
Finland EU Blue Card	3
Finland Specialist	3
United States Employment Third Preference	3
United States H1B Visa	3
Austria Red-White-Red Visa (other key workers)	3
Australia Skilled Independent (1999)	3
Australia Employer Nomination Scheme	2
France EU Blue Card	2
United States Employment Third Preference	2
Germany Research Card	2
Ireland Green Card	2
Norway Skilled Worker Residence Permit	2
France Highly Skilled Immigrant Visa (CCT)	2
Austria Red-White-Red Visa (shortage)	2
Germany Self Employed	2
New Zealand Silver Fern	2
Germany Blue Card	1
Australia Skilled Independent (2013)	1
Ireland, Work Permit	1
UK Tier 2 Points-Based – General	0
Austria Red-White-Red Visa Very Highly Qualified Persons	0

Source: GenderImmi data set (created by author).

gender awareness? Classic feminist explanations related to the broader gender awareness of public policies do not appear applicable, nor do they assist in understanding intra-country variation. In the following chapter, I present and develop a venue shopping account of policy variation from within public policy theory and suggest extensions to an analysis of skilled immigration policy-making. The next chapter also examines alternate theories that might be used to understand variation in gender awareness of skilled immigration policies before defending the venue shopping approach. These theories are then applied to four Australian and Canadian case studies in the second part of the book.

Notes

1 This chapter states the law at 1 July 2013 across all visas, except for the historical coding for Australia and Canada from 1999 and 2002 respectively. It is possible that laws have since changed in various countries and, for this reason, this chapter should not be relied upon for the most recent statement of skilled immigration policies, although the referenced laws in the bibliography direct the reader to the appropriate acts and statutes for further consultation.

2 The codebook will be made available on the author's website following publication of this book (http://sydney.edu.au/arts/government_international_relations/staff/profiles/anna.boucher.php).

3 As I argue in further detail in Chapter 4, this distinction is central within immigration policy as the principal applicant is the lead applicant who must meet the selection criteria. The secondary applicant is reliant upon the principal applicant for admission and, in some countries, ongoing residency status. Only data disaggregated according to principal and secondary admission and gender capture the nuances of gendered immigration outcomes.

4 IRPR Canada, regulation 81; regulation 102.1.

5 Canada: IRPR regulation 81(a); for the skilled trades, the age limit is much higher at 50: IRPR regulation 102.1 a); Australia: DIAC (2012c).

6 Austria: Bundesministerium des Innernes (2013), 'Other Key Workers' (Bundesministerium des Innernes: Vienna); Bundesministerium des Innernes (2013), 'Skilled Workers in Shortage Occupations' (Bundesministerium des Innernes: Vienna).

7 Austria: Bundesministerium des Innernes (2013), 'Other Key Workers' (Bundesministerium des Innernes: Vienna); Bundesministerium des Innernes (2013), 'Skilled Workers in Shortage Occupations' (Bundesministerium des Innernes: Vienna).

8 Employer sponsored: Migration Regulations, 186.231 and 186.221; age limits do not apply for the temporary worker (skilled) subclass 457 visa or for the new General Skilled Migration Visa.

9 INZ [Immigration New Zealand] (2012a), 'Immigration New Zealand Operational Manual: Residence' (Immigration New Zealand), SM4.5; INZ [Immigration New Zealand] (2012b), 'Immigration New Zealand Operational Manual: Temporary Entry' (Immigration New Zealand), WL2.10.

10 Aufenthaltsgesetz 2005, s21(3).

11 Home Office UK Border Agency (2012), 'Tier 2 of the Points Based System – Policy Guidance' (12/12 edn. London: Home Office UK Border Agency).

12 Mussche, N., Corluy, V., and Marx, I. (2010), 'Satisfying Labour Demand Through Migration in Belgium: Study of the Belgian Contact Point of the European Migration Network' (Brussels: Immigration Office/Commissioner General for Refugees and Stateless Persons/Centre for Equal Opportunities and Opposition to Racism).

13 Finnish Immigration Service [Maahanmuuttovirasto] 'The EU Blue Card for Work that Requires High Level Competence' (Helsinki: Maahanmuuttovirasto).

14 European Commission (2013), 'France: What do I Need Before Leaving? Highly Qualified Worker' (EU Immigration Portal).

15 Department of Jobs, Enterprise and Innovation [Ireland] (2011), 'Employment Permits Arrangements: Guide to Green Card Permits' (Dublin).

16 Immigration and Nationality Act 1952, Section101(a)(15)(L); United States Codes, Chapter 8, Sections 214; 1153.

17 Bundesministerium des Innernes (2013), above.

18 8 United States Federal Code (USC) 1153 (3)(A)(i); 8 Code of Federal Regulations (CFR) 214.2(h)(iii)(A); 8 CFR (214.2)(l)(1)(i).

19 DIAC (2012a); Migration Regulations Australia, 1994 2.26AC and Schedule 6D – Part 6D.3 and Part 6D.4.

20 INZ [Immigration New Zealand] (2012b), 'Immigration New Zealand Operational Manual: Residence' (Immigration New Zealand), s11.5.1.

21 8 Code of Federal Regulations 214.2(l)(1)(i).

22 Home Office UK Border Agency (2013), 'Tier 2 of the Points Based System – Policy Guidance' (07/13 edn. London: Home Office UK Border Agency), Part 73, page 19.

23 French Office of Immigration and Integration (2013), 'For the Promotion of Economic Migration'. Paris.

24 Although in the UK and Ireland, it is also coupled with a requirement of employer sponsorship.

25 INZ [Immigration New Zealand] (2012b), 'Immigration New Zealand Operational Manual: Residence' (Immigration New Zealand), SM3.15.1; DIAC (2012c); Immigration Regulations Australia, Schedule 2, regulation 189.211.

26 DIAC (2013c), 'Consolidated Sponsored Occupation List (SOL) Schedule 1 and 2'.

27 The United Kingdom, Ireland and Denmark are not part of the EU Blue Card Directive scheme; however, nonetheless they use wage thresholds to set minimal selection criterion for some of their skilled immigration visas (Kofman 2013: 593).

28 Bundesministerium des Innernes (2013), 'Skilled Workers in Shortage Occupations'.

29 Bundesministeriums, Bundesministeriums für Arbeit und Soziales und des and des Innern (2013), 'Verordnung zur Änderung des Ausländerbeschäftigungsrechts' (Bonn: Bundesministeriums für Arbeit und Soziales und des Bundesministeriums des Innern).

30 Immigration Refugee Protection Regulations (2002), ss75; 87.2(1); for occupational targeting for the FSWP class, see the relevant ministerial instrument powers: CIC (2013d), 'Specific eligibility criteria – Federal skilled workers' (Ottawa: CIC), www.cic.gc.ca/english/immigrate/skilled/apply-who-instructions.asp?expand=jobs#jobs, accessed 14 February 2013. There are certain exceptions against occupational targeting for those with a job offer in Canada, or completion of a Canadian PhD.

31 This is a product of the National Occupational Classification Scheme in Canada and the Australian and New Zealand Standard Classification of Occupations (ANZSCO) that classify care work as semi-skilled or unskilled work. I consider this issue further in Chapters 5 and 6.

32 One argument in support of this change was that such workers would be sourced predominately from the new European Union accession states (Spencer *et al.* 2010: 25–6).

33 IRPR, s112(e).

34 DIAC (2013c), 'Skilled Occupation List (SOL) Schedule 1 and 2' (Canberra: Department of Immigration and Citizenship) www.immi.gov.au/skilled/sol/, accessed 14 February 2013.

35 Danish Immigration Service (2013), 'The Greencard Scheme' (Copenhagen: Danish Immigration Services), https://www.nyidanmark.dk/en-us/coming_to_dk/work/greencard-scheme/greencard-scheme.htm, accessed 14 February 2013.

36 Migration Regulations Australia 1994, regulation 189.213.

37 United Kingdom Border Agency (2013), 'Tier 2 (General) English Language' (London: UKBA), www.ukba.homeoffice.gov.uk/visas-immigration/working/tier2/general/eligibility/englishlanguage/, accessed 13 August 2013.

38 189.213 Schedule 2 Migration Regulations Australia 1994; Reg 1.15C – Migration Regulations 1994. New Zealand requires an *average* of 6.5: INZ [Immigration New Zealand] (2012b), 'Immigration New Zealand Operational Manual: Residence', SM 5.5(1).

39 Danish Immigration Service (2013), 'The Greencard Scheme'.

40 Although Canada does purport to consider these factors as part of its new 'Gender Based Analysis Plus' policy adopted since 2010 (CIC 2011b).

Part II

Gendering skilled immigration policy in Australia and Canada, 1988–2013

3

Gendering the policy process: venue shopping and diversity-seeking

Introduction

The previous chapter identified significant variation both across countries and also within states in the attention paid to gender concerns in skilled immigration selection policies. In particular, I found that Canada ranked higher than Australia for the gender awareness of its skilled immigration policy, although Canada's ranking has been dropping in recent years. Australia, while always ranking lower than Canada, has also fallen in its gender ranking over time (see Table 2.3, last chapter). In the remaining chapters of this book, I develop a theoretical explanation for this variation in policies across Australia and Canada over a twenty-five-year period. I explore this issue through four case studies that also map the major developments in skilled immigration policy over this quarter century. This venue shopping approach proposes that a broad range of interest groups are relevant in shaping the gender awareness of skilled immigration policies. In particular, feminist organisations and immigrant associations ('diversity-seeking groups') can inform policy debates and in some instances policy outputs, when they relate to gender concerns. However, groups must also enjoy the capacity to 'shop' for participation across the key venues of democratic deliberation, in particular parliamentary committees and courts. This chapter focuses on this theoretical account, while also considering several alternate theories: explanations based in broader macroeconomic theory, corporatist interest group accounts and partisan explanations. While I do not deny that these alternate factors play an important role in skilled immigration policy outputs, when it comes to gender awareness, the engagement of diversity-seeking actors is central. However, access to key institutional sites of power is also pivotal for these groups in achieving their goals. This is especially the case within the Westminster-inspired parliamentary systems under examination, which might otherwise present a fairly closed participatory space for economically marginalised groups. Furthermore, governments' capacity to exercise bureaucratic control will also shape participation opportunities. This argument poses an extension of the existing venue shopping scholarship to Westminster-inspired parliamentary systems. First, however, I consider alternate economic, interest group and partisan explanations for variation in skilled immigration policies from a gender perspective.

Understanding skilled immigration policy-making: economic explanations

Orthodox neoclassical economic approaches to understanding immigration policies propose that immigration policy is a product of economic supply and demand. Business cycles and unemployment are viewed as key determinants of immigration policy, with expansive immigration policies predicted during boom periods and restrictive immigration policies during periods of recession (Corbett 1957; Green 1976; LeMay 1989; Martin 1980; Togman 2002: 5). However, when examined longitudinally, the proposed relationship between unemployment and immigrant supply does not always hold (Hollifield *et al.* 2006; Tichenor 2002: 21; Watts 2002: 107). Writing on the Canadian context, Alan Green and David Green (2004: 129) argue that since the mid-1980s and throughout the 1990s there has in fact been a growing gap between actual and predicted levels of immigration selection based on macroeconomic criteria. In particular, while these measures may provide predictions for the size of economic flows they are less helpful in explaining more detailed changes in policy.

This is not to suggest that the economic approach does not provide some important insights into understanding immigration policies and their variation. Gender awareness (or unawareness) of immigration policies might be the unintended consequence of broader economic pressures. We might expect that periods of unemployment or recession could correspond with negative gender effects as other policy priorities emerge. However, such a theoretical argument can only be maintained if similar economic conditions result in similar immigration policies across states. Over the period of analysis, but particularly from 1996 onwards, Australia and Canada experienced similar levels of unemployment, employment growth and employment to population ratios (Richardson *et al.* 2004: 7–10). Yet, future chapters of the book document significant differences in attention paid to gender issues across the two countries, suggesting that economic conditions alone are not central.

Interest group explanations for variation in skilled immigration policies

Interest group approaches focus upon the role of employer associations and trade unions in immigration policy-making. These accounts predominate within the skilled immigration scholarship. I explore two main interest approaches within migration studies – the group politics and the Varieties of Capitalism (VoC) explanations. Group politics scholars emphasise the role of interests in shaping immigration policies.[1] The most important proponent of this view is Gary Freeman, who in a series of papers adopts James Q. Wilson's (1980) theory of group politics. This theory suggests that the political behaviour of interests will depend on the associated costs and benefits of such behaviour. The behaviour can be of an interest group, clientelistic, entrepreneurial or majoritarian quality and policies will accordingly reflect the desires of the relevant group. Gary Freeman (1995) argues that the immigration policy domain is most likely to be characterised by clientelistic behaviour as certain actors have concentrated advantages to gain through political action, while for most the costs of such action are diffuse, and therefore unlikely to provoke a political response. Immigration is predicted to be an area where industry (employers, property developers, industry associations) 'captures' the political agenda and seeks policies that reflect pecuniary concerns.

The idea that interest groups inform policy is relevant for the current focus on the gender awareness of immigration selection policy. As I argue later in this chapter, such interests might include non-corporatist players in the immigration field, including diversity-seeking groups, whom I define as feminist and immigrant associations. Yet, while the group politics approach is useful in drawing attention to the role of interests, there are several potential limitations with this explanation. First, such an approach does not provide a solid account of the initial emergence of interests. In focusing only on the successful action of existing groups, the group politics approach can overlook how differential resources aid or abet the development of interest groups and their subsequent levels of mobilisation (Boswell 2007: 78–9). Further, the group politics approach also ignores possible bias on the part of the state towards groups over time. The effects of uneven distribution of state power are particularly important for women's and immigrant associations who have been historically excluded from the policy-making process (Tichenor 2002: 24). Therefore, paradoxically, while the group politics approach eschews pluralistic assumptions about interest group engagement,[2] examination of broader historical factors that inform the differential negotiating positions of groups is largely ignored. Below, I argue that the venue shopping approach provides a better narrative space to understand the engagement of marginal groups, including diversity-seeking organisations, than existing interest group approaches.

Political economy approaches

Related but distinctive from the group politics approach are the political economy explanations for variation in skilled immigration policies. The VoC approach is situated within this school. It focuses on the importance of economic configurations and employer interests in informing policy (Hall and Soskice 2001) and has been applied to the skilled immigration field (Bucken-Knapp 2007; Cerna 2007,

2009, 2014; Menz 2007, 2008; Wright 2012). The VoC scholarship proposes that business in liberal market economies such as Australia and Canada will have a heightened interest in deregulation through skilled immigration policies, reflecting a broader neoliberal economic production regime (Thelen 2002: 286).

Other political economy approaches focus on the role of trade union and business relations in informing immigration policy outputs, without particular reference to the VoC scholarship. Giovanni Facchini and his collaborators (2007) disaggregate along policy sectors and identify correlative relationships between levels of trade union/employer group engagement and immigrant stock size. Yet, the simplifying assumptions of this model are not always empirically grounded; for instance, trade unions are erroneously assumed to always oppose increased immigration when in fact in recent years they have often supported it (Haus 2002; Watts 2002). In any case, binary characterisations of immigration regimes, as either 'open' or 'closed', or of interest groups as either 'for' or 'against' skilled immigration policy, are limiting. Such a characterisation overlooks vital qualitative differences within open immigration regimes, such as in the balance between skilled and family reunion immigration or the accommodation of gender concerns within selection mechanisms. In addition, the very focus on materialist interests within this approach conceals the importance of non-materialist considerations.

Partisan explanations for immigration policy outputs

Partisan political alignment has sometimes been used to explain variation in immigration policies (Breunig and Luedtke 2008: 128–9; Ireland 2004; Lahav 2004: 133). Under this approach, political positioning of government on the left-right spectrum is a key explanation for differences in immigration policies across states. Yet scholars in settler states rarely advance partisan explanations. In fact, in both Australia and Canada, theorists have frequently assumed bipartisanship in party positions on immigration policy. This is related to the conflict that can arise over immigration issues in ethnically diverse settings like Australia and Canada. The argument follows that as conflict threatens incumbency – through causing splits in voting – it is not in the interest of either side of politics to engage in such behaviour (see Betts 1999: 193–223; Freeman 1995: 884; Hardcastle *et al.* 1994: 112–13; McAllister 1993). Bipartisanship notwithstanding, it is possible that differences in the entire political landscape in Australia and Canada in turn inform policy differences across time in immigration policies. An expert survey carried out by Kenneth Benoit and Michael Laver in 2002–3 measured party positions on immigration on a scale from 1 to 20, with a higher score suggesting a more closed party position towards immigration and greater support for restrictions on immigration. According to this survey, the Canadian Liberal Party had a party position of 5.05 on immigration compared with 6.92 for the Australian Labor Party in 2001. The right-leaning Progressive Conservative Party in Canada had a score of

9.31, compared with 12.0 for the right-leaning Liberal Party in Australia in 2001 (Benoit and Laver 2006).

Benoit and Laver's survey does indeed suggest that the entire Australian political system is positioned more towards a closed position on immigration when compared with that in Canada. Yet, even if we accept that the level of 'openness' or 'closedness' of an immigration regime can be measured on a twenty-point scale using two variables (Benoit and Laver 2006: 228), it is unclear how these broad brushstroke differences in turn affect the gender awareness of skilled immigration policies. Partisan accounts fail to explain qualitative differences in policies. As the analysis in this book suggests, it is also possible to have very high levels of immigration admission and at the same time a selective immigration regime from a gender perspective.

Party ideology might shape government views on gender-aware policy-making. There is a wealth of feminist research, which considers the relationship between party position and gender-aware policies. Although multi-directional, various feminist scholars point to the correlation between gender-aware policies and left-leaning governments.[3] Louise Chappell (2002: 63–4) for instance views the Australian Labor Party (ALP) incumbency from 1983 to 1996 as central to feminist successes over that period. In contrast, the election of the Liberal-National Coalition government in Australia from 1996 until 2007 is said to have resulted in reduced attention to diversity issues (Sawer 2008). In Canada, the two parties closest in their ideological positions to feminist concerns, the National Democratic Party (NDP) and Bloc Québécois, have not held national government. Yet, the Canadian Liberals, who held power from 1993 to 2006, were more progressive on gender issues than the Australian Liberal Party, which was elected in Australia in 1996, although potentially no more so than the ALP that held federal office until 1996. I explore variation across incumbent political parties, across time and across immigration policies in the following chapters.

The venue shopping explanation for gender-aware immigration policies

Despite their important contributions, existing approaches face theoretical and empirical limitations. In particular, these approaches largely overlook the importance of gender, both as an object of policy and as an integral factor within policy processes. I propose an alternate venue shopping explanation that draws upon both neo-institutional and interest group explanations for understanding policy variation. 'Venue shopping' refers to the strategy of policy actors moving between different institutional venues in order to further their political goals. While the focus is generally on the activity of non-state actors, such moves can also be undertaken by government bureaucrats in order to limit the scope of political contestation, or to achieve quicker realisation of policy goals (e.g. Bulmer 2011; Guiraudon 1997).

The public agenda scholarship in which the venue shopping approach is situated, often focuses on changes in the 'policy image', or '[h]ow a policy is understood and discussed' in order to explain policy change (Baumgartner and Jones 1993: 25–6; Daugbjerg and Studsgaard 2005: 103–4; Hunt 2002: 25). As Valerie Hunt (2002: 75) notes, the 'policy image' itself is changed through a redefinition of the central policy problem, which is at least in part a product of a change in the institutional venue in which policy is developed. Institutional venue, or the 'location where authoritative decisions are made concerning a given issue' (Baumgartner and Jones 1993: 31) is central to this conception of change. According to Sarah Pralle (2007: 26) the choice of institutional venue may affect the policy image in three main ways. First, the jurisdiction of an institution may be expanded or contracted in order to shape the decision-making power within that institution. Or alternatively, those who have traditionally been powerful within a particular institution or venue may try to limit the jurisdiction of another venue. Second, groups seeking change in policy may 'shop' for a new venue. For instance, groups may attempt to raise an issue from a regional to a national level, or from the bureaucratic to the legislative arena, in order to highlight its political salience. Third, institutional venues may alter rules of the game, enabling the engagement of some actors and limiting the engagement of others.

Much of the earlier venue shopping scholarship focuses on such activity within the United States' (US) presidential system, although in recognition of potential selection bias (Albaek *et al.* 2007: 3; Boothe and Harrison 2009: 292), this research has recently been extended cross-nationally through the comparative public agenda project (Baumgartner *et al.* 2006, 2011: 947). Studies focus on singular venues, such as the legislature in coalitional parliamentary systems (e.g. Bräuninger and Debus 2009; Breeman *et al.* 2009; Mortensen 2007) or venue shopping within the European Union's intergovernmental system (e.g. Beyers and Kerremans 2012; Guiraudon 2000, 2003; Menz 2010; Princen 2007). Within this expanding comparative scholarship, the peculiarities of Westminster constitutional design have been largely overlooked. This is despite the fact that the broader political science scholarship identifies particular institutional effects of Westminster, in terms of the concentration of power within executive government (e.g. Lijphart 1999; Tsebelis 2000). Studies point to how the presidential system of checks-and-balances offers more opportunities for the engagement of and lobbying by groups, than in the Westminster-inspired system (Mezey 1979; Pierson 2006; Weaver and Rockman 1991). Except in the case of minority government, or where there is strong bicameralism at play, the government of the day in Westminster-inspired systems also controls the legislature (Tsebelis 2000: 457). Further, as Timmermans (2001: 319) notes, these features can limit who participates in the policy process.

Public agenda studies that analyse Westminster-inspired systems do not bring sufficient attention to these important centralising features (Boothe and Harrison 2009: 292; Daugbjerg and Studsgaard 2005; John 2006; John and Margetts 2003;

Penner *et al.* 2006; Pralle 2006a, 2006b). In addition, generally these studies also do not compare across Westminster-inspired systems (see only Studlar 2007: 180) nor pay sufficient attention to the role of bureaucrats themselves as venue shoppers. This is despite the fact that Westminster-inspired systems present a heightened role for the executive in policy processes compared to other systems of government. Nor have venue shopping approaches been considered widely in the immigration policy domain (see only Bendel *et al.* 2011; Guiraudon 2000; 2003; Hunt 2002; Maurer and Parkes 2007; Timmermans and Scholten 2006).

Extending venue shopping to Westminster-inspired systems: diversity-seekers challenge bureaucratic control

In applying the venue shopping approach within Westminster-inspired systems, I start with the assumption that in such systems, government actors will exercise considerable bureaucratic control over the policy process. The capacity for intervention by outside groups in certain key institutional venues is required in order to influence the policy agenda. I identify five factors that may impact upon the capacity of government to bring around changes to immigration policies and of the ability of diversity-seeking groups to intervene to halt or shift policy reform: i) the role of bureaucrats sympathetic to diversity-seeking interests; ii) access to parliamentary committees; iii) strong bicameralism; iv) federalism; and v) strong judicial systems. The book demonstrates variation in these factors across countries, and the four case studies set out in Chapters 4–7.

First, however, two caveats: the focus here is not on the extent of mobilisation by external actors to challenge immigration agendas but rather, on the institutional venues that enable, or disenable, external actors and bureaucrats in achieving policy goals. As such, the supply-side dimension is not explored until Chapter 8, which focuses on this particular aspect of the argument. Second, the theoretical claim is not that bureaucrats seek to circumvent delegated responsibility that underpins parliamentary sovereignty (Rhodes *et al.* 2009: 25–6). Rather, I suggest that the executive-legislative fusion that characterises Westminster-inspired systems eases executive capacity to initiate policy change. As such, bureaucrats in these systems exercise considerable independence in policy reform (Beem 2009: 500–1). The central question is how particular institutional venues may affect the level of control enjoyed by bureaucratic interests, as well as the opportunities for intervention for those external to government.

The role of sympathetic bureaucrats

Turning to this first factor, scholars in both Canada and Australia have emphasised how 'outsiders' in Westminster-inspired systems target the bureaucracy rather than the legislature in order to pursue policy change (Matthews and Warhurst 1993: 89; Mezey 1979: 199–200; Presthus 1973; Smith 2005: 109; Thompson and Stanbury 1979). Bureaucracies may also contain influential 'insiders' who are supportive of the goals of outsiders (Chappell 2002). This form of bureaucratic support for external actors is important because executive venues can easily be transformed into institutional structures that block outside engagement, either through administrative reform, or through intergovernmentalism (Guiraudon 2000: 263–4).

Applying this notion of 'sympathetic bureaucrats', feminist political scientists provide a theoretical rationale for the relationship between the emergence of feminist bureaucrats ('femocrats') within Westminster systems of government, women's policy machinery to buttress these femocrats, and the realisation of gender-aware policies (Chappell 2002; Eisenstein 1996: xvii; Mazur 2002: 4–5; Sawer 1990; Stetson 2001: 271). The scholarship identifies the importance of 'strategic partnerships' (Halsaa 1998) or 'triangles of empowerment' (Vargas and Wieringa 1998) between women in elected office, feminist and women's groups and women's policy officers for feminist policy success. The reasons posited for this relationship are two-fold: political machinery gives feminist actors the opportunity to devote themselves full-time to the women's movement, while state machinery is central to law and policy-making in Westminster-inspired systems, allowing feminists to engage close to the sites of political decision-making (Stetson and Mazur 1995: 5). As such, women's political machinery operates as a challenge to gender norms within the core executive and achieves this disruption through simultaneous 'insider' and 'outsider' activism (Sawer 1990).

To date the role of such women's political machinery in immigration policy-making has not been extensively explored, despite the fact that the establishment of a Gender-Based Analysis Unit within CIC accompanied the enactment of the Immigration and Refugee Protection Act (2002) (Cdn) (see only Abu-Laban and Gabriel 2002; Boucher 2007, 2010; Dauvergne *et al.* 2006). This book analyses the existence of women's political machinery within immigration bureaucracies and examines whether this leads to more gender-aware policies than in contexts without such machinery.

Legislative committees

Outside of alliances with bureaucrats, outsiders may have limited capacity to appeal directly to the executive. In this context, the legislature will take on an elevated space as a relevant institution for venue shopping. Legislative committees have been considered vital in US immigration policy-making in offering opportunities for intervention by outsiders (Hunt 2002: 90–2; Tichenor 2002: 31–4). Committees have also been identified as a key avenue for interest group participation in Westminster-inspired systems, although much will depend on the partisan composition of these committees (Matthews and Warhurst 1993: 89; Pross 1993: 69; Rhodes *et al.* 2009: 200–1; Vromen 2005: 102). The involvement of committees in the policy-making process may be more likely when governments are engaged in legislative as opposed to administrative change, a point which is related to government's strategic choice of regulatory instrument. There are often legal requirements that new acts be referred to committee, which is less the case for regulations that generally must only be tabled in parliament.[4] In the following chapters, I examine a range of regulatory and legislative reforms to assess the relationship between committee involvement and gender-aware policies.

Strong bicameralism

Strong bicameralism is another factor that can ameliorate the tendency towards bureaucratic control in Westminster-systems (Lijphart 1999: 3). In Australia, the upper house of the federal parliament, the Senate, has played an increasing role in Australian politics since the adoption of the system of proportional representational for that house in 1949 (Sharman 1999). Proportional representation has seen the increased representation of minority parties in that chamber. Especially when they hold the balance of power, such parties can block legislation, disallow regulations or negotiate changes with the government of the day (Rhodes *et al.* 2009: 205; Young 1999). Further, in Australia, there is often a connection between parliamentary committees and bicameralism. If the government of the day does not retain power in the Senate, the most powerful parliamentary committees for legislative review will be found there (Thomas 2009: 25). In contrast, in Canada, the Senate of Canada is an unelected body with positions filled by the Governor-General upon the advice of the Prime Minister. This presents a mitigating factor against bureaucratic control in Australia that does not find a counterpart in Canada. This book interrogates the extent to which strong bicameralism in the Australian context introduces a venue shopping opportunity for non-government actors.

Federalism

Federalism is often defined as the constitutionally entrenched and protected division of power between national and sub-national units (Elazar 1987: 34; Riker 1993). Federalist structures are generally assumed to open up veto points, which can be exploited by interest groups (Tarrow 1994: 85; Thomas 2006: 160; Weaver and Rockman 1991: 26). These structures also allow access to one level of government when another is blocked (Baumgartner and Jones 1993: 34, 217, 232; Sawer and Vickers 2001). Federalism contributes to less government control over policy change as policy responses are split across different levels of government. When approval or participation is needed by both federal and state or provincial levels, this reduces the 'capacity for loss imposition' by government (Pal and Weaver 2003: 11).

Federalism can also impact interest group behaviour. As Sarah Pralle (2007: 21) notes, activists may employ federal jurisdictional boundaries to reconstruct issues and find sympathetic ears at alternate levels of government. On the other hand, especially for economically marginal interests such as feminist and immigrant associations, federalism can also contribute to strained alliances and dispersed resources (Dobrowolsky 2000: 24; Jackson 2009: 456; McRoberts 1993: 161, 171). Likewise, under the guise of executive intergovernmentalism, federalism may allow government to move policy issues off the public agenda (Guiraudon 1997: 265–6; see also Smith 2005: 122–3). Clearly, federalism can in some instances present an opportunity for venue shopping, while at other times diminish opportunities due to a shift towards executive politics.

Australia and Canada both have federalist systems. Despite this shared framework there are important differences between the two countries, which are pertinent to analysis of immigration policy. In Australia, a strong vertical fiscal imbalance between the national and sub-national levels (Mathews 1980, cited in Blackshield and Williams 2002: 920) and exclusive national power over immigration (Australian Constitution, s51xxvii) has arguably allowed the federal government to retain significant control over immigration regulation. The states and territories have some involvement in immigration promotion and recruitment; however, the federal government is constitutionally responsible for all aspects of selection policy. In Canada, immigration is a concurrent federal-provincial power and industrial relations a provisional power (Canada Constitution Act, ss95; 92(13)). The provinces are also increasingly active players in skilled immigration policy debates (Boushey and Luedtke 2006: 215; Teitelbaum and Winter 1998: 181, 189). This book investigates whether shared jurisdiction over immigration policy allows for more intervention by feminist and immigrant associations, as well as other social actors, and therefore less governmental control in immigration policy-making than when immigration is a distinctly national policy issue.

Strong judicial systems

The legal system is often identified as an important venue to halt policy change, but also as a venue that opens contestation up beyond government (Albaek *et al.* 2007; Flynn 2011: 383; Guiraudon 2000; Wood 2006). The judiciary may operate as a veto point for interest groups to aid social change in situations where the legislature or executive (or both) is unwilling or unable to act (Dobrowolsky

2000; Pal and Weaver 2003: 325). A distinction is drawn between strong judicial systems with bills of rights and weak judicial systems with greater powers
vested in parliament. Flynn (2011: 382) and Pralle (2006b) have considered the
role of courts in venue shopping in Canada, yet comparative analysis of judicial systems in Westminster-inspired countries is lacking. The key issue is to
whom legal protection extends. In Canada, the Canadian Charter of Rights and
Freedoms, 1982, Art 15(1) provides constitutionally protected rights for discrete minorities, including immigrants who are located within Canada (Carasco
et al. 2007: 153; *Chesters* v. *Canada (Minister of Citizenship and Immigration)*
[2003] 1 FC 361). In contrast, in Australia, there is no bill of rights and judicial review of administrative immigration decisions is significantly curtailed by
statute (Crock 1998: 46).

In addition to bills of rights, I argue that more nuanced aspects of the legal
system, such as the existence of civil class action laws, and standing rules are also
important. As Miriam Smith (2005: 145) notes, with the fiscal restructuring of public institutions there may have been an increased privatisation of collective interests
and the heightened use of litigation as a tool of political action by external interests.
The capacity for individuals to bring legal claims is therefore increasingly relevant.
Standing rules, or the rules governing the right to litigate, can also affect the capacity
for legal intervention. If there is no standing in court, venue shifting to the judicial
venue is obviously barred. As standing rules are defined much more narrowly in
Australia than in Canada, there is reason to believe this might play an important
role in venue shopping. In Australia, standing is restricted to a 'person aggrieved'
by a decision (Administrative Decisions (Judicial Review) Act (1977) (Cth) and this
rule has been interpreted narrowly by the courts (Aronson *et al.* 2009: 767–74). As
a result of this reticent culture, the courts in Australia have not been utilised extensively by feminist and immigrant associations, in areas of social and public policy.
While feminist activists have attempted to have standing rules relaxed in Australia to
enable increased judicial intervention, their calls have not been met by government
which perhaps fears a wave of litigation against administrative decisions (Aronson
et al. 2009: 796–7; Chappell 2002: 145). Australia also experienced restrictions upon
class actions in recent decades (Crock 2006; Gageler 2010: 97).

In Canada, in order to bring a legal claim, an individual must have a 'peculiar grievance of their own beyond some grievance suffered by them in common
with the rest of the public'. While similar in its phrasing, this focus on grievance
has been interpreted much more broadly in Canada than in Australia (*Friends of
the Oldman River Society* v. *Association of Professional Engineers* (1997) 5. W.W.R.
179; Sossin 2008: 394–5). In addition, immigrant applicants both inside and outside of Canada have standing to bring actions for administrative and legal review
of these decisions, including class action claims (IRPA, s72; Federal Courts Act
(1985) (Cdn), s18.14). As we will see, friends of the court interventions are also
common in the immigration field in Canada, suggesting heightened opportunities
for venue shopping in the judicial sphere.

*The engagement of 'diversity-seeking' feminist groups and immigrant
associations within the venue shopping approach*

In their classic study on agenda setting, Frank Baumgartner and Bryan Jones
(1993: 9) argue that the venue shopping approach is an antidote to both pluralistic and elitist conceptions of policy-making. While they do not assume that '[a]ll
disadvantaged actors are small and defenseless' these authors also argue that a
singularly pluralistic understanding of participation undervalues the 'upper-class'
attributes of many engaged actors. Despite this acknowledgement of class and
resource differentials, the role of socio-economically underprivileged groups
in the policy-making process is not central to their analysis (1993: 248–9). For
instance, the authors argue that 'while particular venues may confer up advantage on business or other specific groups, the simple existence of alternate policy venues is more important than the distribution of advantage conferred by
a particular venue' (1993: 35). As such, access to a plurality of venues is seen
to ameliorate inequalities between the power resources of different groups. This
appraisal potentially underrepresents the importance of enduring inequities in
the policy-making process in understanding the impact of interests upon policy
outputs, especially in systems of government with fewer institutional veto points
than the United States.

A variety of interests must be considered when assessing the emergence of
gender-aware policies. In instances when immigration policies pertain to issues
of diversity, it is possible that non-corporatist actors, in particular feminist and
immigrant associations, will attempt to engage in the policy process. As noted in
the introduction, these groups are referred to as '*diversity-seeking groups*'.

While these groups often act separately from one another and cannot be
seen as a coherent lobby, in Canada there is evidence of coalition building
between women's groups and immigrant associations, in particular in instances
where gender-aware policies are realised. There are historical reasons for the
emergence of coalitions across the immigration field in Canada. Vijay Agnew
(1996: 82) argues that the necessity to maintain state funding over the early
1990s forced one of Canada's peak feminist organisations – the National Action
Committee on the Status of Women (NAC) – to 'graft issues of race and class on
to existing agendas'. Similarly, in the immigration sphere, loose conglomerations
of immigration and refugee advocates such as the Canadian Coalition for a Fair
and Just Immigration Policy and the similarly named yet distinct Coalition for
a Just Immigration and Refugee Policy, as well as the Community Coalition on
Immigration and the Toronto Coalition Against Racism, emerged in Toronto
from the late 1980s onwards to tackle common challenges around racial discrimination (interview 21 by author, Canada, 12 September 2008; Coalition
1988; Community Coalition 1987; Hernandez 1988: 164). The Coalition for a
Fair and Just Immigration and Refugee Policy, for instance, comprises individuals working in settlement agencies, ethnocultural organisations, legal clinics

and trade union officials in the Greater Toronto Area (Ethnocultural leader, interview 1 by author, Canada, 7 July 2008). Finally, the Migrant Workers Alliance for Change, comprising activist groups, community legal centres and trade unions, has been active in the area of temporary foreign workers in Canada since the mid-2000s. As will become apparent in future chapters, these coalitions engaged with key gender issues, often led by female members of ethnocultural organisations.

Several organisations also emerged in Canada with a distinctive focus on both gender and immigration issues, such as the National Organisation of Immigrant and Visible Minority Women (NOIVMW) in Canada. In contrast, with the exception of the now defunded Association of Non-English Speaking Background Women of Australia (ANESBWA), these 'diversity-seeking groups' are far less evident in the immigration field in Australia (Vasta 1992). The feminist movement in Australia was strongly incorporated into government agencies over the 1970s and 1980s (Chappell 2002; Sawer 1991) and there has been less of a distinctive ethnocultural dimension within this movement than in Canada. The historical reasons for these differences are explored in Chapter 8.

Conclusion

This chapter has reviewed the major theoretical approaches to understanding variation in immigration policies. The economic, interest group and partisan political approaches offer important insights that provide a theoretical backdrop to this book. Yet, the venue shopping approach offers a preferred explanation for the incorporation of gender concerns, both due to its focus on marginal interests in policy-making and due to a more refined appreciation of institutional variation. In future chapters, I explore the strategic use of institutional venue both by bureaucrats and interests outside of government in shaping the content of skilled immigration policies. The five institutional features identified – sympathetic bureaucrats, legislative committees, strong bicameralism, federalism and strong judicial regimes – provide potential contexts for venue shopping both by bureaucrats and by outsider groups. Where there are many cultural and institutional similarities between Australia and Canada, they do contain variation along these five factors. In the ensuing four chapters, the relative importance of these factors in understanding differences in the gender awareness of immigration policies is examined qualitatively. We move now to the first of the four case studies, changes in the compositional mix of immigration policies that occurred in Australia and Canada from 1988 onwards. These changes saw reductions in the relative percentage of family immigration and increases in the weighting of skilled immigration within immigration programmes in both countries.

Notes

1 Betts 1999; Birrell and Birrell 1981; Birell 1984; Freeman 1986; 1995; 1998; 1999; 2005; 2006; Freeman and Hill, 2006.
2 Lowi (1969) upon whom the group politics approach builds was an elitist rather than a pluralist theorist.
3 O'Connor *et al.* 1999; Beckwith 2000: 440; Chappell 2002: 176–7; Mazur 2002: 44.
4 As I discuss in Chapter 5, the decision to send the regulations to the Immigration and Refugee Protection Act *(Cdn)* to the Standing Committee on Citizenship and Immigration was a first in Canadian immigration policy-making.

4

Changing the mix, 1988–2003: the shift from family to skilled immigration

The ideal migrant is a highly skilled 14-year-old unmarried orphan.
(Departmental official, Department of Immigration, Local Government and Ethnic Affairs Australia, cited in Jenkins 1990)

Introduction

Structural ageing in Western countries creates new challenges for nation states. Labour market gaps are emerging, particularly in the health and knowledge sectors, and yet, there are fewer workers to fill this emerging need (Chaloff and Lemaitre 2009: 10). These demographic trends are particularly dire in parts of Europe, where the European Commission estimates that from 2025 onwards, immigration will be the main source of population growth and where the share of the population of working age will decline from 67.2 per cent in 2004 to 56.7 per cent by 2050 (EC 2005: 3, cited in Cerna 2010: 14). In light of these changes, many nations are turning to highly skilled immigration programmes to meet domestic labour market gaps. Given that there is generally an acceptable upper limit to total immigration, the relative proportion of skilled immigration that a country admits is also determined by the extent to which 'non-discretionary immigration' can be controlled (OECD 2006: 112–25). This 'non-discretionary immigration' includes reunification by immediate and extended family members, inflows of immigrants across free movement zones and humanitarian immigration. In many countries, non-discretionary immigration comprises the bulk of immigration intake and reducing such immigration has proven politically challenging. In the United States, for instance, attempts to reduce non-discretionary immigration and increase skilled labour, have, to date, largely failed (Tichenor 2002). Yet, in other countries such as Australia and Canada, the mix between so-called 'discretionary' and 'non-discretionary' immigration has been successfully altered, in large part due to the bureaucratic control enjoyed by government over policy processes in these Westminster-inspired systems.

Policy-maker preference for 'discretionary' over 'non-discretionary' immigrations stems from the belief that the former is more labour market ready.

According to this conventional argument, family immigrants are either uninterested in, or unable to seek out employment, or dependent on familial or state welfare. For instance, in the US context, George Borjas (1990, 1999) proposes that family reunification immigration should be reduced, and the relative intake of economic immigration increased given the economic cost to the state of the former. Similarly, in the Canadian context, Charles Beach and collaborators (2007) advocate a stronger focus on points-tested immigrants to maximise the economic outcomes of overall immigration programmes. There is broad debate around the economic value of family reunification, with some suggesting that the contributions of family migrants are 'larger and more benign,' than many analysts believe' (Kofman and Meetoo 2008: 163). Alternately, the process of assortative mating whereby individuals marry others with similar educational levels, could mean that as immigration in general becomes more skilled, so too does spousal immigration (Dumont *et al.* 2007).

Implicit in many depictions of a mendicant family class lies an assumption of female economic dependency upon sponsoring male citizens or permanent residents (Dauvergne 2000; EWL 2010). This assumption is in part built upon women's overrepresentation within the family stream. It is also due to both an undervaluation of unpaid labour in which women predominate (Arat-Koc 1999a: 212; Gabriel and Pellerin 2008: 172) and an invisibility of paid welfare and care work as skilled work (Kofman and Raghuram 2006; Kofman *et al.* 2005).

In this chapter, I focus on a secondary question: what does the balance between family reunification and skilled immigration mean for the gender awareness of immigration policy? Does the rebalancing of the family to skill-based ratio of immigration in Australia and Canada make for less gender-aware immigration policies? The relative composition of discretionary and non-discretionary immigration – also known as 'the mix' – must be assessed from a gender perspective. In this chapter, I examine the relationship between compositional mix and gender in Australia and Canada from 1988 through to 2003.

The political and economic arguments in favour of skilled immigration emerged in Australia and Canada from the late 1980s onwards. Government reports from that period demonstrated that skilled immigrants were less reliant on welfare than those entering through family-based streams. These reports also found that skilled immigrants achieved higher rates of labour market engagement than family immigrants. Skilled immigrants earned more money, thereby bringing in more revenue to the tax base. Further, these reports showed that certain types of skilled immigrants – those with local experience and official language skills – were among the best performers economically. Employers more quickly acknowledged the experience of these skilled immigrants who were less likely to be unemployed. If these skilled migrants were less reliant on welfare in the long term, the logic went, increasing the proportion of skilled immigrants in the immigration programme and changing selection criteria to preference the best-performing skilled migrants, would make sound economic sense over the long term. As the laconic quotation from an Australian departmental officer at the onset of this chapter suggests, there were some obvious limits to what selection criteria could be imposed. Yet, the scope of reforms was nonetheless substantial.

This chapter begins by outlining the policy context whereby concerns over the long-term economic (in)activity of the overall immigration programme first emerged in Australia and Canada. It also outlines the key policy changes undertaken in both countries through new levels set for the family reunification and skilled immigration streams. This included cuts to extended family categories: parents and grandparents and in the Australian context, the 'concessional class' that comprised largely adult siblings and working age parents of existing resident immigrants. In the third part of this chapter, I consider the gender implications of the shift towards a more economically focused immigration programme in both countries, drawing upon gender-disaggregated immigration statistics. In the final fourth section, I employ a venue shopping explanation to understand the policy process that emerged across the two countries.

The policy context in Australia: 'rebalancing' of the classes

The historical context in Australia

In 1987, Prime Minister Bob Hawke commissioned the FitzGerald Inquiry into Australia's immigration policy (the 'CAAIP report'). Ross FitzGerald argued that a 'user-pays' logic should be applied to immigration and that government should 'move to restrict the non-survival benefits and privileges available to non-citizens' (CAAIP 1988: xi, 15). In addition to this call for reductions in the welfare dependency of new immigrants, FitzGerald also advocated an economic focusing of immigration selection to improve the public reception of immigration policies (CAAIP 1988: xi, 14). While the report was met with some hostility by the Hawke Labor government, it was to have a central impact upon policy-making under subsequent Labor and Liberal governments (Jupp 2002: 45).

Changes under the Labor Government

An emphasis on higher levels of skill across the immigration programme is first apparent in the CAAIP report. FitzGerald argued that '[s]election methods need a sharper economic focus for the public to be convinced that the program is in Australia's interest', including 'a high proportion of skilled, entrepreneurial and youthful immigrants, with English and other language skills playing a part in selection' (CAAIP 1988: x, xii–xiii). FitzGerald was particularly critical of the concessional class that brought working aged siblings, parents, nephews, nieces and adult children of existing Australian residents into Australia (PAM 1994, Sch 2.1; Migration Regulations 1994, Sch 6A). This class, although points tested, was at the time classified within the family reunification stream. It had a lower pass mark than that for standard skilled immigration and was granted points for familial relationships, which meant that fewer of the points that entrants received were for 'pure' economic factors. By 1988, the concessional class was the largest category within the family reunification stream, with almost 40,000 entrants admitted annually (DILGEA 1989: 9). This class was identified in the FitzGerald Report as one of the main reasons for the declining skill levels of the immigration programme as a whole (CAAIP 1988: 86).

Initially the Labor Party reacted negatively to the recommendations made in the FitzGerald Report (Seccombe 1988: 3). However, as Colin Rubenstein (1993: 155–6) argues, increased pressure from the then Liberal Opposition Leader, Dr Hewson, to reduce immigration intake, promoted policy shifts within Labor. The pass mark for concessional family members was raised from seventy to eighty points. Increasing the pass mark for the concessional family class had the effect of requiring a higher level of occupational skill and reduced the relative importance of points for familial relations. This saw the entrance of concessional family fall dramatically from 38,900 in 1987–88 to 21,325 in 1991–92 and down further to 8,225 in 1992–93 (BIR 1993: 9).

A variety of migratory pressures also contributed to a 38 per cent increase in aged parent immigration from 1986 to 1989. Growing evidence of welfare state reliance among this group led to a perception, according to another former government representative, 'that people were coming in order to ... sponge off the Australian community rather than contribute to Australian employment' (Former senior government figure, interview 21 by author, Australia, 19 October 2009). To slow growth in this subcategory, in 1988, Minister Robert Ray introduced the 'balance of family test' (Ray 1988a: 3753). This test required that the balance of children of the applicant for a parent visa be present in Australia in order for an individual to sponsor their parent. This calculation was tightly implemented and included the children of the spouse of the applicant (Migration Act, s58; Regulation 1.04B). At the same time, Minister Ray introduced statutory provisions into the Migration Act (sections 85–91) which allowed the government to cap the number of entrants who could be processed in any one year, although this 'capping' did not extend to 'preferential family class' members – spouses, children and aged parents over 65 (Ray 1988b: 3040). These changes, accompanied with a refundable bond for the sponsorship of aged parents introduced in late 1991 and the concessional changes mentioned earlier, saw the percentage of the entire family stream as a proportion of the overall immigration programme drop by 8 per cent between 1987 and 1992 (see Table 4.1).

Table 4.1: Permanent entrants to Australia, economic and family streams, 1987–2003

Year	Total (economic and family)	Total family (and as percentage)	Total economic (and as percentage)
1987–88	104,207	69,571 (67%)	34,636 (33%)
1988–89	103,193	59,570 (58%)	43,623 (42%)
1989–90	92,777	49,941 (54%)	42,836 (46%)
1990–91	102,355	53,934 (52%)	48,421 (48%)
1991–92	88,955	48,621 (55%)	40,334 (45%)
1992–93	54,239	32,102 (59%)	22,137 (41%)
1993–94	46,374	33,580 (72%)	12,794 (28%)
1994–95	57,279	37,078 (65%)	20,201 (35%)
1995–96	66,466	46,458 (70%)	20,008 (30%)
1996–97	56,187	36,490 (65%)	19,697 (35%)
1997–98	47,127	21,142 (45%)	25,985 (55%)
1998–99	49,441	21,510 (44%)	27,931 (56%)
1999–2000	52,246	19,896 (38%)	32,350 (62%)
2000–1	55,860	20,145 (36%)	35,715 (64%)
2001–2	59,380	23,344 (39%)	36,036 (61%)
2002–3	66,570	28,066 (42%)	38,504 (58%)

Sources: Table compiled by author using: DILGEA (1987: 35; 1988: 8; 1989: 9; 1990: 13; 1991: 18; 1992: 18; 1993: 18; 1994: 18; 1995: 18); DIMA (1996: 18; 1997: 18; 1998: 18; 1999: 18; 2000c: 18; 2001: 9); DIMIA (2002a: 8; 2003: 8). Note that economic migration includes skilled and business migration.

Changes under the Liberal-National Coalition government

Upon the election of the Howard Coalition government in 1996, further reform of the immigration programme was undertaken. Although there had been some significant cuts to the family stream in the latter years of the Labor administration (1992–96), the family class had continued to grow, while the ratio and size of the skilled stream was cut, leading to a comparatively larger family stream (see Table 4.1). These trends occurred at the same time as concerns over the economic outcomes of the family class emerged. Data from the newly established *Longitudinal Survey of Immigrants to Australia* (LSIA) indicated that at least in the short-term, visa category was highly determinative of labour market performance (Williams *et al.* 1997: 19). LSIA data identified economic benefits to increasing skilled immigration, while an econometric report in 1996 argued that shifting the focus within the immigration programme toward skilled immigration would add A$2 billion to the Australian economy by 2000 (Carrathers and McGregor 1998).

There were ideological dimensions to this shift towards family-based immigration, which coincided with the election of a Conservative national government in 1996. Upon his appointment in 1996, the new Immigration Minister

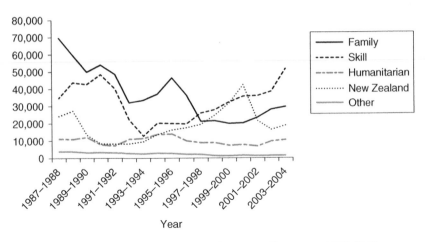

Figure 4.1: Permanent entrants to Australia across all streams, 1987–2003

Philip Ruddock declared that he had 'inherited a migration program that [was] out of balance and out of control' (Ruddock 1996b: 8251). In light of Minister Ruddock's concerns, '[e]very aspect of the family stream was looked at to see whether or not it should be and could be slowed down or limited in some way' (Senior immigration official, interview 26 by author, Australia, 30 October 2009). A flurry of policy options followed to change the mix of the immigration programme. New levels were set in the annual immigration targets, which saw strong reductions in family immigration (Millett 1996; Dore 1997). The concessional class was moved into the skilled category, renamed the 'Australian-Linked Category' and was capped using the capping powers introduced by the ALP in the late 1980s (Birrell 1997: 23). Redefining concessional immigration in this way reduced the family class by around 8,500 entrants and rendered entrants eligible for language testing (DILGEA 1995; DIMA 1996, 1997; Senior immigration officials, interviews 8, 20 and 25 by author, Australia, 24 September 2009, 15 October 2009, 30 October 2009). Finally, the Coalition government passed legislation in 2003 that created a new visa class for aged parent migrants. It imposed not only a health service charge of A$25,000 and an additional A$10,000 Assurance of Support bond for the principal applicant, but also a A$25,000 charge and a smaller A$4,000 bond for any accompanying partner. The bond operates for ten years following entry into Australia (amended through the Migration Legislation Amendment (Contributory Parents Migration Scheme) Bill, 2002). Further, the government changed the law such that the parent class could be capped and entry numbers heavily reduced (Boucher 2013b). As a result of these changes, the family stream was reduced from 70 per cent of overall non-humanitarian intake in 1996 to 38 per cent of intake by 1999 (see Table 4.1 and Figure 4.1 above).

The policy context in Canada: changes in the mix

The historical context: J88 and welfare dependency

Canada over the late 1980s and early 1990s saw similar debates to Australia around the welfare dependency of new immigrants. One senior immigration official observed:

> A lot of people were coming in and going directly on welfare. The provinces started to react. You start having pressures on infrastructure whether it is on schooling, on socials services, that type of thing. And at some point there were huge pressures building on social services and social costs of bringing in large numbers of people. And the family class tend to be a much higher recipient of welfare than the other class. (Interview 16 by author, Canada, 27 August 2008)

In Canada, as in Australia, policy-makers linked the issue of migrant reliance on social assistance to the changing composition of immigration flows in particular increases in humanitarian immigration and family reunification. These trends were compounded by policy changes over the 1980s. In 1987, then Minister for Employment and Immigration, Gerry Weiner, introduced a provision, known as 'J88', which allowed any never-married child of a Canadian resident to be admitted into Canada (EIC 1987: 3, 7). Following the creation of J88, there were significant increases in chain family migration, particularly of parents. A report from 1995 indicates that 'primarily because of previous regulations that permitted never-married children of any age to immigrate as dependents ... [l]andings of parents and grandparents doubled between 1988 and 1992' (CIC 1994a: 9). Senior immigration officials confirmed these multiplicative effects of J88 upon family reunification flows. One immigration official argued that:

> With J88, the mix had really shifted more towards family than we wanted. We realised in '93 there were conversations about 'how do we manage this' ... Even though they changed the regulations in '92, we were still dealing with very large numbers of parents and grandparents. It was virtually crowding out the other categories. (Interview 14 by author, Canada, 21 August 2008)

At the same time as these chain migration trends were under way within the family reunification stream, there was also a movement towards a 'user-pays' logic within Canadian public policy more broadly (CIC 1994b: 3–6, cited in Thobani 2007: 181; Hathaway 1994: 15–16). Debates over the welfare dependency of new immigrants were reinforced by growing reference to the 'mix' of immigration, or the relative balance between the skilled and family reunification streams. From 1965 to 1975, skilled immigrants had made up 50 per cent of permanent intake to Canada, however, from 1976 onwards, coinciding with the diversification of source

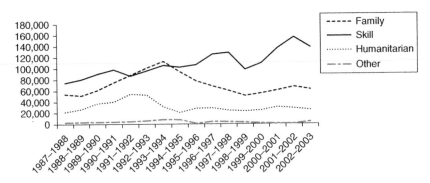

Figure 4.2: Permanent entrants to Canada across all streams, 1987–2003

countries, the family class was increasingly overrepresented (DeVoretz 1995: 2). Despite some small changes in the late 1980s under the Conservative Mulroney government, including rescinding the J88 rule, as Figure 4.2 above makes clear, family reunification numbers were at this stage still very high.

Changes in the mix: the Liberals 1993–98

Changing the mix of the immigration programme became a key policy issue for the Canadian Department of Citizenship and Immigration (CIC) and its new Minister, Sergio Marchi, from 1993 onwards. As in Australia, academic studies informed a perception of declining economic performance on the part of recently arrived immigrants. These reports found that due to reduced human capital among these recent arrivals, new immigrants would not be able to catch up to the earnings of native-born Canadians within a reasonable period (Abbott and Beach 1993; Bloom *et al.* 1995; Li 2003: 83). The title of one seminal study, *Diminishing Returns*, suggested that although recently arrived immigrants were still contributing economically, this was occurring at a reduced rate compared with earlier immigration waves (DeVoretz 1995: 3). A departmental document from 1993 argued:

> There is evidence to suggest that control over the volume and composition of immigration has been eroding. Instead, immigration flows have come to be dominated by persons who are essentially self-selected. This shift has brought with it a concern that the educational and skill advantages formerly enjoyed by immigrants are declining. Only a very small percentage (11 per cent of 24,000 principal applicants) of the immigrants admitted to Canada in 1991 were selected purely on the basis of economic and settlement criteria. (EIC 1993: 2, in Li 2003: 80)

Table 4.2: Permanent entrants to Canada, economy and family streams, 1987–2003

Year	Total (economic and family)	Total family (and as percentage)	(Total economic) and as percentage)
1987–88	127,948	53,840 (42.1%)	74,108 (57.9%)
1988–89	131,645	51,425 (39.1%)	80,220 (60.9%)
1989–90	151,116	60,971 (40.3%)	90,145 (59.7%)
1990–91	172,619	74,686 (43.3%)	97,933 (56.7%)
1991–92	174,477	87,971 (50.4%)	86,506 (49.6%)
1992–93	196,925	101,122 (51.4%)	95,803 (56.7%)
1993–94	218,329	112,666 (51.6%)	105,663 (48.4%)
1994–95	196,506	94,195 (47.9%)	102,311 (52.1%)
1995–96	184,019	77,387 (42.1%)	106,632 (57.9%)
1996–97	193,729	68,359 (35.3%)	125,370 (64.7%)
1997–98	188,331	59,980 (31.8%)	128,351 (68.2%)
1998–99	148,808	50,896 (34.2%)	97,912 (65.8%)
1999–2000	164,527	55,276 (33.6%)	109,251 (66.4%)
2000–1	196,906	60,616 (30.8%)	136,290 (69.2%)
2001–2	222,513	66,795 (30.0%)	155,718 (70.0%)
2002–3	200,154	62,290 (31.1%)	137,864 (68.9%)

Sources: CIC (2009b, 2013d). Note that economic immigration includes skilled immigration and business migration.

In light of these concerns, from 1994 onwards, Minister Marchi began to refer to the need for a more economically focused immigration programme with the 'reorientation' from 1995 onwards 'to applicants who can make an immediate contribution to the Canadian economy' (CIC 1994a: 7–8). This would be achieved 'by increasing the proportion of the economic component in relation to the family; by strengthening selection criteria for economic immigration and by making additional efforts at promoting Canada and recruiting skilled applicants' (CIC 1994a: 7–8). Evidence of a new '60:40' policy of 60 per cent economic and 40 per cent family intake is evident from as early as the CIC 1994 migration report, *A Broader Vision*. In this report, CIC argued that: '[B]eginning in 1996, the balance between economic, family, and other immigrant components will place greater emphasis on attracting those with the capacity to settle quickly and contribute to Canada' (CIC 1994b: 13). The report also identified the need to 'rais[e] selection standards; ... and achiev[e] an appropriate balance between the economic and family components of immigration' (CIC 1994b: 7). As is clear from Table 4.2 and Figure 4.2 above, between 1993 and 1999, family immigration was reduced from 51.6 per cent to 33.6 per cent of the immigration programme at the same time as the skilled intake was gradually increased.

**Changes in the mix: what does changing the mix mean for the gender aware-
ness of immigration policy?**

In Part I of this book, I argued that skilled immigration policy can be designed
to minimise gender bias. Does a shift towards a more skill-focused intake within
the *overall* immigration programme hold gender implications for immigration
policy? This compositional issue is significant given the current global focus on
skilled immigration. When the shift towards skilled immigration was pursued in
Australia and Canada, there was little explicit acknowledgement by policy-makers
in either country of the possible gender implications of these changes, although
these are implicit in policy documents. A CIC report on family immigration from
1994, for instance, noted that 'family class immigrants are more likely than independent principal applicants to be second wage earners and to participate part
time in the labour market. While these attributes would contribute to relatively
lower earnings for family class immigrants, they also diminish the extent of their
economic contribution' (CIC 1994c: 2). What this report fails to identify is possible
reasons for the lower labour force engagement of family reunification immigrants;
in particular the far greater representation of women as principal applicants in
the family class than men and, in turn, the disproportionate engagement of those
immigrants in unpaid work activities, including informal care work that limit
formal labour force engagement.

The principal applicant in both skilled and family immigration streams is the
person who lodges the application, while the secondary applicant is the legal
dependent of the principal, whether or not that person is financially dependent.
Women in both Australia and Canada are underrepresented as principal skilled
applicants – those migrants who meet the points test. As noted, for family reunification, the inverse is true – women are overrepresented as principal applicants;
they often enter as the first-named spouse, parent and extended relative of a male
citizen or existing permanent resident. On this basis we could argue that increasing skilled immigration within the immigration programme mix increases men's
chances of admission and reduces women's chances. However, I shall argue that
the gender implications of the shift in the mix from family reunification to skilled
immigration are more complex than a simple substitution from female-dominated
family reunification to male-dominated skilled immigration.

Women's and men's representation in the skilled and family reunification streams

A preliminary step in assessing this issue is the representation of women as principal applicants in the skilled immigration streams. As Tables 4.3 and 4.4 indicate,
in both countries, from 1996 to 2011, men made up a median of 67 per cent of
applicants who met the points test. It is important to point out that these outcomes do not result from selecting state policies alone. Global gender inequalities
in access to education and training also inform the overrepresentation of men

Table 4.3: Skilled stream principal entrants to Australia, gender disaggregated, 1996–2011

	1996	1997	1998	1999	2000	2001	2002	2003	2004	2005	2006	2007	2008	2009	2010	2011
Female	4063	4143	4308	4190	5911	8130	10,802	12,682	14,781	17,503	17,631	17,354	16,416	14,878	19,604	18,804
	(28%)	(30%)	(32%)	(30%)	(31%)	(32%)	(35%)	(36%)	(37%)	(37%)	(36%)	(33%)	(32%)	(32%)	(35%)	(32%)
Male	10,460	9498	9354	9588	12,982	17,004	20,157	22,639	24,642	29,551	31,366	35,063	34,265	31,638	36,553	40,880
	(72%)	(70%)	(68%)	(70%)	(69%)	(68%)	(65%)	(64%)	(63%)	(63%)	(64%)	(67%)	(68%)	(68%)	(65%)	(68%)
Total	14,523	13,641	13,662	13,778	18,893	25,134	30,959	35,321	39,423	47,054	48,997	52,417	50,681	46,516	56,157	59,684
	(100%)	(100%)	(100%)	(100%)	(100%)	(100%)	(100%)	(100%)	(100%)	(100%)	(100%)	(100%)	(100%)	(100%)	(100%)	(100%)

Sources: Unpublished entrant data provided to author by DIAC (2009b, 2013a). The figures here are aggregated across the various skilled immigration sub-visas.

Table 4.4: Skilled principal applicants to Canada, gender disaggregated, 1996–2011

	1996	1997	1998	1999	2000	2001	2002	2003	2004	2005	2006	2007	2008	2009	2010	2011
Female	12,715	13,117	9900	10,537	12,523	14,472	15,383	14,652	16,765	19,351	18,121	18,623	23,338	24,916	30,751	26,238
	(30%)	(29%)	(28%)	(25%)	(24%)	(25%)	(26%)	(29%)	(30%)	(31%)	(33%)	(35%)	(38%)	(39%)	(40%)	(41%)
Male	29,436	31,852	26,058	31,010	39,603	44,437	42,794	36,553	38,387	42,236	37,562	35,167	37,914	39,045	45,758	38,076
	(70%)	(71%)	(72%)	(75%)	(76%)	(75%)	(74%)	(71%)	(70%)	(69%)	(67%)	(65%)	(62%)	(61%)	(60%)	(59%)
Total	42,151	44,969	35,958	41,547	52,126	58,909	58,177	51,205	55,152	61,587	55,683	53,790	61,252	63,961	76,509	64,314
	(100%)	(100%)	(100%)	(100%)	(100%)	(100%)	(100%)	(100%)	(100%)	(100%)	(100%)	(100%)	(100%)	(100%)	(100%)	(100%)

Sources: CIC (2005: 12–13; 2013g).

and underrepresentation of women as principal skilled immigrants (Boucher 2007: 392; Iredale 2005: 157–8; Purkayastha 2005).

Yet, for reasons discussed in Chapter 1, it is also clear that the selection criteria for skilled immigration will likely be more difficult to achieve for those who engage in part-time work, child rearing and for those with skills in areas of emotional labour and care work. In contrast to their underrepresentation as principal skilled entrants, women are overrepresented as principal family immigrants in Australia and Canada over the same time period. Putting aside children where the sexes are evenly represented in immigration flows, women are overrepresented across all other family class categories. As Tables 4.5 and 4.6 make clear, women on average comprise over 60 per cent of principal applicants in the family stream in both countries. In certain other subcategories, such as the fiancée visa, this figure ranges between 75 and 82 per cent (e.g. CIC 2005; DIAC 2010c).

On the basis of this apparent 'gender gap' between the skilled and family streams, certain commentators have contended that the relative weight of the streams within the immigration programme is a key gender issue. Avvy Yao-Yao Go, principal solicitor from the Metro Toronto Chinese and Southeast Asian Legal Clinic argues that '[a]s you focus more and more on independent immigrants and less and less on the family class, you will see more and more immigrant men coming, as opposed to immigrant women' (Metro 2001: 8; see also Metro 2000: 4). Similarly, immigration law expert Catherine Dauvergne (2000: 302) has stated that 'when the government shifts its migration preferences from the family stream to the economic stream, it shifts its preference from women (however dependently defined) to men'. Similarly, Eleonore Kofman and Veena Meetoo (2008: 167) suggest that a 're-orientation towards family migration and a downsizing of the family component' amounts to a 'devaluation of family relationships [that] is unlikely to be of assistance in the management of the complex human process that is international migration'. Finally, and perhaps most clearly, a report of the United Nations in 1994 argued that choice over immigration mix is central to gender relations within immigration policy:

> [T]hroughout the world, the formulation of migration laws and regulations is influenced by prevailing conceptions of the family and of the roles that different family members ought to play. Women, as spouses or daughters, are traditionally assumed to have primarily non-economic roles under the assumption that their husbands or fathers are responsible for satisfying the family's economic needs. These perceptions are translated into immigration regulations that, in some circumstances, can actually favour female migration by facilitating the admission of dependents. On the other hand, in countries that either restrict or discourage family reunification, or which admit mainly migrant workers, the migration of women will tend to be smaller than that of men. (UN 1994: 69, cited in DeLaet 1999: 4–5)

The assumption that flows from this scholarship is that shifting the immigration programme mix from family to skilled immigration will in turn disadvantage

Table 4.5: Family principal entrants to Australia, gender disaggregated, 1996–2011

	1996	1997	1998	1999	2000	2001	2002	2003	2004	2005	2006	2007	2008	2009	2010	2011
Female	17,948	16,684	16,981	17,153	18,106	20,541	21,859	21,706	21,832	24,414	27,492	27,684	30,640	32,700	30,611	32,221
	(60%)	(62%)	(62%)	(62%)	(61%)	(62%)	(61%)	(60%)	(62%)	(63%)	(64%)	(65%)	(64%)	(64%)	(66%)	(65%)
Male	12,209	10,204	10,410	10,738	11,391	12,856	13,783	14,369	13,517	14,229	15,297	15,058	16,867	18,044	15,955	17,555
	(40%)	(38%)	(38%)	(38%)	(39%)	(38%)	(39%)	(40%)	(38%)	(37%)	(36%)	(35%)	(36%)	(36%)	(34%)	(35%)
Total	30,157	26,888	27,391	27,891	29,497	33,397	35,642	36,075	35,349	38,643	42,789	42,742	47,507	50,744	46,566	49,776
	(100%)	(100%)	(100%)	(100%)	(100%)	(100%)	(100%)	(100%)	(100%)	(100%)	(100%)	(100%)	(100%)	(100%)	(100%)	(100%)

Sources: Unpublished entrant data provided to author by DIAC (2009b, 2013a).

Table 4.6: Family principal entrants to Canada, gender disaggregated, 1996–2011

	1996	1997	1998	1999	2000	2001	2002	2003	2004	2005	2006	2007	2008	2009	2010	2011
Female	28,624	26,356	24,019	26,477	28,725	30,570	33,813	35,681	34,337	34,280	38,280	36,044	35,773	35,394	32,622	30,157
	(58%)	(58%)	(61%)	(61%)	(61%)	(60%)	(62%)	(63%)	(63%)	(61%)	(60%)	(61%)	(60%)	(60%)	(60%)	(59%)
Male	21,153	18,830	15,618	16,971	18,514	20,340	20,781	20,940	20,333	21,652	24,999	23,105	23,645	24,081	22,173	21,103
	(42%)	(42%)	(39%)	(39%)	(39%)	(40%)	(38%)	(37%)	(37%)	(39%)	(40%)	(39%)	(40%)	(40%)	(40%)	(41%)
Total	49,777	45,186	39,637	43,448	47,239	50,910	54,594	56,621	54,670	55,932	63,279	59,149	59,418	59,475	54,795	51,260
	(100%)	(100%)	(100%)	(100%)	(100%)	(100%)	(100%)	(100%)	(100%)	(100%)	(100%)	(100%)	(100%)	(100%)	(100%)	(100%)

Sources: CIC (2005e: 15–16; 2013g).

women more than men. In the following section, I interrogate this argument through empirical analysis of gender-disaggregated immigration statistics.

Cutting the family reunification stream: gender implications

In order to assess the gender implications of cuts to family immigration in Australia and Canada, it is necessary to distinguish between immediate family (spouses, fiancées and children) and extended family (parents, grandparents and adult-age children, siblings, nephews and nieces). With regard to the first category of immediate family members, there were some reductions in this category in Australia between 1996 and 1998, although no analogous cuts in Canada (CIC 2005; DIMA 2000c: 18). However, to argue on this basis alone that there have been gender-unaware policy changes overlooks a key point. While intake of spouses and fiancées was reduced in Australia, there were also increases from 2000 onwards in the intake of secondary applicants (spouses and children) of those principal skilled applicants entering within the skilled stream (see Table 4.7 below). Canada saw similar, although more staggered, increases for secondary applicants within the skilled stream over this same period (see Table 4.8 below). As such, there seems to have been a substitution effect between entrants of immediate family as principal applicants in the family stream to dependents in the skilled stream. While formally a reclassification from family to skill, the end result is substantively similar; women are entering as dependents but of skilled immigrants, rather than dependents of existing residents and citizens.

With regard to the second category of the family reunification stream, the extended family, the gender story is more complex. There is no possible sub-stitution effect between the streams. Extended family cannot enter as accompanying dependents under the skilled category. Rather, they are required to apply separately as reuniting family members, once the original sponsor has settled. A less considered issue is the gender make-up of remaining extended family: adult children, siblings, nieces and nephews. Gender-disaggregated data are not available on entrants arriving as a result of J88 in Canada. This was the provision that allowed unmarried children of any age to reunite with their families. Analysis of the concessional category that operated under similar rules in Australia does, however, provide some insights into gendered admissions of extended family members. As noted earlier in this chapter, this class provided skilled applicants with easier entrance under a modified points test, based on their family connections. The concessional class was located in the family reunification stream, which meant that before 1997, it was not tested for English language skills.

What were the gender implications of the restrictions placed upon extended family classes from the late 1980s onwards? Unpublished data from the Department of Immigration and Citizenship indicate that the concessional class

Table 4.7: Skilled stream, secondary applicants to Australia, gender disaggregated, 1996–2011

	1996	1997	1998	1999	2000	2001	2002	2003	2004	2005	2006	2007	2008	2009	2010	2011
Female	12,168	12,056	12,360	12,686	15,184	16,661	20,394	20,574	21,985	28,835	28,377	33,098	37,419	36,450	34,225	39,076
	(60%)	(58%)	(58%)	(59%)	(59%)	(59%)	(58%)	(57%)	(57%)	(57%)	(58%)	(59%)	(58%)	(59%)	(59%)	(59%)
Male	7984	8749	8873	8888	10,643	11,710	14,698	15,347	16,459	21,447	20,548	23,025	26,677	24,886	23,336	26,988
	(40%)	(42%)	(42%)	(41%)	(41%)	(41%)	(42%)	(43%)	(43%)	(43%)	(42%)	(41%)	(42%)	(41%)	(41%)	(41%)
Total	20,152	20,805	21,233	21,574	25,827	28,371	35,092	35,921	38,444	50,282	48,925	56,123	64,096	61,336	57,561	66,064
	(100%)	(100%)	(100%)	(100%)	(100%)	(100%)	(100%)	(100%)	(100%)	(100%)	(100%)	(100%)	(100%)	(100%)	(100%)	(100%)

Sources: Unpublished entrant data, provided to author by DIAC (2007b, 2013a).

Table 4.8: Skilled stream secondary applicants to Canada, gender disaggregated, 1996–2011

	1996	1997	1998	1999	2000	2001	2002	2003	2004	2005	2006	2007	2008	2009	2010	2011
Female	33,436	36,418	27,719	31,918	41,840	49,002	42,941	36,749	39,439	46,253	31,791	29,211	32,364	32,305	38,123	30,782
	(60%)	(60%)	(61%)	(63%)	(63%)	(63%)	(62%)	(61%)	(60%)	(59%)	(66%)	(65%)	(64%)	(62%)	(61%)	(59%)
Male	22,327	24,261	17,589	19,033	24,632	29,322	26,815	23,098	26,114	31,723	16,032	15,664	18,510	19,647	24,166	21,086
	(40%)	(40%)	(39%)	(37%)	(37%)	(37%)	(38%)	(39%)	(40%)	(41%)	(34%)	(35%)	(36%)	(38%)	(39%)	(41%)
Total	55,763	60,679	45,308	50,951	66,472	78,324	69,756	59,847	65,553	77,976	47,823	44,875	50,874	51,952	62,289	51,868
	(100%)	(100%)	(100%)	(100%)	(100%)	(100%)	(100%)	(100%)	(100%)	(100%)	(100%)	(100%)	(100%)	(100%)	(100%)	(100%)

Sources: 2002–5: CIC (2011a); 2006–11: CIC (2013f).

provided a significant entrance point for women, who were represented at rates 10 per cent higher than in the standard skilled stream (DIAC 2009b). Similarly, women in both countries are overrepresented as aged parents at a ratio of approximately 60:40, with ratios constant across time (CIC 2012c; DIAC 2009b). This finding highlights the fact that skilled immigration selection schemes with familial connections may benefit women as these compensate for their absence of other human capital attributes. This analysis implies more nuanced gender dynamics in mix changes than those suggested by existing commentators. While pointing to potentially significant gender impact in cuts to extended family members, the analysis finds that for immediate family in both countries, there has more likely been a substitution from principal family to secondary skilled applicants.

Increasing admission through the skilled stream

Changes to the mix were also achieved through increasing the intake within the skilled stream. The central gender issue here is that any expansion of economic immigration selection poses the greatest opportunities for applicants with skills that match those selection criteria. Putting aside Live-in Caregivers who are predominately women, this group of eligible applicants is largely male. Entrance as a principal skilled applicant provides advantages over admission as a secondary applicant or as a reunifying spouse. The first is that a principal applicant has his or her skills assessed and accredited prior to entrance, which contributes to higher chances of gaining employment upon settlement (Hawthorne 1996; Mojab 1999). Research by Lesleyanne Hawthorne (2007: 115) demonstrates that principal female skilled applicants in Australia have high rates of employment compared with Australian women, and compared with earlier immigration flows, but it is important to remember that it is the minority of female entrants into the skilled stream that come as principal applicants; the majority enter as spouses. Conversely, research by Sue Richardson and collaborators indicates that secondary applicants have much lower rates of employment when compared with principal skilled applicants (Richardson *et al.* 2004). In the Canadian context, Rupa Banerjee and Mai Phan (2014) and Jennifer Elrick and Naomi Lightman (2014) demonstrate that secondary applicants with professional qualifications have a harder time finding work upon entry into Canada than principal applicants. They also experience lower wage growth than first-named applicants. As women are disproportionately secondary applicants, they are more likely to be affected by these trends than men.

In addition, in Australia, a secondary applicant is tied to the principal applicant for a two-year period following landing on a temporary visa. If the relationship breaks down, the secondary applicant can be refused a permanent visa to remain and can be deported, while the principal applicant can remain (Migration Regulations 1994, regulation 1.23; Crock and Berg 2011: 7.2.2–7.2.4). Recent changes in Canada have emulated this two-year temporary visa policy.[1] While both countries have a rule under which secondary applicants in domestic violence situations are protected from deportation, the reality is that reporting of domestic violence is heavily understated within immigrant communities. Further, requests for use of the domestic violence exemption are discretionary and might be denied by decision-makers (Domestic violence rights advocate, interview 33 by author, Australia, 11 November 2009; CCR 2013).

As Monica Boyd (1991: 6; 1997: 147) argues, secondary categories render a class of 'dependents' within immigrant family units that decreases opportunity for autonomous migration and increases reliance upon romantic relationships. It is here that selecting states have the capacity to open up the opportunities for women to apply as principal applicants through points test design, an issue I explore in detail in Chapters 5 and 6.

For now, it is useful to consider how the policy process in Australia and Canada can be explained. In particular, how was this rapid transformation in the immigration programme in both countries achieved over the late 1980s to mid-1990s? This analysis is instructive not only for understanding policy changes in these two countries but also for other countries, such as the United States, which have struggled to transfer their immigration programme. In the next section of this chapter, I draw upon the theories of venue shopping set out in Chapter 3, to explain the realisation of these policy goals.

The policy process for rebalancing the mix in Australia and Canada

The shift in Australia and Canada away from family reunification towards skilled immigration was achieved through a series of regulatory and administrative policy reforms. In the following section of this chapter, I consider the relevant policy venues where policy changes occurred, and the engagement of groups, both internal and external to government, in this process.

The 'rebalancing' of the family reunification and economic streams was a policy concern in Australia since the FitzGerald Report of 1988. Initially, the relative balance between the family and the skilled streams was achieved through significant reductions in the concessional class (BIR 1993: 9). These changes in the mix continued upon the 1996 election of the Conservative Liberal-National Coalition. Minister Ruddock, after failing in his first few years to convince Prime Minister John Howard to increase the overall migration programme size in order to bolster the relative proportion of skilled flows instead decided 'to push the skill, to control the family stream, and then to work in respect of the humanitarian refugee scheme' (Former senior policy advisor, interview 24 by author, Australia, 23 October 2009). In 1996, Minister Ruddock introduced English testing for the concessional class, through regulation. The opposition parties united in the Senate to disallow this provision (Bolkus 1996: 5258). Following this defeat, administrative measures were instead used to expand the Occupations Requiring English

Table 4.9: Planned immigration levels for the family reunification and skilled streams, Australia, 1989–2003

	Total	Family	Skilled
1989–90	125,000	71,000	54,000
1990–91	114,000	64,000	50,000
1991–92	98,500	56,000	42,500
1992–93	68,800	45,000	23,800
1993–94	62,000	45,000	17,000
1994–95	75,500	47,000	28,500
1995–96	81,800	58,200	23,600
1996–97	72,700	44,700	28,000
1997–98	65,500	30,500	35,000
1998–99	66,400	31,400	35,000
1999–2000	67,000	32,000	35,000
2000–1	91,400	37,900	53,500
2001–2	103,900	43,200	60,700
2002–3	103,900	40,600	63,300

Sources: Table compiled by author. Humanitarian entrants and 'other' categories such as retiree are excluded. 1989–96: DIAC (2010a); 1997–2003: Ruddock (1998, 1999, 2002); DIMIA (2001: 16; 2002b: 17).

(ORE List), a list that set out professions where mandatory English was required. The ORE List was increased to cover 85 per cent of all professions – up from 25 per cent previously (Ruddock 1996b: 8639). As the concessional class was at the same time moved into the skilled stream, it was then also subject to the ORE List. Following the expansion of the ORE List, concessional class entrants fell further from 8,103 in 1996 down to 4,505 by 2003 (DIMA 1997: 18; DIMA 2003). The expansion of the ORE List was in this way a mechanism to achieve significant policy change without legislative reform. It can be viewed as a successful venue move by government from the legislative to the bureaucratic arena, which avoided political blockages in the Senate.

The general setting of immigration levels was also important in informing changes in the mix of the immigration programme. The Migration Act, section 85 empowers the Minister to determine the number of visas in any visa class in any year. This 'levels' process, which occurs by ministerial gazettal rather than legislative change, provides a subtle administrative tool to exercise substantial control over the immigration programme. Section 85 was used during this period to set new levels for the skilled and family streams, which affected their relative distribution in the overall programme. Table 4.9 below shows the planned levels set by the Minister for Immigration in Australia for the immigration programme from 1989 through to 2003.

As is clear from Table 4.9, the levels for the family stream were slowly reduced from 1989 onwards and the entire skilled immigration levels were increased from 1997. While some public consultation is conducted throughout the year prior to the levels-setting exercise, generally informants characterised this process as executive-driven (Former senior immigration officials, interviews 4, 24, 25 and 26 by author, Australia, 18 September 2009, 23 October 2009, 30 October 2009, 30 October 2009).

Further, the power to set levels is accompanied by other delegated administrative powers that are centralised within the immigration ministry. Using combined powers under sections 85, 91 and 499 of the Migration Act, the Minister can issue a Priority Processing Direction that instructs officers to prioritise the processing of certain applications over others. This power, together with that to cease applications in a visa class, played a significant role in enabling the government to shift the composition of the immigration programme. In 1996, Minister Ruddock employed these powers to prioritise processing of applications of spouses of Australian citizens and dependent children and to deprioritise the processing of aged parents (DIMA 2000b; Ruddock 1996b: 8639). According to one former senior immigration official, these prioritisation powers 'become an important tool in … general case management practices and pipeline management practices' (Interview 18 by author, Australia, 15 October 2009).

Finally, levels were also met through resource allocation decisions from 1996 onwards. Processing ports that could deliver skilled migrants were allocated additional resources in order to assess applicants. As one former senior immigration official involved in these policies put it, the Department had to 'take the migration programme, and, without calling them quotas, distribute around, posts all around the world saying "this is how many visas you are going to deliver me…"'. At times this process also involved significant, 'fairly rapid resource transferring going on from initial migration countries, to new migration countries'. This senior official added, 'We never had quotas. But we certainly, you can't manage a migration programme across 60 posts without … giving them an idea. And it's through resource allocation' (Interview 24 by author, Australia, 23 October 2009). These decisions over resources occurred without any changes to the Migration Act or its regulations and without any legislative intervention.

By their own admission, diversity-seeking groups were 'very quiet' on the changes to the mix that occurred from 1988 onwards (Former ethnocultural leader, interview 10 by author, Australia, 2 October 2009). Aside from some initial attempted opposition to the introduction of English language testing for the concessional class, this backlash did not prevent or delay changes in composition. There were some protests by the Federation of Ethnic Communities' Councils of Australia when the levels for the family reunification stream were cut in 1997 and 1998 (ECC NSW 1998; FECCA 1998); however, generally the level of protest was mute (Carruthers and McGregor 1998; Dore 1997; Millett 1997). Importantly from a gender perspective, there was no attention to the particular gender implications

Table 4.10: Planned immigration levels for the family reunification and skilled immigration streams, Canada, 1989–2003

Year	Total	Family	Skilled
1989–90	122,000	57,000	65,000
1990–91	133,000	61,000	72,000
1991–92	168,500	80,000	88,500
1992–93	189,000	100,000	89,000
1993–94	192,000	95,000	97,000
1994–95	220,700	110,000	110,700
1995–96	170,000	90,000	80,000
1996–97	180,200	85,700	94,500
1997–98	179,200	66,200	113,000
1998–99	186,200	58,300	127,900
1999–2000	189,200	58,300	130,900
2000–1	191,700	61,000	130,700
2001–2	191,700	61,000	130,700
2002–3	195,000	58,000	137,000

Sources: Table compiled by author. Upper limited reported for all categories. Humanitarian entrants and 'other' categories such as retiree are excluded. EIC 1989; 1990 – EIC 1990: 2; 1991–93 – EIC 1990: 9; 1994 – CIC 1994d: 1; 1995 – CIC 1994a: 6; 1996 – CIC 1995: 8; 1997 – CIC 1996: 3; 1998 – CIC 1997: 3; 1999 – CIC 1998b: 3; 2000 – CIC 1999c, 7; 2001–2: CIC 2001c: 21; 2002–3 – CIC 2002c: 20.

of these changes, such as women's greater reliance on the concessional or aged parent class. It is clear that bureaucratic control over the policy process limited intervention by outside interests, including diversity-seeking groups, and that the immigration programme was changed speedily and with little critical engagement from such groups.

Concerns over the economic costs and welfare dependency rates of new immigrants in Canada in the early 1990s precipitated the shifts in the immigration mix that I have documented in this chapter. By 1997, planned immigration levels began to reflect an official policy position of 60 per cent skilled immigration and 40 per cent family flows, known as the '60:40 policy' within bureaucratic circles (Senior immigration officials, interviews 13 and 16 by author, Canada, 19 August 2008 and 27 August 2008; see Table 4.10).

These changes in the mix were critiqued by several diversity-seeking groups (Diversity-seeking leader, interview 4 by author, Canada, 19 July 2008; Sarick 1994, citing NAC) as well as by the minority New Democratic Party (Standing Committee 2002: 84). Before a parliamentary committee, Avvy Yao-Yao Go of the Metro Toronto Chinese and Southeast Asian Legal Clinic pointed out that 'since [the Liberals] came to power, the percentage of family class immigrants has been gradually reduced, from over 50 per cent of the overall immigration population in 1992 to under 30 per cent today' (Metro 2001: 5). In 1994, when reductions to family reunification levels were first proposed, a protest was held in Toronto but this did not lead to any change in policy (Rankin 1994).

Ultimately, despite opposition to the 60:40 policy, diversity-seeking groups had little capacity to influence these changes. As in Australia, the Minister in Canada sets levels administratively (IRPA, s 94(2)(b)). While the levels are tabled in Parliament and while there is, as in Australia, consultation with interest groups and provinces over levels setting, the actual decision is determined within Cabinet and achieved through a variety of resource allocation decisions (Macklin 2002: 248; Simmons and Keohane 1992: 439–40). An activist from a key ethnocultural organisation commented on the limited capacity for diversity-seeking intervention in this levels-setting process, given tight bureaucratic control over the process:

> [CIC] didn't have to change anything in writing, it's just had to decide how many staff you are going to put in the visa posting in Cairo, and how many staff you are going to put in the visa posting in Paris. It's as simple as that. That's an internal bureaucratic decision, it's operations. Whereas, you don't have any political will for making these seismic changes in immigration policy and what's really frightening, is the amount of power that bureaucrats wield in situations like these that have far reaching consequences and we've seen that happen. (Ethnocultural leader, interview 27 by author, Canada, 18 September 2008)

Informants within government reinforced the position that levels setting is a fairly closed and bureaucratically driven process. As one senior immigration official noted: 'It is not a very transparent process in the sense of those instructions to the offices are not part of the report tabled in parliament' (Senior immigration official, interview 13 by author, Canada, 19 August 2008). In the mid-1990s, when the 60:40 policy was initiated, backlogs became a central method to manage the composition of the immigration programme. Instructions could be provided to various processing ports regarding which backlogs to focus on. One senior immigration official noted that changes to the mix were essentially achieved through 'the use of levels basically and putting more ... the resources where we were getting the greater number of skilled immigrants and things like that. As you are shifting your mix, you also need to look at where the application mix is and where you have your resources' (Former senior immigration official, interview 16 by author, Canada, 27 August 2008). Growing backlogs, especially of aged parents, were raised as a concern by a number of diversity-seeking groups but there was little that they could do about this issue, related as it is to administrative resource allocation (i.e. Ethnocultural leader, interview 21 by author, Canada, 12 September 2008). In short, through a series of resource decisions, Canada, like Australia, was able to achieve significant changes in its immigration programme mix over the mid to late 1990s. In both countries, considerable bureaucratic control over the policy process allowed government to achieve these goals, with limited intervention by outsider groups.

Conclusion

By the mid-1990s, the immigration programmes in Australia and Canada had been transformed, with a far greater percentage of immigrants entering through skilled immigration channels than a decade earlier. While this chapter does not dispute the economic arguments in favour of these changes in selection, it highlights some of the gender concerns inherent in the shift towards skilled immigration. It finds that while a shift towards skilled immigration will mean that more men than women are principal applicants (as men are overrepresented as principal applicants in skilled entrance), this alone does not mean that the shift has negative consequences for gender. This is because the skilled stream also provides opportunities for the entrance of immediate family members, as dependents of secondary applicants within the skilled stream. When conducting a gender analysis it is therefore necessary to differentiate between categories of the family class, in particular between immediate and extended family entrants. For the latter, changes in the mix raise gender concerns. As we have seen, parent and aged parents, as well as the concessional class, are all categories where women predominate. Across these categories, there was reduced admission from the late 1980s onwards.

Some of these policy trends continued in the latter part of the 2000s, particularly in Canada. Between 2007 and 2010, the proportionate percentage of family migration in Canada decreased from 19 per cent to 14.5 per cent (Alboim and Cohl 2013: 27). Further, in 2011, the Canadian government placed a moratorium on future applications under the permanent parent and grandparent category in light of a considerable backlog of places. In 2013, a new moratorium was introduced until 1 January 2014, and a new annual limit of 5,000 applications per year was established. The government also tightened asset testing for sponsors of parents and grandparents to ensure that they have the means to support family members (Black 2013b). At the same time as restricting permanent entry for the elderly, a new 'Super Visa' was created that allows a parent or grandparent two years of entry on a temporary basis over a ten-year period (Alboim and Cohl 2013: 28). These changes further curtailed the immigrant rights of extended family rights and mirror those in Australia in the early 2000s. They could intimate even greater shifts towards skilled immigration in the permanent mix in Canada in the future.

Note

1 These rules were only introduced in Canada in 2012 (IRPR regulations 70–72) but have been in place in Australia since 1996: Regulations 1994, Schedule 2, subclauses 801; 802.

5

New selection grids: points tests and gender effects, 1993–2003

Introduction

Points tests or 'quantitative assessments of human capital' (Papademetriou 2008) are a popular mechanism by which to select skilled immigrants. Applicants must aggregate points received for different criteria to meet a 'pass mark' for admission. Canada and Australia are leaders in points tests, having adopted them in 1962 and 1973 respectively (Hawkins 1989). Australia and Canada were also the first countries to refine their points-test systems from the 1990s onwards. In Australia in 1999 and in Canada in 2002, new points tests were adopted that placed more emphasis on language, education and, in the Australian case, work experience than previous selection grids. In both countries, these new points tests also reduced the emphasis on familial connections within skilled immigration selection, by removing or limiting points gained from 'sponsorship' by family members already resident in Australia and Canada. This hinted at the growing demarcation between the skilled and family streams outlined in the previous chapter.

Despite similar policy trajectories there were also important differences between Australia and Canada with their new points tests. The Australian selection grid placed more emphasis on occupational requirements and targeted skills, whereas the Canadian test allocated higher points for education and general human capital endowment. There were also concomitant gender differences. The Canadian points test was the first to be subject to a Gender-Based Analysis (GBA), a significant development that was accompanied by the establishment of a Gender-Based Analysis Unit within the Department of Citizenship Immigration Canada. Australia did not undertake any similar gender auditing of its new points test, nor did it establish a unit specialised in gender assessment of policy. In this chapter, I argue that the Canadian points test contained more gender-aware dimensions than its Australian counterpart. In the first section of this chapter, I outline the key policy developments in Australia and Canada from the 1990s onwards that led to the adoption of new points tests. I then consider the gender implications of these changes, both through analysis of the relevant policies and through the presentation of gender-disaggregated data. In the final section, I examine differences in policy processes in the two countries, in particular the greater degree of bureaucratic control exercised in Australia and the heightened role played by diversity-seeking groups in the policy process in Canada.

The policy context in Australia

Following the FitzGerald Inquiry in 1988, a Skilled-Independent category
was introduced for skilled immigration admission into Australia. In its structure, it most closely approximated a points test designed by a public servant
in Canada in 1962. At this time, compulsory language testing was introduced
for those skilled occupations requiring English and the 'Occupations Requiring
English' (ORE) list, discussed in Chapter 4, was created (Birrell 1997: 32).
However, despite these policy changes, there were ongoing concerns over the
welfare dependency of new immigrants. On this basis, upon his appointment as
Minister for Immigration in 1996, Philip Ruddock brought attention to revising
skilled immigration selection and commissioned an external review to study
the existing selection grid. The External Reference Committee recommended
in its *Review of the Independent and Skilled-Australian Independent Categories*
that greater points be allocated under the points test for 'the core employability
factors of skill, age and English language ability' (DIMA 1999: 2). The Review,
initiated in late 1998, culminated in a new points test introduced in mid-1999.
This new points test increased the requirements for education, work experience
and arranged employment, with differences between the points test before and
after the 1999 reforms outlined in Table 5.1.

An important feature of this new points test was a move away from a general
human capital towards an occupationally targeted model. During this period, a
Migrant Occupations on Demand List (MODL) was introduced which allocated
up to five bonus points for those occupations where there was strong economic
demand. Decisions over the content of the MODL list were determined by the
Department of Education, Employment and Workplace Relations (DEEWR), initially on an annual basis (DIMA 1999: 5). The shift from a targeted to a specialised model was based on research conducted in the mid-1990s by academics Bob
Birrell and Lesleyanne Hawthorne (1997, 1999) and, later, data coming through
the first wave of the *Longitudinal Survey of Immigrants to Australia* (LSIA). These
studies indicated that since the mid-1980s, entrants in certain occupations did
well economically after arrival, whereas for others, in the words of one senior
departmental officer, 'the labour market results were hopeless' (Senior immigration official, interview 8 by author, Australia, 24 September 2009). On the basis
of these deteriorating economic outcomes, a targeted model of skills selection
was seen to better deliver those workers who matched the current needs of the
Australian economy (Birrell 1998; Birrell and Hawthorne 1997, 1999).

The cut-off age to receive maximum points under the new selection grid was
also reduced significantly from pension age (of sixty-five for men and sixty for
women) down to thirty years for both sexes. The points test was heavily weighed
towards the young with a strong tapering off in points for those over thirty. At the
same time, English language requirements were also heightened. While there was
no increase in the points allocated for English, following the review, mandatory
language testing was introduced and the required language ability was increased

Table 5.1: The Australian points test for skilled immigrants, before and after the 1999 reforms

	Before reforms	After reforms
Points		
Occupation (based on general occupations list)	80	0
Occupational/training based factor – based on particular skill	0	60
Education	0	15
English ability	20	20
Australian work experience	0	10
Age	30	30
Demographic	0	0
Relatives in Australia	15	15
Relative an Australian citizen for at least five years	10	0
Relative's employment situation	10	0
Arranged employment	0	15
Spouse's education	0	5
Bonus points	0	5
Total	165	175
Pass mark	**110**	**120**

Source: Tabled compiled by author using Migration Regulations 1994, Schedule 6, consolidated on 1 July 1999; Migration Regulations 1994, Schedule 6A, consolidated on 10 December 1998.

across all bands of the International English Language Testing System (IELTS) examination.[1]

With the exception of some additional points for spouses, there was no acknowledgement of possible gender issues in the design of the new points test. A recommendation to move away from a 'principal/secondary applicant' model and instead assess the points of migrating couples was rejected during a 1989 regulatory consolidation of the points test and was not revisited in the 1998 reforms (Academic expert, interview 12 by author, Australia, 8 October 2009). When considering part-time work experience of less than twenty hours per week, the External Reference Committee noted that '[w]hile it is not necessary to be employed on a full-time basis to perform the full range of duties of an occupation, it is unlikely that a person working only a few hours would be able to demonstrate this' (DIMA 1999: 61). The gender implications of this decision went unassessed.

Policy context in Canada over the 1990s and 2000s

In the early 1990s, policy-makers began to call for a new approach to skilled immigration selection (Ruddick and Burstein 1993: 24). Immigration Minister Sergio

Marchi's 1995 *Immigration Report to Parliament* emphasised the need for 'education, official language ability, decision-making skills, motivation and initiative' of selected immigrants (CIC 1995: 9). The proceeding report, *Not Just Numbers*, reinforced the desire for heightened human capital endowment among skilled immigrants (ILRAG 1997: 6.1). Departmental consultations provided additional evidence in favour of a 'human capital' model that focused on general skills, such as education and language (CIC 1999a, 1999b, 2000). A review by the Standing Committee on Citizenship and Immigration followed from 2001 through to 2003 and the new points test was published in the regulations to the new immigration act, the IRPA.

At the same time as the legislative process leading to the new immigration act, the IRPA, was under way in Canada, CIC both established a Gender-Based Analysis Unit and introduced a gender-auditing tool, known as Gender-Based Analysis (GBA) in the draft bill and accompanying regulations. These gender-aware changes were a response to political pressure from diversity-seeking groups in Canada, as well as support within the Women's Caucus of the Canadian Liberal Party and then Minister for Immigration, Elinor Caplan, who was a strong advocate of gender issues (Former Liberal Party parliamentarian, interview 37 by author, Canada, 19 May 2009; Former GBA officer, interview 9 by author, Canada, 8 August 2009). Inspiration was taken from gender mainstreaming initiatives at the United Nations level that flowed on from the Beijing Platform for Action for Equality, Development and Peace. Importantly, the GBA Unit was established within the powerful Strategic Policy Branch of the immigration department and was headed by a high profile public servant, Sandra Harder. This placement enabled horizontal influence by the GBA Unit into other departmental sections that contributed to the new immigration legislation (Boucher 2010: 193).

Further, as a product of calls from minority member Judy Wasylycia-Leis of the New Democratic Party within the Standing Committee of Citizenship and Immigration, the government also introduced a provision in the immigration act that ensured an annual GBA would be incorporated into the Minister for Immigration and Citizenship's Annual Report to Parliament. The rationale behind this provision was to establish ongoing monitoring of gender issues within the immigration portfolio, beyond the initial gender audit of the IRPA.

The differences between the points test before and after the 2002 IRPA reforms are depicted in Table 5.2.

As Table 5.2 makes clear, the *IRPA* points test saw a 40 per cent reduction in the points allocated for occupational skill. This is understandable on the basis that the new points test represented an attempt to move in the opposite direction of Australia – away from a specific, targeted model of skill towards an assessment of general human capital. The emphasis in Canada under the new selection grid was on education, language and work experience. Correspondingly, the points for education were increased by 14 per cent, the points for language by 15 per cent and there was a 20 per cent increase in work experience points. The GBA Unit within

Table 5.2: Canadian Federal Skilled Immigrant points test before and after the Immigration and Refugee Protection Act ('IRPA') (2002) reforms

	Before reforms	After reforms
Points		
Occupation (based on general occupations list)	10	0
Occupational/training-based factor – based on particular skill	18	0
Education	16	25
Languages (English and French)	15 points in total	24 points in total
First language	9	16
Second language	6	8
Work experience	8	21
Age	10 (ages 21–44)	10 (ages 21–49)
Demographic	10	0
Relatives in Canada	5	5
Arranged employment	10	10
Adaptability	10 points in total	10 points in total
Spouse's work	0	5
Spouse's education	0	5
One year's work in Canada	0	5
Two years' work in Canada	0	5
Arranged employment	0	5
Relative in Canada	See above	5
Pass mark	70	67

Sources: Table compiled by author using IRPR, ss78–83, consolidated on 11 June 2002; Immigration Regulations (1978) (Cth), Schedule 1, 2001 consolidation.

CIC lauded the shift under the 2002 points test from a specific to general human capital model as a gender-aware achievement (CIC 2001a, 2002a).

There were also debates in Canada over the political dimension of defining 'skill'. Departmental analysis of the statistical *Immigration Database (IMDB)* had found that professional occupations such as management, teaching and medicine performed best economically (CIC 1998a: 52). Yet despite what departmental analysts presented as an empirical fact, discussions within the Standing Committee on Citizenship and Immigration ('the Committee') from late 2001 to early 2002 challenged a simple economic assessment of 'skill'. Feminist activists were concerned that the definition of skill encapsulated in the new points test reflected prevailing gendered market biases. The West Coast Domestic Workers' Association, for instance, argued that the 'evaluation system unjustly discriminates against women as it introduces selection criteria emphasising higher education and experience in highly-skilled, male-dominated professions' (WCDWA 2002: 1). In doing so, the selection criteria 'exacerbate[d] the discrimination that women face in their country of origin' where those women 'may not have

the opportunity to obtain higher education or pursue professions in their origi-
nating country' (WCDWA 2002: 4). The Association also noted that the points
test 'reproduces the gender bias associated with traditional skill evaluation
approaches, which do not recognise child care or domestic labour as learned
expertise worthy of compensation' (WCDWA 2001: 6). In its submission to
the Standing Committee on Citizenship and Immigration, the National Action
Committee on the Status of Women recommended that in order to ameliorate
the gendered effects of the point test, the Live-in Caregiver Program (LCP)
should instead be assessed under the federal skilled worker points test (NAC
2001: 4; see also Intercede 2001: 1). The GBA Unit within CIC was also cogni-
zant of these gender concerns, noting in its first analysis of the draft regulations
that '[t]here is a substantial sociological and economic literature that criticizes
the definition and understanding of "skill" as reflecting traditional male occupational experiences' whilst also stating that 'the overriding goal of the selection
system is to select skilled workers who will make the greatest contribution to the
labour market' (CIC 2001a).

As discussed in Chapter 1, acknowledgement of gendered life course differences
is a key component of gender awareness in skilled immigration policy design. The
2002 points test recognised both non-continuous work experience and part-time
work. The acknowledgement in the IRPA points test of work experience gained
over a ten-year period was a direct product of engagement by the GBA Unit (CIC
2001b: 4518–19). Concessions were also granted under the new points test on the
basis of age despite analysis from the *IMDB* that found that age correlated with
strong reductions in earnings at the 'tail ends' of working life (CIC 1998a: 31–2;
Senior immigration official, interview 13 by author, Canada, 19 August 2008).
After debates in the Standing Committee, the cut-off was increased from the originally planned forty-five to forty-nine. The change was the product of calls by the
Standing Committee to then Minister for Immigration, Denis Coderre, and pressure from employer groups (senior immigration official, interview 13 by author,
Canada, 19 August 2008). A forceful submission by the Canadian Chamber of
Commerce to the Standing Committee for instance reveals concern that the productivity of older workers also be recognised (Trister 2002; see also Industry leader,
interview 31 by author, Canada, 22 September 2008).

Points for a second official language (either French or English) were increased,
although unlike in Australia, language was not set as a mandatory threshold criterion. Empirical evidence coming through the *IMDB* identified the centrality
of language skills to the economic performance of new immigrants and recommended mandatory language testing (CIC 1998a: 20–8). Mandatory language
testing using certified international language examinations, similar to those in
place in Australia since 1999, was also proposed by the external advisory report,
Not Just Numbers (ILRAG 1997). There was evidence that this would lead to better economic settlement outcomes for skilled immigrants. Speaking before the
Standing Committee, Meyer Burstein from CIC noted '[l]anguage ability is [more]

strongly correlated with settlement success and with contribution and income and taxes … than almost any other measure you can think of' (Standing Committee 1995: 23). However, following opposition including public protests from ethnocultural groups in Vancouver and Toronto in early 1998, then Immigration Minister Lucienne Robillard quietly backed down from her government's position of introducing mandatory language testing (Former senior immigration official, interview 16 by author, Canada, 27 August 2008; Ethnocultural leaders, interviews 18 and 33 by author, Canada, 3 September 2008 and 25 September 2008; Howard 1998; Walker 1999). One senior bureaucrat within CIC described the events:

> After *Not Just Numbers* was published, there was a ministerial consultation tour with Minister Robillard and there was a lot of protests and media articles, particularly in British Columbia, and the Chinese community tended to see language standards as a negative for them because, generally speaking, knowledge of English or French was somewhat lower in the Chinese community that it was say, in the Indian or Filipino community … and the government very quickly backed away from it. (Interview 65 by author, Canada, 14 August 2013)

As a result of this opposition, the IRPA points test was not as stringent with regards to language testing as the Australian model.

A final important development in Canada was the setting of the pass mark at sixty-seven rather than eighty. The pass mark is of crucial importance to those applicants who are borderline cases; those who might have low levels of points in one category but can compensate in another. This argument was made by a variety of diversity-seeking groups in seeking that the pass mark be lowered. The Coalition for a Just Immigration and Refugee Policy, for instance, argued that a pass mark of eighty would increase the 'weight on education and language proficiency and will have an adverse impact on applicants from non-English and non-French speaking countries' (CJIRP 2002: 9). Similarly, the National Association of Women and the Law noted that raising the pass mark to eighty 'only makes the gender bias of the existing points test worse' (NAWL 2002: 1). Historically, feminist activists in Canada have favoured a lower pass mark for female applicants to ameliorate against other discriminatory aspects of the points test (Macklin 1992: 742–6).

As noted, policy-makers in Canada originally intended to increase the pass mark from sixty-seven to eighty points. However, following complaints within the Standing Committee that the pass mark was too high, it was reduced to seventy-five (Standing Committee 2002: 11–12; Coderre 2002; Thompson 2002). Even once the pass mark was lowered to seventy-five, many participants were unhappy that it was to apply retroactively (IRPA, s190).[2] Despite some limitations to the retroactive application of the new points test, at the time of the IRPA's promulgation in June 2002, the pass mark would still have barred 425,000 applicants awaiting processing (Standing Committee 2002: 11–12; Coderre 2002; Van Rijn 2003). Ben Trister from the Canadian Bar Association pointed out that retroactivity would have had the biggest impact upon those from developing countries given that existing backlogs were the longest in those countries (cited in Clark 2002).

Lawyers within the Immigration Section of the Canadian Bar Association brought a series of legal actions, including *Dragan* v. *Canada* [2003] that struck down the retroactive application of the IRPA points test. Further, a class action was initiated using new laws that had recently been adopted in Canada (Senior immigration lawyer, interview 34 by author, Canada, 25 September 2008). Counsel for the applicants filed an action for 104,000 individuals requesting a writ of mandamus – a form of public injunctive relief – that prevented the Minister and his delegates from rejecting any applications that had been lodged before 1 January 2002 (*Borisova* v. *Canada* [2003]). This case was successful. Following the decision, the pass mark was lowered to sixty-seven, which was the level at which it had been set prior to the 2002 changes. The backlog of 425,000 applicants who would otherwise have had their applications rejected was instead processed under the old, easier pre-IRPA points test (Van Rijn 2003).

The gender implications of the points tests in Australia and Canada

The structure of skilled immigration points tests may help or hinder the admission of female principal applicants. Differences between the Australian and Canadian points tests provide an instructive comparison of how the design of skilled immigration selection policy matters for gender awareness. If we return to the issue of life course factors canvassed in Chapters 1 and 2, it is clear that there are differences across the two countries. In Australia, for applicants whose occupational skill was assessed at sixty points or above, the 1999 points test required twelve months' work experience in the eighteen months immediately preceding application. For applicants whose occupational skill was in the lesser range between forty and fifty-nine points, the points test required two years of work experience in the three years immediately preceding application. In both cases, continuous work experience was required. Under the Canadian points test introduced in 2002, fifteen points were granted for one year's experience and two points for each additional year up to a maximum of twenty-one points for four years' work experience. This experience could be gained over a ten-year period (IRPR, s75(2); s80). The Regulatory Impact Assessment Statement for the revised points test noted that the previous requirement that work experience be obtained within five years was altered because it was thought that it had an 'adverse impact ... on female applicants, many of whom may have taken family-related breaks in their employment history' (CIC 2002a).

As noted in Chapter 2, cut-offs for age are also of central importance from a gender-awareness perspective given that it generally takes women longer than men to reach key career milestones. The young were rewarded under both the Australian and the Canadian schemes, although this was especially the case in

Australia where age comprised up to 25 per cent of the pass mark and the cut-off for maximum points for age was thirty years (Regulations, Schedule 6, Part 2). In contrast, in Canada the cut-off for maximum points for age was set at forty-nine years (IRPR, s81).

The two points tests also treat part-time work differently. The Canadian selection grid identified the preponderance of women in part-time paid work and attempted to remedy this through its recognition. As the first gender analysis on the IRPA noted, including part-time work over a longer period and for a larger range of age groups 'is potentially advantageous from a gender perspective because it recognises the greater likelihood of women's involvement in part-time employment' (CIC 2001a). In contrast, in Australia, part-time work experience of less than twenty hours per week was not recognised within the points test (Migration Regulations 1994: Schedule 6A reg 2.26A(7)).

As was discussed in Chapter 1, feminist scholars argue that neoclassical economic understandings of 'skill' are gendered. This relates to the way in which occupational areas where women predominate, such as emotional labour, are rarely deemed skilled. In both countries the points tests defined 'skill' according to common understandings of 'professional skill' linked to both educational attainment and training. The Australian Regulations stated that the applicant must have a 'usual occupation' with a degree or diploma recognising that occupation (Schedule 6: 6101–09). This meant occupations that fitted within the Australian and New Zealand Standard Classification of Occupations (ANZSCO) codes 1, 2, 3 and 4 were included. This covers Mangers, Professionals, Technical and Trade Workers and Community Service Workers. Categories 5, 6, 7 and 8 that cover Clerical and Administrative Workers, Sales Workers, Machinery Operators and Drivers and Labourers were all excluded from these lists. Similarly, in Canada, the applicant must possess one year's work experience and educational qualifications in a managerial, professional or technical profession to be eligible for skilled immigration entry (skill levels A, B and O) (IRPR, s75(2)). On this basis 'intermediate level, clerical or supportive functions' and 'elemental sales or services and primary labourer occupations' were excluded (CIC 2002a: 6). Aside from primary labourers, these are all occupations where women strongly predominate. 'Emotional labouring' occupations in Canada such as care work (young and aged), house-keeping, commercial cleaning and retail work were all excluded from the point tests as those occupations were not included within the regulatory definitions of 'skilled occupations'.

Despite these similarities in the gendered definitions of 'skill' in both Australia and Canada, there were important differences between the two countries' schemes in terms of the extent of skills targeting. Under the points test introduced in Australia in 1999, applicants received between forty and sixty points depending upon their particular occupation (Regulations, Schedule 6A, Part 1, 6A11–3). As noted above, five points were allocated to applicants listed on the MODL, and an additional five points for those working in a MODL profession for six months in the two years preceding application (Regulations, Schedule 6A, Part (7) 6A71–2; Part 8, 6A81(b)). Canada in contrast did away with an occupationally based specific skills system in 2002, in place of a general human capital model. The Regulatory Impact Assessment Statement (RIAS) of the IRPR points test predicted that 50 per cent of relevant occupations were excluded under the older specific skill test (CIC 2001b). Both the GBA unit and the selection unit within CIC lauded the new general human capital points test because it expanded the pool of potential applicants, including female applicants, who might otherwise have not achieved the pass mark (CIC 2001a, 2001b: 4519). What has been the gender impact of a general human capital model in the Canadian context? The 2011 GBA of the Federal Skilled Worker Program found that women's representation as principal applicants increased by 8 per cent between 2003 and 2008. Further, an Evaluation of the Federal Skilled Worker Program in 2010 found that the IRPA reforms had led to a diversification of occupational classifications compared with the previous targeted points test (CIC 2010b).

Earlier chapters have discussed how consideration of the intersection of gender and ethnicity is important for the gender awareness of policy design. Language testing is a central concern for applicants from Non-English and Non-French Speaking Backgrounds, a point that was raised by several diversity-seeking activists in Canada (Interviews 1, 22 and 25 by author, Canada, 7 July 2008; 15 September 2008; 17 September 2008; CJIRP 2002). As these informants noted, the potential intersectional impact here is ethno-linguistic rather than strictly ethnic. Immigrants from former British colonies, even if racialised, do not suffer the same linguistic disadvantage as those from other countries where English is not spoken. As one feminist activist argued, if women were entering the Federal Skilled Worker Program '[t]hey're coming from the southern Asian regions …. And, one of the main advantages is [that in] the school system, English … is … mandatory' (Ethnocultural leader, interview 8 by author, Canada, 29 July 2008). For those entrants from outside the former British colonies, there are intersecting gender and ethnicity concerns resulting from the new points test. This is because in both Australia and Canada, language requirements increased with the reforms discussed in this chapter.

The intersecting gender and ethnicity dimension emerges in respect of women's lesser second language skills when compared with men. Findings from the *Longitudinal Survey of Immigrants to Australia*, for instance, indicate that women have lower levels of English proficiency than men across all major visas classes (Richardson *et al.* 2004: 64). This would suggest that women who are not native English speakers are more likely to be affected by increased language requirements. Further, earlier Australian studies demonstrate that this effect is particularly heightened for women from certain key source countries, such as China, Cambodia and Vietnam (Lennon *et al.* 1995: 9–10). Analogous gender-disaggregated data of language skill across visa categories is not available for Canada. However, Monica Boyd and Xingshan Cao's (2009: 69, 71) analysis of census data for settled immigrants in Canada indicates that women have lower levels of self-assessed language skills than men when their home language is neither English nor French. Further, CIC's 2010 review of the Federal Skilled Worker Program indicates that admissions into that visa class have seen a significant drop from 28 per cent to 16 per cent in entrants from China and a worsening trend for other parts of Eastern, South-East and South Asia since the 2002 reforms were introduced (CIC 2010b: 5, 25). In Australia following points test reforms, the percentage of entrants from Non-English Speaking Backgrounds dropped from 80 per cent of entrants in 2000–1 to 66 per cent by 2004–5 (Birrell *et al.* 2006: 27, Table 1.7). Existing evidence suggests that there were ethnic-linguistic biases in place in the points tests as a result of language testing.

Understanding the policy process in Australia and Canada

Both the Australian and Canadian points test reforms raise salient gender issues. Yet, in the Canadian context, the engagement of the Gender-Based Analysis Unit coupled with attention to gender issues by diversity-seeking activists appears to have informed different points tests than its Australian counterpart, with greater sensitivity towards gender concerns. General human capital, a comparatively lower points test pass mark with fewer threshold criteria, more accommodation of older immigrants, more flexibility around work experience time periods and part-time work as well as less stringent language testing were all features of the Canadian points test that appear to have had gender-aware effects. What explains the difference between the two points tests from a gender-awareness perspective? In the final section of this chapter, I explore key differences between the two case studies using the venue shopping approach.

Institutional venue appears to have shaped not only the policy process in the two countries but also the content of the eventuating policies. In Australia, the process was largely bureaucratically driven and determined, within a short eighteen-month period. The external review did not result in any major changes from a model proposed earlier by the Department of Immigration and Multicultural Affairs (Senior immigration officials, interviews 8 and 25 by author, Australia, 24 September 2009 and 30 October 2009). As one senior policy official noted, the policy changes 'largely stemmed out of the department. And we presented [the External Committee] with options. And they debated the options and then, on that basis of that debate, we went forward with options to the government' (Interview 25 by author, Australia, 30 October 2009).

A notable feature of this policy process in Australia at this time is the extent to which decisions were made and justified on the basis of key academic and statistical studies. The external review members presented reliance on the available studies as 'evidence-based policy-making' (DIMA 1999: 19) and this representation went virtually unchallenged by interest groups. For instance, the decision to introduce mandatory English language requirements, to raise the overall standards for English and to make language a threshold requirement for all skilled applicants, was based on research from the *LSIA*. The findings of the survey indicated that the most economically successful immigrants were those with the highest English language skills (Senior immigration officials, interviews 8 and 25 by author, Australia, 24 September 2009 and 30 October 2009). Concerns had been raised from the late 1980s onwards over the employment outcomes of those without high English skills (Birrell *et al.* 1992: 27, 43). In their submissions to the review, a few ethnic associations unsuccessfully opposed the introduction of mandatory English language testing, claiming that it would preference applicants from English-speaking countries. Generally, however, these groups found the economic arguments in favour of the new provisions difficult to rebut, and mandatory language testing was successfully introduced (FECCA 1998; Ethnocultural leaders, interviews 10 and 38 by author, Australia, 2 October 2009 and 6 March 2010).

In Canada, in contrast, the policy process was protracted, spanning almost one decade. While the new points test in Australia was seen as a response to economic needs, in Canada, political compromise, largely achieved within the Standing Committee on Citizenship and Immigration, meant that economic factors were not the only policy consideration for government, as the following quotation from one senior policy official within CIC indicates: 'If the policy was only a gender issue, it may have looked radically different just as if it had been really seriously only an economic issue, or if it was only a process to bring in people with language abilities. The realities are that policies are trying to achieve different objectives all at the same time' (Interview 13 by author, Canada, 19 August 2008).

This quotation highlights important differences between the ability of policy-makers in the two countries to promote an economically focused and rationalised points test. To adopt the ideas developed in Chapter 3, it indicates different levels of bureaucratic control by the two immigration ministries over the policy process. Three key venues were important in minimising bureaucratic control over the policy process in Canada and also opening opportunities for the engagement of diversity-seeking groups in that process, that were not present in the Australian context.

First, the establishment of the GBA Unit within the Canadian immigration department can be seen as the institutionalisation of diversity-seeking machinery within government. This case study provides some support for the argument that feminists within government ('femocrats') are important in developing gender-aware policies, both independently of external actors and in collaboration with them. The GBA Unit did positively shape the departmental culture on gender issues and did have an impact upon some of the gender-aware dimensions of the Canadian points test such as points for part-time and non-continuous work (Senior CIC policy officials, interviews 3 and 9 by author, Canada, 16 July 2008 and 8 August 2008). The Unit also challenged some of the existing assumptions around economic immigration policy. For instance, for a former departmental officer, the

GBA Unit offered a significant new voice within CIC. She noted: '[W]e'd always say in the points test, we made it very, very clear that ... the world wide labour market is gendered, period. You know we did try to make those categorical statements ... which were also an analytical point being made that had never been made before in that kind of legislative analysis' (Interview 46 by author, Canada, 1 October 2009).

Yet the Unit appears to have had less impact on other dimensions of the points tests, such as the increased points for language, or the very definition of 'skill'. One of the most important changes to the points test – the shift towards a general human capital model – was unrelated to work by the GBA Unit. In fact, the central rationale for introducing general skill was to respond to changing labour market conditions (CIC 2001b: 4507). The old occupations-based model had been under significant criticism since the independent inquiry, *Not Just Numbers* in 1997, both for its inflexibility to changes in labour market demand and due to lags between certification of labour needs and the actual processing of immigrants (CIC 1998b; ILRAG 1997: 56–7; Senior policy officers, interviews 9, 13 and 46 by author, Canada, 8 August 2008; 19 August 2008; 1 October 2009). Research from outside of the immigration policy domain, including a prime ministerial advisory council, *Stepping Up: Skills and Opportunities in the Knowledge Economy*, provided a strong impetus across labour policies for a movement away from a 'static' understanding of skill, as epitomised by the occupational-based selection approach, towards a broader, more 'dynamic' human capital model (CIC 2000: 1). The Canadian Bar Association and internal government agencies, such as Industry Canada, were also important in lobbying for this change in policy (Senior immigration officials, interviews 13 and 16 by author, Canada, 27 August 2008 and 27 August 2008). As such, this change was unrelated to engagement by the GBA Unit.

The GBA Unit did, however, leave an enduring legacy through the annual gender reporting mechanism. As a former GBA officer noted this provision is 'very important' because it provides 'accountability to Parliament on an annual basis' (Former GBA officer, interview 46 by author, Canada, 1 October 2009). Further, the establishment of the GBA Unit was itself a response to calls by diversity-seeking groups within the Standing Committee on Citizenship and Immigration for more attention to gender issues within the draft legislation. As such, the Unit provided an important branch between social activism and government activity.

Any limitations in Canada's GBA must also be assessed against the comparative record in Australia. There was a Women's Desk within the Australian immigration department between the mid-1980s and 1996 that was responsible for some gender analysis of 'women's specific areas', such as domestic violence and statistical reporting on women (Cox 1992: 39; DIEA 1986; DILGEA 1991). However, the Women's Desk never had the prominence or the oversight over general policy issues of the GBA Unit within CIC. From 1993 onwards, the Women's Desk was moved to a component within the Social Justice Division of the Department and, from 1996, its function was mainstreamed, meaning that there was no longer a distinct individual within the Department dealing with gender issues, including those raised around the new points test. The Australian Immigration department acknowledges the importance of gender issues in its 'non-discriminatory immigration policy statement' (DIAC 2009a); however, this document does not define 'gender awareness' or 'gender equity' and barely mentions gender anywhere in its other public documentation.[3]

Second, aside from these femocrat structures, legislative committees were identified in Chapter 3 as another central method by which actors external to government can challenge bureaucratic control of immigration processes. These committees adopted different functions in the two countries with regard to changes in the points test. In Australia, the Senate committees were not engaged in the review of the points test. In Canada, the Standing Committee on Citizenship and Immigration provided a vital venue for both diversity-seeking and other actors to affect policy change. The inclusion of a GBA requirement in the new immigration act and the expansion of the cut-off for maximum points for age were both Committee amendments. It was also the first time that regulations were submitted to the Committee for assessment and, in doing so, a participatory space was created for the engagement of a broader range of actors in regulation-making than had previously been the case (Former opposition parliamentarians, interviews 2 and 5 by author, Canada, 15 July 2008 and 20 July 2008). Given that in immigration policy, much of the 'meat' is in regulation and not legislation (Dauvergne 2005: 12–16), this was a particularly important achievement that found no counterpart in Australia. It is worth noting that actors engaged in the process in Canada did have differing views on the relative role of the Committee in shaping the details of the new points test. According to one opposition parliamentarian, for instance, majority government vitiated against a powerful committee system: 'The government decides who shows up and who they are going to hear and in the end, even if they hear all these people, whoever writes the bill decides what they are going to put in it. It is better than nothing but it is not totally honest' (Interview 11 by author, Canada, 13 August 2008). Notwithstanding these limitations, it is clear that policy-making in this legislative space opened the field of contestation in a way that was simply not the case in Australia. For instance, CIC consulted with 250 groups and individuals, as well as receiving 850 submissions over the IRPA reforms (CIC 2002b). In Australia, in contrast, thirty-seven submissions were made to the External Reference Group (DIMA 1999: Attachment B).

Third, differences in judicial regimes also played an important role across the two cases. When diversity-seeking groups in Canada failed to achieve a substantial lowering of the pass mark, legal opportunities were available to challenge the retroactive application of the points test. The implications of the *Dragan* and *Borisova* decisions for subsequent government actions in Canada are significant and considered in detail in the following chapter. According to Lorne Waldman, Counsel for the immigrant applicants in *Borisova*, '[t]he class action is a very powerful weapon, and gives us [lawyers] a new avenue of recourse when the government acts unfairly' (cited in Jimenez 2004). At the same time as these developments occurred in Canada, class action possibilities were closed down in the immigration field in Australia and there were no significant legal challenges to the new points test (Crock and Berg 2011: Chapter 19).

Finally, there were also differences in levels of diversity-seeking engagement across the two cases. In Canada, diversity-seeking groups were active in parliament around the development of the new points test. These groups played a vital role in raising attention to the need for a gender analysis of the new points test. The magnitude of submissions to the Standing Committee requesting a GBA of the new points test, for instance, supports the relevance of diversity-seeking activity in entrenching GBA in the immigration context.[4] However, diversity-seeking groups were less important in informing the particular content of the points test. According to the former leader of one women's organisation: 'I don't think [the GBA Unit] asked us to comment, no. I remember trying to call them, asking how it was going alone, we were not consulted on that, no. They kind of took the ball and ran with it, completely distanced themselves from the women's groups who promoted it. So it was a frustrating exercise' (Interview 10 by author, Canada, 12 August 2008). Nor were all of the recommendations of feminist groups adopted in the new selection grid, such as the need for a redefinition of 'skill' to acknowledge women's work. However, the importance of engagement of these diversity-seeking groups at the agenda-setting stage in bringing about the establishment of the GBA Unit should not be underestimated. In Australia, where no such groups were active in the debates over the points test, gender concerns were absent from both the policy process and eventual policies.

Conclusion

Over the late 1990s and early 2000s, both Australia and Canada attempted to reform their points tests for skilled immigration selection, such that the tests were more closely aligned with economic need. While there were divergences in the overarching policy approach – Australia moved towards a more targeted occupational model whereas Canada placed emphasis on general human capital – a strong economic rationale underpinned government thinking in both countries. In Australia, the immigration bureaucracy efficiently implemented its 'evidence-based' policy agenda, and there was little political debate over the new selection model that was adopted within eighteen months of its initial proposal. In Canada, the policy process was protracted over almost one decade. The process was also politically thwarted and the eventual selection grid was challenged on legal grounds. Australia successfully reduced the cut-off for age under the new points test, introduced mandatory English testing and raised occupational requirements and standards. The Canadian government, in contrast, was forced through political challenges before the Standing Committee on Citizenship and Immigration, to increase the age cut-off, introduce gender mainstreaming mechanisms, remove mandatory language testing and lower the pass mark. While the Canadian immigration department was able to increase the focus on human capital with the 2002 points test, it came with significant political compromises, including on gender grounds.

The distinction between specific skills versus general human capital identified in this chapter takes on increased importance in the next phase of reforms in Australia and Canada. More recently, both countries have increased occupational targeting within their points tests systems. In 2008, Canada disbanded its previous commitment to general human capital in favour of a 'demand driven' model that closely emulates earlier developments in Australia. Concerns over perverse outcomes with the Migrant Occupation on Demand List led to further changes to skilled immigration in Australia. In both countries, the policy process was also marked by increased bureaucratic control. The next chapter traces these policy developments and assesses the implications of these changes from a gender perspective.

Notes

1 DIMA 1999: 52; Migration Act (1958), Schedule 6, Part 3, 6303–4; Schedule 6A, Part 3, 6A31-6A33.

2 As evidenced by the archived submissions of: CAMC 2002: 4; CJIRP 2002: 8; CME 2001: 3; Green 2002: 10; NOIVMWC 2002: 1; UCC 2002: 4.

3 A single document entitled 'DIMA gender equity statement' can be located from 2002. This document refers to a departmental 'Gender Equity Coordinator Network'; however, no further details of this can be found and it was not raised in any of the interviews conducted with senior departmental officers, despite deliberate questioning about gender issues (DIMA 2000a); Various interviews by author, Australia: 4; 5; 8; 18; 19; 20; 24; 25; 26; 27 and 32.

4 See for instance: CJIRP 2000; Intercede 2000, 2001; Metro 2000: 4; 2001: 8; NAC 2001: 1; PWCBC 2001: 1; NAWL 1999, 2000: 5; 2001: 9; VSW 2001; Former Canadian parliamentarians, interviews 2 and 5 by author, Canada, 15 July 2008 and 20 July 2008.

6

Targeting skills during the global financial crisis, 2007–13: gendered winners and losers?

The hallmark of a quality skilled migration programme is the ability to target those applicants who have skills in need. The imperative to do has become a lot sharper ... as Australia got drawn into the whirlpool of the Global Financial Crisis. (Senator Chris Evans, Minister for Immigration and Citizenship, 8 February 2010)

Introduction

With the onset of the global financial crisis, governments in both Australia and Canada undertook major reforms of their points tests. In Australia, controversy over a perceived reliance on permanent skilled independent immigration channels by former international students precipitated these policy changes. Reforms ultimately led to a renewed selection grid that focuses more strongly upon both formal language abilities, as well as a shift towards employer sponsorship, or what the Minister for Immigration and Citizenship, Chris Evans, called a 'demand driven system' (Evans 2010). In Canada too, key occupations in demand were targeted more carefully, resulting in a move away from the general human capital model introduced under the IRPA. Language testing was made mandatory. As in Australia, the link between employer sponsorship and permanent skilled immigration was tightened. Regulatory changes altered the ways in which immigration policy is made in Canada, moving towards greater bureaucratic control; not dissimilar from the trends documented in Australia in previous chapters. In both countries, these changes increased the role of employers in the selection process, raised the economic rationale of the selection grids and, arguably, also reduced the capacity of government to legislate in ways that might improve the gender awareness of immigration selection policy.[1]

This chapter sets out the policy process in Australia and Canada around these major reforms, followed by an analysis of the gender implications of the policies themselves, relying in part upon hitherto unpublished gender-disaggregated data. In the final section of the chapter, I assess how reduced diversity-seeking engagement in Canada, accompanied with a centralisation of decision-making processes, was central to understanding the policies adopted. In Australia, diversity-seeking groups were all but absent from debates and concomitant policies lacked an attention to gender awareness.

The policy process in Australia (2007–13)

The election of a Labor government in Australia in 2007 was a political watershed after eleven years of Liberal-National Party rule. However, despite the broader ideological shift this change in government represented, the reforms in the economic immigration arena have been consistent with the policy trajectory established by the earlier Conservative government. Under the Rudd–Gillard ALP governments (2007–13) the size of the skilled immigration programme not only increased, but selection criteria also became more economically stringent. In February 2010, the Minister for Immigration and Citizenship, Senator Chris Evans, announced an overhaul of the selection scheme for general skilled immigration (DIAC 2010e). By 2009 the Migrant Occupations on Demand List (MODL) had become a weaker predictor of labour market need in the Australian economy (Senior immigration officer, interview 19 by author, Australia, 15 October 2009). Driven by the desire for permanent residency, many international students were enrolling in technical college courses in Australia that gained high points on the MODL, leading to an escalation of applications in certain key occupations, in particular cooking and hairdressing. As Lesleyanne Hawthorne (2014: 5) noted, '[f]ormer international students at the time had a 99 per cent chance of skilled category selection, unless they failed health or character checks' (see also Birrell *et al.* 2006: 31, 76). In announcing reforms to the MODL, Chris Evans argued that '[u]nder the previous government's policy settings, Australia's skilled immigration programme has been delivering too many self-nominated migrants from a narrow range of occupations with poor to moderate English language skills who struggle to find employment in their nominated occupation' (Evans 2010).

In light of the global economic recession, the Australian government was concerned with developing a more occupationally targeted skilled immigration scheme (Kukoc 2011: 6). Although former international students were not performing badly compared to the overall immigration programme, evidence from a new Continuous Survey of Immigrants to Australia did demonstrate that they were not doing as well economically as those entering through employer-nominated skilled immigration schemes (DIAC 2010d; see also Birrell *et al.* 2006: 79–80). Changes to the skilled immigration system in May 2009 did away with the MODL and replaced it first with an interim 'Critical Skills Occupation List' (CSOL) and later in May 2010, with a new Skilled Occupation List (SOL). This new list narrowed the range of professions under which individuals can apply from 486 to 188 (DIAC 2010e; Hawthorne 2014: 10). Decision-making over the content of the SOL was also moved from the Department of Education and Workplace Relations to a newly appointed statutory body, Skills Australia (now the Australian Workplace

Productivity Agency), which while still reporting to the Ministers for Employment and Immigration, comprises an independent board of industry and trade union representatives, as well as academics (AWPA 2013).

Following a department review in 2010, in 2011, a new points test was introduced for the Skilled Independent stream; the main points-tested visa. This new test increased English language requirements from the 1999 reforms. IELTS Level 8 – a level many native speakers would not achieve – is now required to receive the highest number of points, while IELTS 6 operates as a threshold criterion (Migration Regulations, Schedule 2, 186.232). The new test also requires more extensive work experience in a skilled occupation and rewards doctorate level qualifications with higher points. Finally, the points for different age levels are recalibrated under the new test such that those in the age bracket twenty-five to thirty-two receive maximum points (DIAC 2011c).

Changes to processing rules also ensured that those selected where chosen under the new rather than the old selection rules. Using the Priority Processing Direction power that had previously been employed by Philip Ruddock (discussed in Chapter 4), Immigration Minister Chris Bowens prioritised the processing of some economic visas over others (DIAC 2012b). At the same time, 'cap and cease' powers allowed all pre-2007 applications to be nullified, meaning that they were automatically rejected (Senior immigration official, interview 53 by author, Australia, 12 November 2013). It is important to note that the new points test did not apply to all immigrants under General Skilled Migration. Over this period, government also increased the proportion of permanent skilled immigration for which employers initiated the selection process, from 29 per cent of skilled entrants in 2007–8 to 53 per cent in 2010 (DIAC 2010a). Nonetheless, the points test still applies to a large component of permanent skilled immigration and therefore remains an important policy tool to examine in this chapter.[2]

The creation of SkillSelect, an online database for skilled immigration applicants in 2012, further changes the nature of permanent skilled immigration selection in Australia, transforming entry for qualified applicants from a right to a possibility. While previously an immigrant who met the points test had a statutory right to qualify for entry, the applicant now lodges an 'expression of interest' (EOI) to be considered for future processing by immigration officials. Assuming the applicant meets the pass mark cut-off, he or she is then scored against the appropriate points test. Depending upon how the individual ranks against other applicants, he or she may then either receive an invitation to formally apply, or may receive an invitation from an Australian employer for a job. Further government control over supply of skilled immigrant flows is provided through occupational ceilings that can cap the number of EOIs granted for processing in any given year (DIAC 2012d). One former senior immigration official likened SkillSelect to university admission where the pass mark 'varies according to what course, it goes up and down' (Interview 43 by author, Australia, 11 October 2013). This method fundamentally changes the basis for entry and the reliability of likely admission: the EOI system renders the applicant competitive against other applicants rather than simply subject to a pass mark threshold.

Generally, SkillSelect has been lauded in Australia as producing a more efficient supply of skilled immigration into the country and reducing processing times. One senior immigration official commented: 'People have their skill assessment, their English language, everything good to go at the EOI stage. When they want to apply for a visa and there's a job or a sponsor identified … it's a seamless process. That makes it a much faster matching service' (Interview 54 by author, Australia, 12 November 2013). Yet, against these benefits, SkillSelect also represents a reduction in administrative transparency and raises some potential diversity concerns, as I discuss later in this chapter.

The policy process in Canada (2008–13)

The period from 2008 until 2013 also saw a rapidly increased economic targeting of skilled immigration in Canada, mostly under the directorship of Immigration Minister Jason Kenney, who held the position over that period. In 2008, the Canadian government created the new 'Canadian Experience Class' that offered permanent residency to immigrants with either highly skilled temporary work experience or international student status. This visa requires at least two years of full-time experience (in a skilled worker area) or one year of full-time work experience for a graduate from a Canadian university. The applicant also needs to be proficient in English or French, with recent changes increasing language requirements (IRPR, reg 87.1; CIC 2012d). Entry into the new visa class rose from 2,545 in 2009 to 9,348 in 2012 (CIC 2012b).

At the same time as the Canadian Experience Class was created, government sought to introduce new powers to manage the growing backlog within the Federal Skilled Worker Program (FSWP). The legal cases against the retroactive application of the points test in 2003, discussed in Chapter 5, as well as under-allocation of resources to various visa processing posts, contributed to exponential growth in the backlog. In particular, the *Borisova* and *Dragan* legal cases had allowed for 'dual assessment' of applications under both the old and new rules and extended average processing time from twenty to fifty-five months (CIC 2010b: 56). By November 2007, this backlog numbered around 850,000 people and was growing quickly (Goar 2007). In her report to parliament in 2007, then Immigration Minister Diane Finley declared that 'looking ahead, actions to control application intake and bring down the inventory are critical' (CIC 2007).

In 2008, an amendment to the Immigration and Refugee Protection Act (Bill C-50) empowered the Minister for Citizenship and Immigration to issue instructions that establish orders and categories for the assessment of off-shore immigration applications (IRPA (2002) (Cdn)), s87(3), (6); CIC 2008c). Essentially, this bill gave the immigration minister in Canada statutory powers similar to those that have been in place in Australia since the late 1980s to cap and queue immigration applicants in the skilled class (as discussed in Chapter 4). The introduction of these provisions through budget legislation – rejection of which would have acted as an election trigger – highlights the political salience of Bill C-50, especially compared with the uncontroversial nature of analogous reforms undertaken in Australia many years earlier.

Since 2008, a variety of ministerial instructions have been issued for the FSWP. These included instructions to limit applications into thirty-eight key occupations (CIC 2008c). Those who did not have an occupation on the list were offered a full application refund, while those with occupations on the list could have the processing of their applications fast-tracked (Javed and Keung 2008). In effect, the ministerial instructions secured a reversion to a specific skill selection model. Further changes introduced through instruction included the imposition of mandatory third party language testing for principal applicants (CIC 2010c) and the placement of caps upon the number of applicants within each occupation that would be processed (CIC 2010c, 2011c). The combined effect of Bill C-50 and the ministerial instructions was to increase bureaucratic control over selection rules and to minimise the role played by other arms of government in the development of skilled immigration policy. By way of example, a group of federal skilled immigration applicants that did not qualify under the new list initiated a legal action in 2011. Yet, ultimately this action was unsuccessful as government action was permitted under the broad remit of the new rules (Keung 2011, 2012).

Despite the policy changes, by 2011, the backlog of applicants from pre-July 2011 was still around 314,000 applicants (Standing Committee 2012: 7). In the 2012 Budget Bill, *C-38*, a provision was introduced that allowed for the retroactive application of new rules to old visa classes. This provision effectively gave the Minister the power to cull the backlog of those applications preceding 2008 that did not meet the new selection rules (Alboim and Cohl 2013: 1). The focus was on processing efficiency. According to Immigration Minister Jason Kenny, these changes 'finally unshackle[d] Canada from the outrageous backlogs and wait times of the past. The system [had] become dysfunctional' (Canadian Press 2012). A court case, *Tabingo* v. *Canada* (2013), was brought to challenge the backlog cull as a breach of the Canadian Charter of Rights and Freedoms, on the grounds that 92 per cent of the culled applicants were located in ports in Africa and Asia, compared with 8 per cent in ports in Europe and the Americas. This was argued to violate the section 15(1) Equality provision of the Charter. Lawyers also proposed that the section 7 Liberty and Security principle of the Charter was violated on the grounds that applicants had endured psychological stress awaiting processing (Chase 2013; Schmitz 2013). In April 2013, the Federal Canadian Court rejected this case finding that the government's actions to cull the applicants were within the bounds of the Charter of Rights and Freedoms (*Tabingo* v. *Canada* FC 377 2013, paras 103–37). The case was again rejected on appeal.

At the same time as these legal challenges to the backlog were under way, the Immigration Minister introduced a new points test that resulted in higher thresholds for language and restricted points for age and work experience. Despite concluding that the post-IRPA skilled workers had done well economically, a departmental evaluation found that those with a job offer did even better, earning 74 per cent more than those without a job offer (CIC 2010b: 45, 47). This finding contributed to an overall stronger focus on Canadian employment offers within the new selection grid. The number of years needed to gain the maximum points for work experience was also raised from four to six (CIC 2012d).

The level of language testing was also increased and made subject to the Canadian Language Testing Benchmark Level 7.[3] Departmental analysis found language testing to be central to the economic performance of new entrants with those scoring in the top levels for language allocation earning around 39 per cent more than those in the lower levels. The new reforms also placed greater emphasis on youth. Citizenship Immigration Canada found in its evaluation that 'immigrants who were less than 30 years old at landing earned 27 per cent more than people 50 years of age or older' (CIC 2010b: 46). The departmental evaluation also found that younger immigrants had far lower rates of unemployment than those over forty-five and, accordingly, the upper limit for maximum points for age was reduced from forty-nine to thirty-five (CIC 2012d). Changes were introduced to the way in which spouses gained points as secondary applicants under the Adaptability Section, with language aptitude rather than education set as a relevant factor for allocation of those points (CIC 2012d).

The 2013 changes separated the skilled trades from the professional skill areas and created a new Federal Skilled Trades class. The creation of this new visa category was primarily in response to growing demand for workers in the trades (CIC 2008b). The new Federal Skill Trades Class only permits admissions with National Occupational Classification (NOC) Skill Level B (technical occupations and skilled trades) and delineates the occupations included within this category.[4] Generally, English language requirements are easier under this new category than in the FSWP, in acknowledgement of the fact that trade occupations require lesser language skills than professions (CIC 2012d; Senior policy official, interview 48 by author, Canada, 15 July 2013). Finally, in 2013, at the time of completion of this book, Canada is also moving towards a SkillSelect EOI system, which proposes to place even greater emphasis on employer sponsorship than the Australian model (Koslowski 2014).

The gender implications of points tests reform in Australia and Canada

In both Australia and Canada, the period since 2008 is marked by an increased targeting of points tests for permanent skilled immigration as well as a stronger alignment of points test design with employer demand. What are the gender implications of these changes? In the following section of this chapter, I consider this question through the examination of several indicators of gender awareness developed in Chapters 1 and 2. First, I assess the dilution of the GBA function in Canada since 2005. Second, changes in treatment of life course issues under the points tests in both countries are considered. Third, I address the increased language requirements in both countries and possible intersectional issues. I also outline the shift away from the general human capital model towards occupational targeting and the implications of the adoption of an EOI system in both countries.

Changes to women's political machinery in the immigration field in Canada

In 2005, the GBA Unit within CIC was dismantled and replaced with one policy officer. This officer no longer conducts the GBA that is published in the Annual Report to Parliament; rather, the officer provides guidance to the various branches of CIC in undertaking analyses, which together form the annual GBA. A cross-branch GBA committee assists with this activity (CIC officer, interview 9 by author, Canada, 8 August 2008). While the 2005 change has been cast as a reduction in the capacity of the GBA Unit by many activists (Members of non-governmental organisations, interviews 4 and 10, Canada, 19 July 2008 and 12 August 2008), it can also be seen as the mainstreaming of the GBA function within the Department, in turn allowing for attention to gender issues by a wider range of bureaucrats (CIC officer, interview 3 by author, Canada, 16 July 2008). The location of the GBA officer in Strategic Planning may also be seen to have a positive effect on future gender-based analyses. Marian Sawer's (1996: 20) assessment of gender mainstreaming units in Australia supports the idea that a centralised bureaucratic location for gender mainstreaming, close to the point where important decisions are made, is essential for such units to impact upon policy design.

A new GBA policy was developed by CIC in 2010 and launched in 2011 (CIC 2011b). According to CIC (2011b) '[w]hile the previous framework set the groundwork for GBA at CIC, the new policy reflects government-wide approaches to GBA by integrating gender and diversity issues across the program and policy continuum, while also continuing to build capacity and provide targeted support'. Since 2011, a federal Canada-wide *Departmental Action Plan on Gender-Based Analysis* also requires that all memoranda to Cabinet and Treasury Board submissions include a GBA component (CIC 2011b). The newest iterations of GBA therefore indicate a move towards considering a broader range of equality issues than simply gender, with the 2012 GBA noting that '[a]pplying GBA involves the consideration of the intersections of gender and other diversity factors, including ethnicity, religion, nationality, class, age and sexual orientation' (CIC 2012c). As one policy officer argued, this shift towards an intersectional analysis is consistent with the Canada-wide policy of 'GBA Plus', a 'sort of Status of Women branding of intersectionality' (Policy officer, interview 59 by author, Canada, 7 August 2013).

Despite these positive developments, the reduction in departmental capabili-ties does appear to have contributed to a dilution of the relative importance of gen-der analysis in the skilled immigration policy process in Canada. In some recent years, the GBA in the annual immigration reports has amounted to the replica-tion of gender-disaggregated data with less of the clear feminist analysis than that which underpinned the GBAs in earlier years (see further Boucher 2010). Analysis of important gender issues, such as investigation of the gender implications of the shift away from the human capital model, have not been undertaken by CIC in these reports (Policy officer, interview 59 by author, Canada, 7 August 2013).

In Australia over the same period, there have been no developments in the gender mainstreaming area with the immigration portfolio. Despite the reelection of a Labor government in 2007, much of the feminist machinery that was estab-lished under the Keating and Hawke Labor governments was not resurrected. The Rudd–Gillard governments demonstrated considerable policy continuity to ear-lier Conservative governments in their approach to women's political machinery.

Accommodating life course issues

In previous chapters, I have argued that policy attention to the differing life course experiences of men and women is essential in rendering skilled immigration policies more gender aware. In this regard, some differences emerge between the Australian and Canadian points tests. In Australia, the points for age were recali-brated in such a way that maximum points are now allocated for those between the ages of twenty-five and thirty-two. The central rationale behind these changes was to balance the need to attract youthful individuals with a longer working life against the potential contributions of those individuals with significant work expe-rience and educational achievements (DIAC 2010c). This newly prioritised age bracket also overlaps with the key child bearing years for women, raising consider-able gender discrimination concerns. However, this point was not acknowledged in the policy documents that supported the increased points for age. Further, as under previous iterations of the points test, non-continuous work experience is acknowledged, but part-time work is not (Migration Regulations, Schedule 2 186.212; PAM Guidelines point 10).

In Canada, more attention was paid by policy-makers to the central issue of the interaction of life course events, skill qualifications and gender. The capacity to gain work experience over a ten-year period that had been a feature of the original IRPA selection grid was retained under the new selection grid 'to be inclusive for those with family caregiving requirements' (CIC 2012d; IRPR, reg80). Further, reduction of the relative importance of work experience within the new selection grid was seen to have gender-aware effects 'since care-giving responsibilities can reduce the potential for applicants to accumulate years of work experience' (CIC 2012d). On the other hand, the regulatory impact assessment for the skilled trades class noted that the requirement within that new visa for applicants to achieve two years of work experience within a five-year period could have 'a negative gender-based impact given that requiring the experience to be recent could negatively impact those who had to leave the workforce for family care responsibilities' (CIC 2012d; IRPR, reg87.2(3)(b)). Despite this fact, government retained this requirement because 'work experience is a critical factor for assessing the ability of applicants in the skilled trades to become economically established' (CIC 2012d). Generally CIC acknowledged that there is a male imbalance of 80 per cent in the trades, meaning that the disadvantage to female applicants might not in practice be that great (CIC 2012d).

Heightened language requirements

Previous chapters discussed the relationship between increased language proficiency requirements and gender awareness. The argument follows that raising the difficulty of language tests, and rendering such requirements mandatory, also increases the gender inequality of selection grids insofar that access to secondary language training is more difficult for female than male applicants. In both Australia and Canada, language proficiency emerged as a central predictor of labour market success and earnings. On this basis, language requirements were increased in Australia (Migration Regulations, Schedule 2, 186.232). In Canada, mandatory language testing was introduced first via ministerial instruction and, in 2013, through regulatory amendment (IRPR, reg 79(3)). The relative weight of language in the points tests also increased considerably in both countries.

The GBA to the reforms in Canada noted that 'increased language requirements could place greater burdens on women than men given women's lesser earning power'; however, argued that 'it is not expected to act as a barrier in most cases' (CIC 2012d). No further analysis was undertaken on the topic. In contrast, the Fairness Commissioner of Ontario (Office of the Fairness Commissioner 2012: 4) objected to mandatory language testing on the basis that it might exclude some applicants from certain countries. The Canadian Labour Congress (CLC), Canada's peak trade union body, was also highly critical of the increased language requirements and argued that 'they will likely result in an increased representation of immigrants from English or French speaking source countries at the expenses of people from other regions of the world' (CLC 2012: 1). This argument would seem to correspond with CIC's own evaluation of the IRPA changes, which demonstrated that those increases to language testing had a disproportionate effect on applicants from China, East, South-East and South Asia (CIC 2010b: 5, 25).

In Australia, formal statistical analysis of source country impacts of language testing was not undertaken, in part because it was not viewed as a relevant policy question. According to one former ministerial advisor: '[F]rom our point of view that wasn't the driver, that wasn't the issue at all. The issue was we had evidence that when they're in country, … [immigrants'] ability to participate in their chosen field was primarily driven by their language skills' (Interview 49 by author, Australia, 24 October 2013). A senior departmental official also noted that: 'I don't think we're interested in going down that path [of investigating the effects of increased language testing] because we have a universal non-discriminatory programme but I think it's more about has the higher level of English led to better labour market outcomes?' (Interview 51 by author, Australia, 11 November 2013). As such, the focus in Australia was on labour market outcomes post-arrival rather than selection effects upon source country diversity, although one former senior immigration official did accept that '[w]here we ended up was a test that was possibly more biased towards English speaking degree holders [and] native English speaking degree holders' (Interview 43 by author, Australia, 11 October 2013).

Targeting skill and the move away from the general human capital model

As a result of excess supply into the permanent skilled immigration pool in both countries, governments moved towards more targeted models of selection. In both countries, this saw a narrowing of the number of occupations considered for the purposes of skilled immigration. In Canada, these changes were more substantial with a reduction from the full NOC A, B and C list of 351 occupations to an enumerated list of thirty-eight occupations in 2008 and since July 2013, twenty-four occupations.[5] In Australia, the number of occupations was reduced from 486 occupations[6] in 2008 to 188 under the 2013 SOL (Department of Employment Australia 2013; DIAC 2008b). It should be recalled that the Canadian GBA Unit in 2000 had been in favour of a general human capital model which encompassed a broad range of occupations, whereas the previous specific occupational model was seen as 'discriminatory against women because it identified different categories that were more gendered' (Former GBA officer, interview 46 by author, Canada, 1 October 2009). In Canada, the 2010 evaluation of the FSWP indicated that the IRPA reforms from 2003 to 2008 had resulted in an increased occupational diversification within the Federal Skilled Worker scheme. Of the intake over this period, 69 per cent worked in five NOC groups, compared with 81 per cent of the pre-IRPA intake (CIC 2010b: 25). This suggests a real shift towards a general human capital model that occurred under the IRPA reforms, which could have contributed to the significant increases in women's representation. Female applicants made up 25 per cent of pre-IRPA principal applicants in 2001 compared with 39 per cent of post-IRPA applicants by 2011 (CIC 2010b: 24).

Given these trends, it is important to investigate empirically what effect occupational narrowing has had upon gender diversity within permanent skilled immigration intake into both countries. In Canada, the 2010 GBA notes that women's representation in the more targeted FSWP actually increased after 2009 once occupational targeting was introduced, although women were concentrated in fewer professions than men (CIC 2010a).[7] Later analyses by CIC corroborate the finding that while policy developments since 2009 reinforce horizontal gender segregation they do not appear to restrict women's representation as principal skilled applicants, which has continued to grow since 2008 (CIC 2012c; see also Table 4.4 of this book). This may in large part relate to strong increases in the representation of nursing and vocational instructors – both occupational areas where women dominate (CIC 2012c: 32). Table 6.1 documents the top ten occupations for male and female applicants in 2007 and in 2012 accordingly, in order to capture the effects of occupational targeting in Canada. The data from 2012 are confined to those applicants who entered under new ministerial instruction rules and exclude entrants processed under the old rules following court rulings.

Table 6.1 reveals some interesting trends. First, it is clear that following the introduction of ministerial instructions, far fewer immigrants are entering through the FSWP than previously. This is apparent by comparing the totals for 2012 against those for 2007, and relates to the increased use of other channels for entry, in particular temporary immigration, which is considered in the next chapter. Perhaps more relevant for current purposes, is that a greater number of immigrants are entering through the top ten professions in 2012 than in 2007 and that occupational concentration has become greater for female than it is for male entrants. From a gender perspective, it is also clear that, while both men and women are represented in the top ten professions in both years, women make up a smaller percentage of overall principal skilled applicants. This is consistent with the trends discussed in previous chapters. Finally, it is clear that key occupations in which women predominated in 2007, such as administrative assistants and secondary school teachers, are now excluded by the ministerial instruction and do not make up the top ten professions. That said, women's representation has increased both in nursing and the medical profession more broadly, meaning that overall the relative percentage of female principal applicants entering has not fallen.

In Australia, women's representation within the skilled immigration visas has dropped from a high of 37 per cent of principal applicants in 2004–5 to 32 per cent by 2011–12 (DIAC 2013b; Table 4.3 of this book). However, we need to interrogate whether this reduction is a product of occupational targeting or other factors. Table 6.2 documents the top ten occupations for men and women in 2008 and in 2012, before and after the occupational targeting occurred.

Table 6.2 demonstrates clear 'his and her' occupations for male and female entrants into Australia; there is strong horizontal segregation between the sexes in how they negotiate occupational pathways to skilled immigration. Like in Canada, there is an increased concentration of the percentage of occupations represented in the top ten occupations, although this is greater than men than for women. Reductions in women's representation as principal applicants across the broader

Table 6.1: Changes in top occupations for male and female principal skilled independent applicants across time in Canada

	2007		2012	
	Men	Women	Men	Women
1	University professors and lecturers (1,890)	University professors and lecturers (910)	Computer and information systems managers (925)	Registered nurses (735)
2	Electrical and electronics engineers (1,135)	Financial auditors and accountants (540)	University professors and lecturers (640)	College and other vocational instructions (435)
3	Mechanical engineers (920)	Administrative assistants (485)	Financial managers (430)	University professors and lecturers (370)
4	Computer programmers and interactive media developers (890)	New worker (CIC) (430)	Specialist physicians (430)	Financial auditors and accounts (355)
5	Advertising, marketing and public relations managers (860)	Secondary school teachers (410)	General practitioners and family physicians (400)	General practitioners and family physicians (275)
6	Civil engineers (790)	Registered nurses and registered psychiatric nurses (370)	College and other vocational instructors (360)	Specialist physicians (240)
7	Information systems analysts and consultants (720)	Administrative officers (365)	Financial auditors and accounts (355)	Licensed practical nurses (230)
8	Software engineers and designers (700)	Advertising, marketing and public relations managers (340)	Restaurant and food service managers (290)	Financial managers (225)
9	Financial auditors and accountants (650)	Elementary school and kindergarten teachers (310)	Construction managers (235)	Biologists and related scientists (195)
10	Computer programmers (625)	Business development officers and marketing researchers and consultants (265)	Architects (230)	Dentists (190)
Total	9,180/ 28,050 (33%)	4,425/13,205 (34%)	4,295/8,040 (53%)	3,250/5,360 (61%)

Source: CIC (2013g).

Table 6.2: Changes in top occupations for male and female principal skilled independent applicants across time in Australia

	2008		2012	
	Men	Women	Men	Women
1	Software and applications programmers (2,913)	Accountants (2,164)	Cooks (3,092)	Accountants (2,167)
2	Accountants (2,332)	Registered nurses (872)	Software and applications programmers (3,064)	Cooks (1,014)
3	Cooks (904)	Software and applications programmers (644)	Accountants (1,977)	Registered nurses (813)
4	Industrial, mechanical and production engineers (877)	Hairdressers (469)	ICT business and systems snalysts (1,304)	Software and applications programmers (765)
5	Metal fitters and machinists (825)	Cooks (332)	Industrial, mechanical and production engineers (538)	Hairdressers (587)
6	Civil engineering professionals (738)	Secondary school teachers (226)	Civil engineering professionals (452)	ICT business and systems analysts (378)
7	Electricians (706)	Pharmacists (207)	Generalist medical (391)	Secondary school teachers (295)
8	Electronics engineers (478)	Social professionals (182)	Other engineering professionals (359)	Social professionals (280)
9	Electrical engineers (475)	Civil engineering professionals (142)	Electronics engineers (302)	Generalist medical practitioners (272)
10	Motor mechanics (444)	Generalist medical practitioners (142)	Computer network professionals (274)	Bakers and pastry cooks (250)
	10,692/15,309 = 69%	5,380/9,562 = 56%	11,753/15,598 = 75%	6,821/9,626 = 70%

Source: Unpublished data from DIAC (2013b).

General Skilled Migration category may therefore relate to other selection factors, discussed in more detail below.

Non-recognition of care work and emotional labour

An important factor in both countries is which occupations are excluded from the occupational lists. As discussed in the previous chapter, the gender critique follows that the statutory restriction of skilled immigration to certain occupational skill levels excludes the majority of emotional labouring occupations in which women predominate. For instance, no care professions are included under the current list in Australia except for child care managers (DIAC 2013b).[8] This exclusion is despite the fact that care workers are projected as the single fastest growing occupational area in the vocational sector in Australia (AWPA 2012: 45). Policy proposals to lower the occupational classifications in the Australian case for certain sub-classes of General Skilled Immigration (DIAC 2011a) were rejected in a departmental review.[9] Similarly, one senior immigration official noted that with care work in particular, the key reasons for exclusion from the list relate less to under-supply and more to 'pay and conditions' (Interview 48 by author, Australia, 24 October 2013). Australia continues to largely eschew semi-skilled immigration in order to prevent the exploitation of lower paid workers,[10] while in Canada, carer occupations classified as 'low-skilled' and 'semi-skilled' have been brought in through temporary immigration programmes. This analysis suggests that it is centrally national skills classifications rather than occupational targeting that excludes female-dominated occupations from skilled immigration. The differential treatment of the skilled trades and the caring professions in Canada is instructive here. As noted earlier, in 2013 a new Federal Skilled Trades class was introduced to respond to growing structural needs for these workers. Not only can trade workers enter on a permanent basis, they can also enter with a lower level of English testing than general skilled immigrants (CIC 2012d; IRPR, regs 74(1) and 87(2)(d)). Further, the lack of university credentials required for most trades positions was not presented as an impediment to entry of trade occupations on a permanent basis, although it has been cited as a reason for the exclusion of care occupations (Senior policy officer, interview 48 by author, Canada, 15 July 2013). The treatment of care work under temporary low-skilled schemes in Canada is considered in detail in Chapter 7.

The move towards EOI and an increased role for employers

The adoption of an EOI system in both countries can be viewed as a move towards employer-based skilled immigration selection. As one industry representative in Canada noted 'what EOI does is it … basically brings an immigrant in directly to an employer' (Interview 52 by author, Canada, 23 July 2013). Comprehensive evaluation of this system in Australia is hindered by the fact that it has only been in place for one year at the time of completion of this book. However, in New Zealand where the programme originated in December 2003, analysis by Richard Bedford (2012) indicates that EOI has led both to a reduction in entry from China over the last decade, and a sharply increased representation of immigrants from English-speaking nations. Bedford (2012) also indicates that the migrants most successful under the EOI system are those at the upper rankings of the permitted pass mark. As such, concerns about the interaction of pass mark levels and gender-based exclusions discussed in Chapter 5 would appear to take on heightened significance under an EOI system.

Employer-sponsored visas are also prioritised under Australia's skilled immigration programme processing rules (DIAC 2012b). Analysis of the employer-sponsored sub-class visa within Australian General Skilled Immigration gives us some indication of how the gender outcomes of permanent skilled immigration might fare differently when employers have a greater role in the selection process. Unpublished gender-disaggregated data from the Australian Department of Immigration and Citizenship reveals that while women comprised 35 per cent of principal skilled independent visa holders in 2011–12, they comprised only 29 per cent of employer-sponsored visa holders and only 27 per cent of state- and territory-sponsored visa holders (DIAC 2013b).[11] Ongoing examination is necessary to monitor gender trends as employer sponsorship continues to grow in importance in both countries.

Understanding the policy process in Australia and Canada

Recent developments in permanent skilled immigration policy in Australia and Canada indicate a convergence both in policy design and process. In both countries, selection grids for skilled immigration have become more targeted and aligned to projected occupational needs. Both countries place an increased emphasis on language proficiency and employer-determined selection in their recent reforms. In both countries, the policies that resulted also aligned closely with those originally proposed by policy-makers, suggesting a high degree of bureaucratic control over the policy process. Immigration policies themselves increasingly formed a part not only of the immigration portfolio but also of broader Cabinet deliberation. For instance, the focus on labour market outcomes in the new 2013 selection grid in Canada reflects a government-wide commitment to long-time economic contributions of citizens, a goal that was clearly articulated in the 2012 Canadian Budget, *Economic Action Plan 2012* (CIC 2012d).

Governments in the two countries have also adopted a more centralised approach to skilled immigration policy-making. Looking first at Australia, the recent changes were not debated in parliament. Instead, changes were achieved through regulatory reforms, ministerial processing and prioritisation powers (DIAC 2010b) The use of prioritisation powers allowed immigration officials to 'drop out those people who … passed the points requirements but [were] not deemed to be the highest priority skill needs' (Senior immigration official, interview 53 by author, Australia, 12 November 2013). Further, although the Australian policy process was already quite centralised within the immigration ministry by 2007, the introduction of occupational caps for the processing of skilled immigration visas further empowered the Minister to limit occupations with excessive supply (Evans 2010; Senior policy official, interview 51 by author, Australia, 11 November 2013).

The changes in Canada reflect a clearly stated government objective to compete with Australia for the 'best and the brightest'. Defending the need for occupational targeting, then Immigration Minister Diane Finley argued that '[w]hen we compare ourselves to the United Kingdom, Australia, and New Zealand, we are the only country that does not use some kind of occupational filter to screen applicants. This weakens our ability to select applicants who will be best placed to succeed in our labour market' (Finley 2008: 1530). The tightening of the policy process in Canada largely resulted from the creation of ministerial instruction powers through Bill C-50 (the Budget bill of 2008). In tying the passage of these immigration powers to the passage of the Budget – which itself ensured supply and therefore the ongoing maintenance of the minority government – the passage of these controversial powers was ensured (Campion Smith 2008). These subsequent policy changes saw a shift in the policy-making process from the legislative to the administrative venue, and indeed, to the ministerial office. These powers were pivotal in managing the inventory of applications and in targeting selection to the most desired immigrants. One senior immigration official noted that '[w]ithout the ability to limit intake we were at the mercy of global demand and Canada is a very desirable place to live' (Interview 47 by author, Canada, 11 July 2013).

At the same time, however, this increased bureaucratic control over the policy process also appears to have had a negative impact upon the gender awareness of the ensuing policies. For instance, the 2008 *Annual Report to Parliament* states that a GBA was conducted of Bill C-50 (CIC 2008a). However, it is unclear whether this GBA was performed prior to or after the publication of the ministerial instructions (IRPA, section 14.1).

In Chapter 3, I identified five factors that may impact the capacity of government to bring around changes to immigration policies, as well as the capacity of diversity-seeking groups to intervene to halt policy reform. In the final section of this chapter, I consider the role of three of these factors in shaping the current case study: i) sympathetic bureaucrats; ii) legislative committees; and iii) strong judicial regimes. The other two factors, bicameralism and federalism, are less relevant in the current case study.

Recent policy trends in permanent skilled immigration fields in Australia and Canada identify a diminished role for sympathetic bureaucrats in assisting the ambitions of diversity-seeking groups. In Australia, there was no documented awareness of gender issues either in publicly available documents or in departmental decision-making. When asked about gender and race assessment of the new points test, one former senior immigration official commented that '[g]enerally speaking, the Department ... doesn't try to adjust the system to positively or negatively affect gender or ethnic origin; it tries to have a neutral system' (Interview 47 by author, Australia, 18 October 2013). However, this informant also clarified that the department did not track the demographic outcomes of points-test-selected immigrants, so there was no way of identifying if the system was 'neutral' in its policy design.

As noted earlier in this chapter, the GBA Unit within CIC was dismantled in 2005 and its function mainstreamed across the department. In light of these changes, it is unsurprising that the GBA function did not have a major impact upon Bill C-50 or the subsequent reforms to the points test. Interviews with immigration policy officials in the skilled immigration field in Canada in 2013 also demonstrated a diminished appreciation for the role of GBA in policy design, when compared with interviews undertaken in 2008. For instance, while immigration officers could confirm that a GBA was undertaken for the 2013 FSWP points test (Interviews 48 and 59 by author, Canada, 15 July 2013 and 7 August 2013), they were unclear who had undertaken this analysis or how, if at all, it informed the eventual policy design. Similarly, gender issues were not raised in the departmental evaluation of the ministerial instructions power, despite the relevance of this change for gender issues (CIC 2011a). Officers in the Research Branch of CIC had not undertaken gender analysis of the possible effects of recent skilled immigration reforms upon women, although previous GBA analysis highlights possible areas of concern and although relevant data were available to undertake such analysis (Senior policy officials, interviews 54 and 58 by author, Canada, 25 July 2013 and 6 August 2013).

In the previous chapter, legislative committees were identified as a central venue for diversity-seeking engagement in the policy process. In Australia, these major reforms were implemented without the engagement of a parliamentary committee (DIAC 2010f: 3; Senior policy officer, interview 52 by author, Australia, 12 November 2013). Immigration Minister Senator Chris Evans did establish an independent Skilled Migration Consultative Panel to provide advice to the government on skilled immigration issues; however, this was by invitation only and did not include diversity-seeking groups (DIAC 2008a).

In Canada, the development of ministerial instruction powers represents a paradigm shift in the policy process when compared with earlier IRPA negotiations. There is no legally guaranteed avenue for stakeholder input on future ministerial instructions. Nor is there requirement for consideration of ministerial instructions before a parliamentary committee (Green 2008: 1115). Although Immigration Minister Diane Finley argued that instructions would be subject to a policy of consultation, this policy was not entrenched statutorily (Finley 2008: 1535). Janet Dench from the Canadian Council of Refugees summarised the concerns of many diversity-seeking groups with regards to Bill C-50.

These amendments will allow the minister to issue 'instructions' without any parliamentary supervision or mandatory consultations. The fact that the rules for accepting immigrants can be determined and changed by ministerial fiat will create uncertainty, a lack of transparency and make the immigration selection process vulnerable to inappropriate political pressure. (Dench 2008: 1550)

Diversity-seeking groups also argued that Budget Bill C-50 has had a withering effect upon participatory immigration policy processes in Canada. One community activist argued that Bill C-50 has seen a reduction in 'consultation time, when they [CIC] hold consultations and the number of people who can appear' (Community activist, interview 27 by author, Canada, 18 September 2008). The introduction of Bill C-50 itself was only briefly debated before the Standing Committee on Citizenship and Immigration after complaints by that committee over a lack of engagement. The ability of activists to address gender issues during this truncated process was severely limited. Analysis of all committee transcripts reveals that there was no discussion in the four days of hearings on gender issues. Although the 2008 GBA in the *Annual Report to Parliament* states that a GBA was conducted of Bill C-50, it was not available for review prior to the Budget. Further, race and ethnicity issues, similar to those raised around the time of the Immigration and Refugee Protection Act, were canvassed by activists, but appear not to have shaped the ultimate ministerial instruction (Non-governmental organisation member, interview 36 by author, Canada, 4 May 2009; Boudjenane 2008: 1530; Ferreira 2008: 1535).

This change in consultation approach that followed Bill C-50 was also apparent with the regulatory reforms around the new points test in Canada. In comparison to the first round of IRPA reforms, the new selection grid was not subject to Standing Committee review, rather invitation-only consultations (Keung 2011). Unlike the public consultations for the IRPA for which transcriptions of debates were available publicly, there were no transcripts from the consultations. While CIC officers argued that the consultations, including new online consultations, resulted in 'a common line ... a consensus across what we heard from Canadians' (Senior immigration official, interview 48 by author, Canada, 15 July 2013) there was no way to verify this given a lack of public documentation. The closed policy process in turn meant that there was less media attention to the reforms than had been the case around the IRPA. Some diversity-seeking activists critiqued the remit of the consultation, arguing that the focus on the economic success of new immigrants minimised the capacity to draw attention to other policy issues. For instance, one activist argued that within this discursive context 'it's kind of hard to say "we don't want you to pick people that succeed". We just have a problem with how you define "success" and what you think are factors that contribute or inhibit somebody's so-called "success rate" ' (Interview 64 by author, Canada, 13 August 2013).

Judicial regimes were identified in previous chapters as a last port of call when diversity-seeking engagement in other venues has failed. In Australia, given standing rules in the immigration arena, and enduring limits placed upon administrative review of immigration decisions, there were few legal challenges to the points test. Indeed, government avoided possible legal challenges by increasing the scope of grandfathering provisions for potential applicants (Senior immigration official, interview 52 by author, Australia, 12 November 2013). The move towards an

EOI system in Australia further limits the capacity for legal intervention against skilled immigration policy decisions. Through the EOI system, the entire process of skilled immigration is now excluded from merits review as the 'EOI is not a visa application' (DIAC 2012d) and, as such, not a 'decision under an enactment' for the purposes of public law assessment. Further, a skilled immigration applicant does not have access to information about their ranking in the EOI system, rendering the decision somewhat opaque (DIAC 2012c; Mares 2011).

In Canada, there are ongoing attempts by lawyers working in collaboration with diversity-seeking groups to challenge government policy. These cases related to attempts to reduce or eradicate the backlog of federal skilled worker applicants. However, the cases, including the class action 'unfaircic.com' failed in large part due to the broad powers conferred on government via Bill C-50 and Bill C-38 that allowed the minister to both cull the backlog and to choose the order in which applications are processed (CBA 2008: 1; CCR 2008; OCASI 2009). As such, the increased bureaucratic control achieved through the budget bills and subsequent amendments to IRPA also resulted in a commensurate narrowing of venue shopping opportunities.[12] The significance of this outcome should not be underestimated. Without backlog culling, the number of outstanding applications would have risen to 1.5 million by 2015 applicants and taken fifteen years to process (Black 2013a).

Changes in the engagement of diversity-seeking groups across time

The theoretical framework set out in Chapter 3 identified the presence of diversity-seeking groups as an important feature in terms of shaping gender-aware skilled immigration policies. In Australia, I find that diversity-seeking groups were largely absent from the reforms of the points test from 2008 through to 2013. With the exception of the Federation of Ethnic Communities' Councils of Australia (FECCA), diversity-seeking groups were missing from discussions over the new points test, and FECCA's involvement was in itself limited to a single discussion paper (FECCA 2010). Nor did FECCA comment on the adoption of SkillSelect and the EOI system (Ethnocultural leader, interview 50 by author, Australia, 25 October 2013). No women's groups were involved in the consultations over the new points test. A variety of international students associations did lobby against the changes to the points test; however, one senior immigration officer noted that these groups lacked a clear spokesperson and were not a consolidated counterforce to policy developments (Interview 54 by author, Australia, 12 November 2013).

Despite a narrowing in consultation methods in Canada since the IRPA, the number of organisations consulted was still significant. Key diversity-seeking groups such as the Canadian Council for Refugees and the Ontario Council of Agencies Serving Immigrants were involved in the policy process. However, in contrast to the IRPA consultations, the engagement of diversity-seeking groups did not translate into policy changes in the current case study. For instance, some diversity-seeking organisations felt that a focus on age ignored other possible reasons for employer preference for younger workers, such as the reduced cost of entry-level wages (CLC 2012: 7). However, the reduction in age thresholds was retained as a key component of the new points test. Other groups opposed the reduction in points for international work experience, arguing that this overlooked the ways in which racial discrimination played into employer appraisal of experience (i.e. CLC 2012: 9). Yet, this policy also remained. Many organisations were concerned about raising the bar for official languages, suggesting that it could have racialised effects in terms of selection and preference those from European nations. The CLC argued that the new skilled trades class presented 'gender bias' and that 'equalising points' should be offered for women in that class (CLC 2012: 2).

Yet, despite this opposition, other interests presumed increased importance in this second round of points test reforms. In particular, employer groups enjoyed a heightened role in the policy process. This trend towards increased employer participation in and influence over skilled immigration policy-making corresponds with an increased use of skilled immigration to meet broader labour market gaps and broader industrial policy. Evidence from elite interviews indicates that employers were consulted in length over the reforms in both countries. In Canada, for instance, the new Federal Skilled Trades class was a direct response to employer group requests (Industry representatives, interviews 52 and 53 by author, Canada, 23 July 2013). In Australia, the entire policy focus has shifted towards the Employer Nomination Scheme, which gives increased selection power to employers (see also Wright 2014). At the same time, the relative importance of other interest groups in the policy process diminished.

Conclusion

Recent reforms to permanent skilled immigration in Australia and Canada demonstrate increasing convergence in policy approaches. This convergence relates to 'lesson learning' on the part of Canada from experiences in Australia. For instance, in preferencing the young under its new selection grid, Canadian policy-makers drew an analogy to developments in Australia in the late 1990s (CIC 2010b: 50). The adoption of the EOI system in Canada in 2014 was a direct response to the Australian EOI policy (Senior immigration official, interview 47 by author, Canada, 11 July 2013).

Perhaps the most significant change in the skilled immigration field in the last ten years, however, relates less to the convergence of permanent immigration points tests than the rise of temporary foreign labour programmes. Temporary labour categories are 'demand driven and also given processing priority' in both countries (Alboim and Cohl 2013: 59). New policy instruments such as the EOI system provide a mechanism for existing temporary skilled immigrants to apply for permanent status. These processing factors, combined with a changing economic context, have contributed to sharp increases in temporary economic immigration in Australia and Canada since the mid-2000s. Yet, these changes have gone largely unexamined from a critical gender perspective. The next chapter analyses these trends in temporary skilled immigration, locating developments within structural economic changes such as resource booms in the western states of both nations and accompanying skill gaps, and highlighting the underexamined gender components of the reforms.

Notes

1 In both countries there were developments in provincial or state-based skilled immigration that, while important, are beyond the remit of this chapter.
2 In the financial year 2011–12, 71,819 immigrants entered through the Skilled Independent stream and 46,554 through the various employer-sponsored visa sub-classes (DIAC 2013a). Yet, all skilled immigration sub-class visas other than labour agreements and the employer nomination stream (both classified under employer sponsorship) require points testing (DIAC 2011a).
3 CLB Level 7 is equivalent to IELTS Level 6 used in Australia (Senior immigration official, interview 48 by author, Canada, 15 July 2013).
4 The key Federal Skilled Trade Professions are: Industrial, Electrical and Construction Trades; Maintenance and Equipment Operation Trades; Supervisors and Technical Occupations in Natural Resources, Agriculture and Related Production; Processing, Manufacturing and Utilities Supervisors and Central Control Operators; Chefs and Cooks; and Bakers and Butchers (CIC 2012a).
5 For those applicants without a prior employment offer in Canada, or enrolment in a PhD programme in Canada: CIC 2011c, 2013f. The July 2013 list includes the following occupations: Engineering managers, Financial and investment analysts, Geoscientists and oceanographers, Civil engineers, Mechanical engineers, Chemical engineers, Mining engineers, Geological engineers, Petroleum engineers, Aerospace engineers, Computer engineers (except software engineers and designers), Land surveyors, Computer programmers and interactive media developers, Industrial instrument technicians and mechanics, Inspectors in public and environmental health and occupational health and safety, Audiologists and speech-language pathologists, Physiotherapists, Occupational therapists, Medical laboratory technologists, Medical laboratory technicians and pathologists' assistants, Respiratory therapists, Clinical perfusionists and cardiopulmonary technologists, Medical radiation technologists, Medical sonographers, Cardiology technologists and electrophysiological diagnostic technologists (CIC 2013c). Gender-disaggregated data for the entire of 2013 are unavailable.
6 This number includes the occupations for the Employer Nomination Scheme sub-visa. For Skilled Independent migration alone, there were 162 occupations listed in 2008.

7 'The top five occupations for women are primarily in areas of education, financial management, and nursing; the top five for men are in the areas of information technology, education, financial management and health-care professions (physicians) ... In the case of women, the top five occupations represent 72.2 per cent of total female principal applicants under the FSWP, whereas they represent only 56.6 per cent for men' (CIC 2010a).

8 This analyses the lists in place at July 2013.

9 The review considered the possibility of allowing semi-skilled occupations to enter with the Employer-Sponsored sub-class visa of General Skilled Migration (DIAC 2011a: 24).

10 The limited exceptions to this exclusion of low- and semi-skilled labour are discussed in Chapter 7.

11 This visa is used where a state or territory government initiates the sponsorship process, essentially playing the role of a public employer.

12 The legal reason for this would appear to be that Bill C-50 amended the IRPA to allow government discretion in whether it issued a visa to an applicant who qualified for processing under the Federal Skilled Worker class. Previously, the Minister and his or her delegates were mandated to process the application through the use of the word 'shall' in the relevant regulations. As a result, the legal scope for challenge to a non-decision was delimited through Bill C-50 (see Crépeau 2008: 1055).

7

Mining booms and Nanny-Gate: the gendered terrain of temporary economic immigration, 2007–13

Introduction

Since the mid-1990s, the Australian and Canadian governments increased temporary immigration to the extent that by 2013 it exceeded permanent immigration in both countries. Structural ageing and the move towards a knowledge economy inform these changes. Large-scale resource sector booms from the early 2000s onwards also spurred particular, unique labour demands, in part met through temporary economic immigration. Notwithstanding their peculiar experiences with resource wealth, Australia and Canada are in many ways exemplars of a broader prioritisation of temporary economic immigration currently under way by immigration countries, including in the US, the UK and New Zealand (Chaloff and Lemaitre 2009: 36). According to the OECD, temporary worker flows within the region were 1.9 million in 2011 (OECD 2012b: 22). Given the scope of this movement, Stephen Castles (2006) has gone so far as to suggest that we may be observing the resurrection of a guest worker model in democratic immigration states. Yet, despite these broader trends, the shift towards temporary labour in Australia and Canada is significant not only due to the magnitude of the expansion, but also because these setter states have traditionally eschewed temporary immigrant labour in favour of permanent settlement (Campbell and Tham 2011: 4; Freeman 1995).

The field of temporary economic immigration is vast and covers many areas, not all of which I can fruitfully address in this chapter. For instance, a significant component of the debate relates to whether temporary immigrants displace domestic labour. Central to this academic discussion is the unresolved question of whether the control relationship that an employer exercises over his or her sponsored immigrant worker can in turn contribute to a downward pressure on wages for both domestic and foreign workers (e.g. Birrell and Healy 2012; Campbell and Tham 2013; Ruhs and Anderson 2010). Similarly, there is the empirical question of whether trade union groups have resisted the shift towards temporary immigration in a protectionist fashion, or indeed, in solidarity with migrant workers, trade unions have pushed for extended labour protections for domestic and foreign workers alike.

Some discussion of these themes is unavoidable insofar that it is central to the political debates around temporary economic immigration. However, in this chapter, I focus upon two distinctive issues that are most relevant from a gender perspective. First, I consider what kind of economic immigrant is permitted entry on a temporary work basis. In Australia, temporary economic immigration is largely skilled, although there have been some small movements towards unskilled and semi-skilled immigration since 2011. In Canada, by contrast, the low-skilled component of the Temporary Foreign Worker Program (TFWP) eclipses the high-skilled component. Second, I consider the portability opportunities for temporary economic immigrants in both countries from temporary to permanent status. I demonstrate that low-skilled temporary immigration has facilitated women's entry in the Canadian case but has also limited portability. In Australia, there are high levels of portability between temporary and permanent skilled visas; however, I demonstrate that intake into these visa categories is male-dominated. In Canada but not in Australia, diversity-seeking activists have also been engaged in the temporary economic immigration policy space. This chapter first describes the policy processes in Australia and Canada. It then analyses the policies from a gender perspective. The final part of the chapter assesses the policy processes that took place, including the extent of engagement of diversity-seeking groups in the two countries.

The policy process in Australia

Temporary economic immigration into Australia takes many forms including working holiday makers, New Zealand citizens who enter Australia on a temporary basis, international students who are entitled to work and temporary skilled visa holders, most often known as '457 visa' holders. The 457 visa is the focus of this chapter, although I do also refer to some relatively new labour agreements for low- and semi-skilled labour that bring in a number of 457 visa holders under a single contract.

The creation of the 457 visa was first recommended in the 1995 Roach Inquiry into the Temporary Entry of Business People and Highly Skilled Specialists. This inquiry also called for a skill focus in the 457 programme (MCA 2013: 36; Roach 1995). Although the recommendations of the Roach report were adopted by the then Labor Keating government, they were not introduced until the election of the Howard Coalition government in 1996 through the Migration Regulations (Amendment) Act 1996 (Cth). The 457 visa requires nomination by an approved employer sponsor (Migration Regulations, 2.17). Since mid-2013, there has also been a labour market test, which requires the employer to demonstrate that there is no Australian citizen or permanent resident equipped to fill the position

(Migration Act, 140GB(2)). Annual grants of 457 visas have grown significantly from 22,630 visa grants in 1996–97 to 125,070 grants in 2011–12 (DIAC 2013d). At June 2013, the stock of 457 visa holders in Australia was 162,140 individuals (DIAC 2013a).

The 457 visa programme was deregulated in important ways under the Howard Coalition government in 2003. In that year, a labour market testing requirement in place since 1996 was removed and replaced with a less stringent minimum salary level (Tham and Campbell 2011: 13). Despite the fact that these deregulatory changes occurred under the Coalition, it has in fact been since the election of the Labor government in 2007 that numbers in the 457 programme increased most sharply. The heightened reliance upon the 457 visa under the Rudd–Gillard Labor government can be located within several key public policy and structural trends in Australia at this time. Uptake in the programme occurred during a period of both strong domestic employment and emerging sector-based skills gaps. Employer groups claimed that these pressures were particularly apparent in the resource-rich states of Queensland and Western Australia and in the areas of construction, mining and tourism. The Mineral Council of Australia, for instance, argued that a lack of workers was leading to delays in projects and mothballing of the labour force (External Reference Group 2008: 5, 12, 18; see also JSCM 2007: 1–2).

In light of these strong economic and employer group pressures, temporary skilled immigration was given processing prioritisation in the 2011–12 Federal Budget with an additional A\$10 million allocated to this end (DIAC 2011b). At the same time, the Rudd–Gillard government made a series of regulatory changes that provided further protections to temporary migrant workers. These included:

i) the indexation of the Minimum Salary Level (renamed the Temporary Skilled Migration Income Threshold (TSMIT)) to ensure that migrants were not paid less than natives;
ii) the introduction of market-based minimum salary levels for 457 visa holders for the same reason;
iii) raising the IELTS language requirements from 4.5 to 5 to ensure that those with low English abilities were not exploited on the labour market;
iv) rendering language testing compulsory for all visa holders except high-income earners; and
v) introducing a requirement that individuals entering into occupations deemed to be 'high risk' for exploitation from employers undertake a formal skills assessment.

The 457 visa only permits entry of applicants with skills in Australian and New Zealand Standard Classification of Occupations (ANZSCO) Levels 1–4 (Managers, Professionals and Technicians, Trade Workers and Community and Personal Service Workers). The relevant occupations are gazetted and listed on the immigration website (DIAC 2013c). Six hundred and forty occupations are listed from a full possible ANZSCO range of 1,342 (MCA 2013: 8). This compares with only 188 occupations under permanent skilled immigration, rendering temporary immigration far more expansive in its potential range. Nonetheless, it is also clear that the focus within the 457 visa category is still squarely on those occupations that ANZSCO defines as 'skilled' (JSCM 2007: 53). The prevailing focus on high-skilled workers in Australia is a product of the TSMIT (a salary threshold) as well as the requirement that the salary paid to an incoming 457 visa holder be 'no less favourable than that paid to an Australian citizen or permanent resident perform-ing the same job' (Tham and Campbell 2011: 16).[1] In 2013, the TSMIT was set at A\$51,400, which is higher than the average Australian income for a single full-time earner (DIBP 2013b; Evans 2009a: 6).

Some industry groups (and elements within government) have attempted to create low- or semi-skilled modes of entry within the 457 visa class. In 2013, the Australian Council of Chamber and Industry (ACCI 2013: 8–9, 19) called for the 'as-needed' inclusion of low-skilled and semi-skilled occupations in the 457 programme. The Aged and Community Services Australia Association (ACSA 2010: 6) also argued that the scope of the 457 visa should be extended 'to include suitable short-term skilled and non-skilled workers who can provide care services in areas of critical labour under-supply'. According to this association, the defini-tions of 'skill' and salary threshold within the 457 visa process created obstacles for the entry of much needed care workers into the Australian economy (ACSA 2010: 34). Further, the Australian Productivity Commission (2011: 383) in its review into the care needs of older Australians recommended reducing the 'regu-latory burdens and costs associated with employing care workers from overseas' to meet the 'future demands for care workers due to the ageing of Australia's popula-tion'. On this basis, employer groups have argued that exceptions should be made to the TSMIT to allow workers to enter into some sectors or regions on lower salaries than currently permitted (e.g. External Reference Group 2008: 34).

With two major exceptions, the Australian federal government has rejected these arguments in favour of low- and semi-skilled migrant labour. The two excep-tions to this are Enterprise Migration Agreements (EMAs) and Regional Migration Agreements (RMAs). The creation of EMAs was a recommendation from the 2010 National Resource Sector Employment Taskforce into the specific labour needs of the mining sector (Maher *et al.* 2012), which itself was precipitated by employer demand. For instance, a 2006 report, *Staffing the Supercycle* by the Chamber of Minerals and Energy, argued that while there were skill gaps across the skill spec-trum as a product of the mining boom, 'the projected gaps are largest in occu-pational classifications with low skill levels' (cited in External Reference Group 2008: 37). EMAs were announced in the 2011 federal budget with the intention to provide semi-skilled workers on a temporary five-year basis onto key mining and resource projects (Needham 2011). The first EMA was reached in 2012 with the Roy Hill iron ore project owned by mining magnate Gina Rinehart. This was intended to employ foreign workers in scaffolding and boilermaking (Tham 2012). Following public outcry over this agreement with Rinehart, who is a controversial figure in Australia, the agreement was withdrawn and remains unfinalised (Maher *et al.* 2012; Sloan 2012).

RMAs were announced at the same time as EMAs with the intention to provide semi-skilled labour on a temporary five-year basis to key areas in Australia. Workers on RMAs would not necessarily be involved in only mining sector work but rather across a broad range of occupations (DIBP 2013a). One former political advisor noted that another policy rationale behind RMAs was to bring more immigrants into regional areas, in light of political concerns over urban overflow (Interview 45 by author, Australia, 16 October 2013). RMAs are negotiated between government and local designated representatives (Phillips and Spinks 2012: 7) and, as of 2014, the first RMA is being piloted in the Northern Territory capital of Darwin (Hind 2014).

The policy process in Canada

The TFWP has a lengthier pedigree in Canada than does the 457 visa in Australia. The low-skilled component can be traced back to the formation of the Seasonal Agricultural Worker Program in 1973 and the Live-in Caregiver Program (LCP) in 1970.[2] The skilled TFWP, founded under a different name in 1973, originally focused on the entry of academics, business executives and engineers (Nakache and Kinoshita 2010: 4). This programme was formalised into the High-Skilled TFWP in 2000, while the so-called 'Low-Skilled Pilot', which provides entry opportunities for a wide variety of low-skilled occupations, was created in 2002 under the IRPA and utilised from 2007 onwards (Reitz 2012: 527). One key difference between Australia and Canada is that although both share a strong domestic demand for care workers, in Canada, this demand is at least partially met through the LCP. Unlike other low-skilled visas, the LCP offers clear pathways to permanent residency for former temporary immigrants.

The contextual factors behind the rise of temporary immigration labour in Canada are similar to Australia. Changing economic circumstances and labour shortages in the resource, tourism, hospitality and health sectors played into the policy setting (CIC 2009a). Trade unions contended that there was insufficient investment in the domestic workforce by employer groups (i.e. CLC 2011); however, this point remains contested. As in Australia, employer pressure for increased temporary economic immigration was particularly strong in the resource-rich states, of Alberta and British Columbia (Vanderklippe 2011). Regional disparity in economic growth also played a role. One senior immigration official commented there were 'vast differences between regional economies in Canada'. He added that 'there's no way that the economic growth and expansion in the West … could have been achieved without temporary foreign workers' (Interview 47 by author, Canada, 11 July 2013).

The entry of temporary foreign workers eclipsed permanent workers in Canada in 2007 (Nakache and Kinoshita 2010). The stock of temporary foreign workers quadrupled from 81,921 in 1999 to 338,213 in 2013 (CIC 2013e). Over 40 per cent of these entrants went into the Western provinces of Alberta and British Columbia (CIC 2009a). Focusing on flow data, from 2011–13 alone, 213,573 temporary workers entered Canada (CIC 2013g). It is important to point out that the greatest expansion has been in low-skilled temporary immigration labour, and approximately half of current temporary foreign workers resident in Canada possess secondary school training or below (Boyd 2014: 11; Reitz 2012: 527). In fact, Naomi Alboim and Karen Cohl (2013: 46) estimate a 2,119 per cent increase in low-skilled temporary workers in Canada since 2002, compared with a 192 per cent increase for the LCP and a 207 per cent increase for high-skilled temporary workers. In this sense, at least at the time of writing this book, the skill level of temporary economic immigration differs substantially between Canada and Australia. Further, as I explore in detail later in this chapter, the expansion of the low-skilled programme has resulted in far greater rates of female and non-Western temporary immigration into Canada than Australia.

The high- and low-skilled streams within the TFWP mirror the division under the Canadian National Occupational Classification (NOC) discussed in previous chapters. NOC Levels O, A and B gain entry into the high-skilled stream, while NOC Levels C, D and unstated are restricted to the low-skilled stream (CIC 2013b: 66). In either case, in order to apply for a visa to sponsor a temporary foreign worker, an employer must request a Labour Market Opinion (LMO). Processed by the Department of Employment and Social Development Canada, this LMO determines whether the employment of a migrant is likely to lead to job creation or retention for Canadian citizens and permanent residents, whether it will create a transfer of knowledge or skills to a Canadian, and whether it fills a labour market shortage that a Canadian cannot fill (IRPR s203(3)(a–c)).[3] For the low-skilled TFWP category, there are additional rules that must be met by the employer sponsor around 'wages, working conditions, round trip transportation costs, medical coverage [and] assistance with finding suitable accommodation' among other factors (CIC 2013b: 47). Once the LMO is granted, an employer must also apply for a work permit from CIC, after which the immigrant may enter Canada.

The fast growth of low-skilled temporary immigration in Canada since 2007 has raised concerns over foreign worker exploitation. These concerns precipitated a public review before the Standing Committee on Citizenship and Immigration in 2009. Following the review, a series of reforms was announced, including:

i) new methods to assess the genuineness of an employer's offer to a Temporary Foreign Worker (TFW);
ii) additional contractual requirements for Live-in Caregivers;

iii) blacklisting of employers who misused the TFWP;
iv) total duration of four years for a TFWP visa after which no authorisation to work be provided for another four years (SOR/2010–172, s3; CIC 2009a).

The changes to the LCP were particularly important from a gender perspective given that intake into this low-skilled visa comprises over 95 per cent women as principal applicants (CIC 2012b). Reforms to this programme from 2009 through to 2011 were precipitated by a political scandal in Canada known as the 'Ruby Dhalla affair' or alternately as 'Nanny-Gate' (Brazao 2009). A senior Canadian Member of Parliament from the Opposition Liberal Party, Ruby Dhalla, was revealed to have kept care workers in her home and, according to some accounts, her family both requested unreasonable work from these caregivers and provided insufficient remuneration for their efforts.[4] These allegations were not unique to the Dhalla case and resonated with several decades of claims by caregivers activists that had drawn attention to underpayment, overtime work and, at times, physical and sexual assault of caregivers by their employers (e.g. Arat-Koc and Villasin 1990; Macklin 1992).

'Nanny-Gate' coincided with the broader public inquiry into the TFWP. Former caregivers to Dhalla, advocates in the Caregivers Action Centre of Toronto, Dhalla herself and members of the Ontario Liberal government were called to give evidence before the parliamentary Standing Committee on Citizenship and Immigration (Alphonso 2009; Delacourt 2009). These events brought significant attention to the plight of caregivers in Canada and, in 2009, a series of regulatory changes occurred within the programme, in addition to the broader changes mentioned earlier. These included:

i) new rules that increased the amount of time during which a caregiver could accrue relevant work experience for the purposes of conversion of permanent residency status;
ii) tightening the contractual requirements around compensation and pay owed to live-in caregivers;
iii) heightened penalties against employers who misused the system; and
iv) providing some acknowledgement for the overtime worked by caregivers (CIC 2009b).

In addition to these federal changes, at the provincial level in Ontario where the scandal took place, activists were successful in achieving some important changes to provincial labour laws as they affected caregivers. This was encapsulated in the Employment Bill for Protection of Foreign Nationals (Live-in Caregivers and Others) 2009. Also known as 'Bill 210', this legislation resulted in high financial and jail penalties to be charged against the imposition of illegal recruitment fees upon caregivers (Brazao 2009).

Gendering temporary economic immigration in Australia and Canada

On the face of it, temporary economic immigration programmes may not present distinctive gender issues from those canvassed in previous case studies on permanent skilled immigration. However, if we return to the discussion of gender awareness in Chapters 1 and 2, it is clear that the heightened role of employers in temporary economic immigration selection does raise peculiar gender concerns. Pertinent questions emerge: do women who aim to enter into highly skilled temporary economic immigration channels face gender discrimination on the grounds of employer preference for male applicants? Is highly skilled temporary immigration more difficult for women given the focus within skilled temporary routes upon 'high-skilled' occupations where men predominate? Do women instead enter through low-skilled temporary channels? What role do existing male-dominated career networks play in leading employers to select men over women (Walby 2011)? Given the increased capacity for employer discretion within temporary economic immigration selection (as the employer generally sponsors the immigrant) does statistical discrimination play a greater role here than in government-orientated selection methods, such as points tests? Finally, the emphasis on 'soft skills' within employer recruitment should also be factored in once employers take on the key selection role. In this context, 'gender may be viewed as a "proxy for productivity" and competence rated highly when employees are the "right" gender for the job' (Grugulis and Vincent 2009: 599).

A variety of feminist scholars have argued that temporary skilled immigration offers different opportunities for men than it does for women. For instance, Christina Gabriel (2008) suggests that existing male-dominated networks offer greater pathways for male than female applicants through free trade and intra-company transfer visas. Siew Ean Khoo and collaborators (2008) document highly skewed male to female ratios (5:1) within temporary skilled immigration flows into Australia. Similarly, Jathika Badkar and co-authors (2007: 148) find a strong predominance of male entrants within temporary skilled immigration into New Zealand that increases from the child rearing age of twenty-nine upwards. Others, such as Eleonore Kofman (2004: 654) and Rhacel Perrenas (2000: 654) argue that women from non-Western countries face a double burden when applying for temporary skilled status, as their qualifications are often not recognised by employers. Elizabeth Oliver (2009) provides a possible causal argument for women's underrepresentation when she proposes that temporality has a greater effect upon women than men, given that temporary status may require the deferral of major life decisions, including pregnancy, which present different implications for women than they do for men. Her qualitative study demonstrates that skilled immigrant women may forgo temporary skilled visa opportunities that interfere with social reproduction and child rearing.[5] Finally, comparing across immigration systems, the UNDP's Hanna Zlotnik (1995: 231) finds that women predominate in immigration countries that favour permanent settlement over temporary migrant labour. Therefore, a substantial migration scholarship identifies potential gender bias within temporary skilled immigration streams.

Table 7.1: Grants to principal 457 visa holders in Australia, gender disaggregated, 2008–9 through to 2011–12

	2008–9	2009–10	2010–11	2011–12
Male	37,000 (73%)	24,650 (71%)	35,420 (74%)	51,640 (76%)
Female	13,650 (27%)	10,140 (29%)	12,660 (26%)	16,670 (24%)
Total	50,650 (100%)	34,790 (100%)	48,080 (100%)	68,310 (100%)

Source: DIAC (2013d).

Table 7.2: Grants to principal high-skilled temporary foreign workers in Canada, gender disaggregated, 2008–9 through to 2011–12

	2008–9	2009–10	2010–11	2011–12
Male	52,220 (79%)	54,566 (80%)	57,393 (80%)	64,343 (81%)
Female	13,647 (21%)	13,966 (20%)	14,441 (20%)	15,506 (19%)
Total	65,867 100%)	68,532 (100%)	71,834 (100%)	79,849 (100%)

Source: CIC (2013f).

Although the causal mechanisms that lead to these gendered outcomes are difficult to unravel, analysis of gender-disaggregated data from the 457 visa class in Australia and the high-skilled TFWP in Canada does reveal low representation of women:

In both countries, as Tables 7.1 and 7.2 indicate, women's make-up as principal applicants in the skilled temporary streams is substantially less than their representation under the permanent skilled streams in both countries (cf. Chapter 4, Tables 4.3 and 4.4). When women do enter as the lead temporary skilled applicant, it is largely in nursing and associated occupations (e.g. DIAC 2013d). This analysis supports earlier gender-disaggregated studies of the 457 visa in Australia, which found that in all occupational groupings other than nursing, women are highly underrepresented as principal 457 visa holders (Khoo *et al.* 2008).

In contrast to this pattern across skilled temporary immigration, in the low-skilled pilot category in Canada, women are highly represented:

As Tables 7.2 and 7.3 indicate, women comprised 19 per cent of highly skilled temporary entrants in Canada in 2011–12 but 38 per cent of low-skilled immigrant stock in the same year (CIC 2013d; f). The analysis clearly demonstrates that low-skilled temporary visas provide greater entry opportunities for women than highly skilled temporary visas.

Table 7.3: Grants to principal low-skilled temporary foreign workers in Canada, gender disaggregated, 2008–9 through to 2011–12

	2008–9	2009–10	2010–11	2011–12
Male	65,056 (59%)	65,322 (59%)	70,199 (59%)	89,715 (62%)
Female	45,820 (41%)	45,196 (41%)	48,533 (41%)	55,006 (38%)
Total	110,876 (100%)	110,518 (100%)	118,732 (100%)	144,721 (100%)

Source: CIC (2013f).

These data bring us to a discussion of skill stratification and gender within temporary economic selection policies. In Australia, debates around the skill levels required for 457 entry have focused upon the potential exploitation of low- and semi-skilled temporary workers. As noted, there is pressure from employer groups to expand the 457 visa class into the area of unskilled labour, or alternately, to reclassify unskilled occupations as 'skilled' in order to render those occupations eligible for admission under the 457 visa rules. The most notable example of this was expansion into the areas of meatpacking under the Howard Coalition government. However, following several controversial incidences involving exploitation of migrant meatpackers (O'Malley 2006), Labor reduced the capacity for low-skilled workers to enter through 457 channels through the introduction of the TSMIT.

This focus on higher skill levels in Australia is intended to protect more vulnerable workers from exploitation. According to Barbara Deegan (2008: 23) who ran the Labor government's inquiry into the integrity of the 457 visa class, those occupations closer to the bottom of the TSMIT should be the focus both 'from an exploitation perspective and in relation to integrity issues'. A Joint Standing Committee on Migration review of the 457 visa in 2007 also recommended the maintenance of a focus on skilled occupations for entry under the visa (JSCM 2007: xvii), while the Immigration Minister at the time, Senator Chris Evans, noted that low-skilled immigration was more likely to bring in immigrants from source countries with low levels of English who 'are more capable of being exploited, less understanding of the society they come to' (cited in Healy 2008: 4). The key approach to protection of low-skilled foreign workers in Australia since 2008 has been to exclude such immigrants from entry. A less clearly articulated aspect of the public debate – but one which came through strongly in elite interviews – was an ideological concern among the Labor government over potential conflict between low-skilled immigrant labour and domestic unskilled workers (Former political advisors, interviews 45 and 49 by author, Australia, 16 October 2013 and 24 October 2013). This concern also resonated with that of the peak trade union organisation, the Australian Council of Trade Unions (ACTU), which argued that the 457 visa was being used to push down the wages of Australian workers (ACTU 2007).

As noted earlier in this chapter, some industry associations in Australia have called for the entry of care workers on low-skilled visas. Yet, here again, the TSMIT has presented a policy obstacle. One senior policy advisor noted that the fact that most aged care worker salaries did not meet the TSMIT rendered the exclusion of that occupation from the 457 visa list 'a salary issue not a labour shortage issue' (Interview 51 by author, Australia, 11 November 2013). Further, both representatives from the aged care sector and government officials argued that the shorter period of educational training for care professionals militated against its characterisation as a 'skilled occupation' (Interviews 48 and 49 by author, Australia, 24 October 2013). This brings us back to the classic feminist critique that embodied knowledge (such as care work) is often undervalued on the labour market (e.g. Kofman 2013, 2014).

This focus on skilled temporary immigration performs a protective function for both domestic and international workers. Yet, at the same time, it also excludes many women and racialised immigrants from entry. It is important to note that this situation may change in the future with the introduction of the RMAs. These agreements could cater to occupations in which women predominate, such as care work, tourism and hospitality. RMAs could be one way to bring in workers 'who don't fit the 457 requirements [as] they don't fit within the minimum pay issue [or] … the occupational skill areas for 457s' (Industry group representative, interview 40 by author, Australia, 9 October 2013). At present, the focus on high skill levels in Australia, while playing an important role in terms of minimising exploitation of foreign workers, also reduces migratory opportunities for women.

In Canada, as noted earlier, a broader spread of skills has led to strong representation of women in the low-skilled TFWP category. Further, as the biggest increases in temporary immigration have actually been in NOC levels C, D and unstated this policy has led to a greater representation of women principal applicants, albeit with fewer rights upon entry, an issue I now turn to.

Pathways to permanent residency: portability between temporary and permanent status

The relationship between temporary and permanent residency influences not only whether an immigrant has a right to stay but also how the immigrant is viewed by the host society: as a future citizen or as a temporary guest. A central issue therefore is whether there are portability rights for those on temporary visas onto permanent status. If there are limitations upon such portability, a secondary question is whether these play out for some visa holders over others, including along gender lines.

In Australia, most temporary economic immigration is skilled and, traditionally, the pathways from temporary to permanent residency have been fairly clear. Employers may sponsor temporary economic immigrants for permanent status and, indeed, the growth of the Employer Nomination Scheme in recent years suggests that portability from temporary to permanent skilled status is increasing rather than decreasing. As Lesleyanne Hawthorne (2011: xvi) notes, by 2009 'an unprecedented 70 per cent of Australia's labour migrants were employer-sponsored, entering through the temporary and permanent skilled immigration streams'. On these grounds, the 'two-step' immigration process, as it is termed by government, can be viewed as a policy success. However, some commentators have cautioned against such an assessment. Peter Mares (2013) argues that despite the growth of the Employer Nomination Scheme, employer discretion is increasingly important in ensuring portability. He argues: 'The more the 457 visa becomes the first step in a two-stage migration process, the more the second step – employer sponsorship for permanent residency – becomes a potential lever of power in the workplace.' Industrial relations expert Barbara Deegan also noted in her report on the topic in 2008 that those temporary migrants who 'have aspirations towards permanent residency' are 'vulnerable to exploitation as a consequence of their temporary status' (Deegan 2008: 23). Nonetheless, there are high rates of portability between temporary and permanent status and at present few obstacles to transitioning on the part of temporary workers. On this basis we can conclude that for those female applicants who successfully gain a 457 visa, there are good opportunities for permanent residency, albeit ones heavily controlled by employers.

In Canada, the issue of portability is more complex as there are not clear pathways between low-skilled temporary status and permanent landing. Due to the low- and high-skilled division in the TFWP, there is a growing stratification between low-skilled immigrants who enjoy few rights of portability and high-skilled temporary foreign workers who can become permanent either through sponsorship under the FSWP or the Canadian Experience Class.[6] Given that both permanent programmes require occupational skill levels A, B and O, they necessarily exclude former temporary low-skilled foreign workers from application (Sweetman and Warman 2010: 59). As one activist put it: '[t]he National Occupational Classification pre-determines exclusion and differentiated rights' (MWAC activist, interview 63 by author, Canada, 13 August 2013).

There is also a gender dimension to this issue. Analysis in 2009 by the Canadian Council for Refugees (CCR) demonstrated that while 38 per cent of temporary workers generally would be eligible for the Canadian Experience Class, only 20 per cent of temporary females would be due to the latter's clustering in C, D and unstated NOC categories (CCR 2009). Further, steps in 2012 to make the FSWP more selective, as documented in Chapter 6, move portability options for temporary low-skilled workers further out of grasp. Recent reforms to the Low- Skilled Pilot that restrict renewal of temporary visas for four years exacerbate this stratification. As one diversity-seeking activist noted, these changes mean 'the door is open a crack and then it just kind of slams shut. It's going to be really hard for workers in low-skilled positions to get in' (Interview 56 by author, Canada, 31 July 2013). Provincial Nominee Programs offer settlement opportunities for low-skilled temporary foreign workers (Nakache and D'Aoust 2012). Yet, these programmes are restricted in number by the federal government, and generally do not provide the clear portability channels that exist for skilled labour. There is a legitimate concern that low-skilled workers unable to transit to permanent residency could become undocumented (Standing Committee 2009b: 24–5).

According to some diversity-seeking groups, this lack of portability in Canada significantly increases the risk of exploitation for low-skilled workers by employers. For instance, the Adult Entertainment Association Canada (AEAC 2009: 9) argues that the low-skilled TFWP has seen a rotation of dispensable adult sex workers in Canada. Consistently, a variety of diversity-seeking groups proposed that clear pathways to permanent residency should be available for both low- and high-skilled temporary workers (e.g. Mainland of Nova Scotia 2008: 9; Parkdale Community Legal Centre 2008: 2–3). Yet, government explicitly rejected creating these pathways for low-skilled temporary immigrants in its response to the Standing Committee Report (Government of Canada 2010). One senior immigration official, while acknowledging that '[t]he question of pathways to permanent residence is another perennial one' argued that the government was 'not sure about how resilient those [low-skilled] individuals are within the community and labour market' (Interview 61 by author, Canada, 7 August 2013). On this basis, clear portability for low-skilled workers has to date not been incorporated into policy with the exception of the LCP.

Caregivers who enter through this visa scheme enjoy high rates of portability to permanent residency at approximately 90 per cent (Brickner and Straehle 2010: 311, citing Government of Canada 2009: 3781). Nonetheless, given the overwhelming representation of women in this visa class, their initial temporary status could itself be viewed as discriminatory on gender grounds, especially when compared with the immediate permanent status conferred upon skilled immigrants. On this basis, diversity-seeking groups argued before the Standing Committee in 2008 and 2009 that the LCP should be a permanent visa subsumed within the general federal skilled worker points tests (e.g. CDPCJ 2008: 7; Intercede 2000: 13; PINAY 2008: 5; TWAG 2009: 3). The argument follows that offering immediate permanent residency to caregivers would remove the exploitation that some tolerate in order to meet the work conditions for permanent status (Standing Committee 2009b: 7). Alternately, activists proposed that the live-in requirement should be removed from the visa and made sector- rather than employer-specific. This, it was argued, would also minimise exploitation by individual employers, as it would reduce dependency upon one sponsor (Chow 2009; PINAY 2008: 6; Quash 2009; Standing Committee 2009b: 5). The federal Canadian government rejected all of these recommendations in its response to the Standing Committee hearings (Government of Canada 2010).

The creation in 2009 of open work permits for caregivers does, however, improve the conditions for those workers on transitional visas. As CIC's gender analysis (CIC 2012a: 16) notes, '[o]pen work permits allow flexibility in employment and support the caregiver's establishment in Canada as they wait for the processing of their permanent residence permit'. The 2009 changes were also important in providing some acknowledgement of overtime worked by caregivers, by allowing up to 10 per cent of such work to be counted towards the hours required for the application for permanent residency (CIC 2009b).

Intersectional issues

In addition to these gender considerations, it is also important to interrogate what the shift towards temporary employer-sponsored models means for racial diversity within immigration selection. The fact that employers now possess increased decision-making power could hold important implications for selection, given what we know about patterns of homophily that play out in recruitment. This vexed (and controversial) question is difficult to examine exhaustively, given data restrictions. However, in both countries it is clear that the source country profile of temporary employer-sponsored skilled visas differs substantially from permanent government-selected immigration streams. Speaking of the Australian experience, Lesleyanne Hawthorne (2011: 157) notes that while '[f]rom 2005/6 to 2008/9 [only 17 per cent of] General Skilled Migrants Principal Applicants were selected from the major English Speaking Background nations' in the same years for the 457 visa 'five of the major English Speaking Countries featured in the top 10'. This was also the case in 2011–12, with Ireland attracting the greatest increase in 457 nominations (DIAC 2013a: 123).

Similarly in Canada, country-of-origin stratification operates between the low- and high-skilled streams of the TFWP. As Nandita Sharma notes of the low-skilled category (2006: 129), '[t]he proportion of workers from Asia and the Pacific has increased, while that from Europe and the United States has dropped. In skilled categories however, almost 70 per cent still originate in Europe ... while almost 60 per cent from Asia and the Pacific and 85 per cent from the Americas (outside of the United States) are in the lower-skilled categories'. As such, any restrictions on the low-skilled temporary programme will affect certain minorities disproportionately. This brings me to a discussion of the tension within low-skilled temporary immigration policy between the scope for intake of such immigrants, compared with the rights which they possess upon entry.

A gendered and racialised 'rights versus numbers' trade-off?

In his book *The Price of Rights*, Martin Ruhs (2013) provides compelling evidence that in high-income countries, there is a trade-off between the rights conferred on temporary immigrants and the numbers that are permitted entry. In particular, Ruhs (2013: 120) argues that such nations 'grant more rights to high- than low-skilled migrant workers because they consider these policies to be in their best national interest'. As such, states develop a policy justification for conferring fewer rights on low-skilled migrants, which they may nonetheless still offer entry to on a large-scale basis. Ruhs' thesis operates convincingly in the Canadian case, where as noted above, the numbers in the low-skilled TFWP pilot (who possess fewer rights) heavily exceeds those in the high-skilled foreign worker programme.

Even in Australia, where rates of temporary unskilled immigration are low at present, we can see how such an argument might play out: the care sector in Australia suffers both from poor wages and considerable churn of workers. This has the effect that domestic supply of labour into the sector is low and campaigns for wage increases by care workers are often unsuccessful (Trade union representative, interview 34 by author, Australia, 11 November 2009). As such, any move towards increased provision of care workers through immigration will face the possibility of further reduced salaries for temporary migrant workers. On the other hand, such a development could open significant opportunities for new pathways of immigration for citizens from some of Australia's closest neighbours, including Indonesia, where there are large populations of semi-skilled workers eager to gain mobility rights into the Australian labour market (Senior immigration official, interview 56 by author, Australia, 29 November 2013).

On the basis of this empirical trade-off, Ruhs (2013: Chapter 7) develops a moral defence of temporary labour immigration programmes with some reduced rights for low-skilled immigrants. As he notes (2013: 165), there are no easy moral choices but such an approach avoids 'rights fetishism' and also acknowledges other factors such as those of 'agency, choices and interests of migrants'. Yet, aside from the empirical and moral application of the rights versus numbers argument, it is clear from the analysis in this chapter, that there is both a gendered and racialised dimension to this trade-off; one which is under-analysed in Ruhs' work. Low-skilled pathways offer entry opportunities for female immigrants (and often racialised minorities from the Global South) that do not exist under a system skewed towards the highly skilled. On the other hand, low-skill visas also often limit the rights of such workers and lead to stratifications across immigrant groups along gender and source country lines (see also Benería et al. 2012: 6–9). This chapter does not claim to resolve this moral issue; I merely observe that when assessing the gender awareness of the Australian and Canadian temporary economic immigration policies, it is necessary to consider how these policies sit on either side of the rights versus numbers trade-off. In the remaining section of this chapter, I consider the differences in the policy process around temporary skilled immigration in Australia and Canada.

Understanding the policy process in Australia and Canada

The policy framework for admission of temporary economic immigration into Australia and Canada differs significantly. For one, Canada brings in far more unskilled temporary economic migrants than Australia. Employers have led the growth in 457 visas in Australia, although trade unions have been successful in bringing about some regulatory changes to this visa that both protect migrant workers and restrict the entry of low-skilled workers that might compete otherwise with domestic labour. In Canada, policy developments have also been employer-initiated; however, trade union groups and diversity-seeking activists have mobilised around the Low-Skilled Temporary Pilot.

In both countries, a remarkable feature of the policy process is the extent to which this expansion has occurred through bureaucratic and market-driven rather than legislative channels. According to one trade union leader in Canada, the incremental nature of the reforms ensured that the changes 'did not raise alarm bells' with the general public (Interview 53 by author, Canada, 23 July 2013). The uncapped nature of the programme in both countries has allowed this growth to occur and not be subject to the annual planning levels discussed in Chapter 4. Prioritisation of funds to process temporary visas in both countries also contributed to rapid expansion of the programme in both Australia and Canada (Alboim and Cohl 2013: 59; Evans 2009b).

Another dimension unique to the temporary arena is the extent to which business secrecy has reduced the transparency of policy processes. For instance, in Canada, Labour Market Opinions are not made public due to privacy concerns (Labour group representative, interview 53 by author, Canada, 23 July 2013). In Australia the full details of EMAs are also not publicly available (Taylor 2012). One senior official from the Department of Employment explained the rationale behind this secrecy:

> The advice from Immigration was that a lot of things were commercial-in-confidence, and my understanding is that the companies were concerned that if a lot of this information became public, or in fact, everything was handed over to unions, etc., that it would affect bargaining positions in wage negotiations, or their commercial position relative to their competitors ... (Interview 41 by author, Australia, 9 October 2013)

Commercial-in-confidence rules in turn meant that when opposition parliamentarians requested information about the EMAs, they were refused (Senior policy official, Department of Employment, interview 41 by author, Australia, 9 October 2013). Attempts by the minority Greens Party to introduce legislation that would have increased ministerial oversight over the EMA process were also rejected by Parliament (Parliament of the Commonwealth of Australia 2013: 2662). Further, the rules governing the EMAs are set through guidelines rather than regulation (Tham 2012), further reducing parliamentary scrutiny.

Interest groups' engagement in the policy process

Within this closed policy context, what capacity have diversity-seeking groups had to influence the process? In Australia, aside from trade union groups, there has been limited engagement by diversity-seeking groups in debates over the 457 visa. While the Federation of Ethnic Communities' Councils of Australia (FECCA) did provide a submission to a 2006 inquiry into the 457 visa, it was otherwise inactive in the area of temporary skilled immigration (FECCA 2006). When asked why FECCA was not more involved in debates around temporary skilled immigration, one ethnocultural leader explained that 'because of its variable nature, [the 457 visa] hasn't formed a key part of how we've advocated'. He also noted that focusing on representing new labour from overseas would conflict with another constituency for that organisation; that of 'young people from non-English speaking backgrounds ... who are unemployed' (Interview 50 by author, Australia, 25 October 2013). This divide within the Australian ethnocultural sector between older and newer waves of migration and intergenerationally, is addressed further in Chapter 8.

A critical gender dimension was also absent from the debates over the 457 visa. In fact, the most active interest groups in general have been employer associations and peak industry bodies (Industry representatives, interviews 40 and 46 by author, Australia, 9 October 2013 and 17 October 2013). It is also these peak industry associations who have pushed for increased unskilled and semi-skilled modes of entry. Yet, the gender dimension is not addressed in such endorsements by business, with the focus of such claims instead on the creation of a flexible labour force (e.g. ACCI 2013: 8–9, 19).

Likewise, in Canada, employer groups have been highly engaged in pushing for increased temporary immigration. One captain of industry related this increased role for employers to the changing demographic circumstances faced by Canada:

> I think what's happened with the onset of the demographic sort of lump in the boa as they say, is 'oh my goodness, we've got to start using immigration as part of the solution to dealing with our future labour market demands'. We're better at talking to the players, because how do you match the two without getting some idea or indication or what requirements are? All of a sudden labour market intelligence became the thing. (Interview 51 by author, Canada, 23 July 2013)

As such, employer expertise and engagement in labour market policy began to play a larger role in immigration selection as immigration itself adopted a larger position within broader economic policy. Multiple reports by industry groups also drew attention to the need for temporary labour (e.g. CCC 2011) and policy officials within CIC identified the importance of consultation with employer groups during the key period of TFWP expansion (e.g. Senior immigration official, interview 61 by author, Canada, 7 August 2013).

Yet, against this context of rising employer engagement in policy-making, Canada has also experienced a renaissance in diversity-seeking activism and coalition building in the temporary economic migration field. Activism around the LCP has had a long history in Canada, stemming from the early 1980s, when portability rights were secured for caregivers. The earlier activism is well documented by Canadian scholars, including the importance of coalition building to create alliances and push for changes, especially in British Columbia, Quebec and Ontario (Choudry *et al.* 2009: 84; Macklin 1992; Pratt 2004: 108). Yet, coalitions have also featured in more recent campaigns around the TFWP. The Toronto-based Migrant Workers Alliance for Change (MWAC) that comprises a number of legal centres, workers' centres and trade unions based in that city[7] was formed shortly after the Ruby Dhalla affair (MWAC member, interview 68 by author, Canada, 22 August 2013). As a member of MWAC noted, the alliance grew rapidly, coinciding with the fast increase in temporary foreign workers in Canada: 'It's suddenly become one of the major priorities of many large private sector unions, public sector unions, labour congresses around Canada, and racialised labour alliances and associations' (MWAC member, interview 70 by author, Canada, 22 August 2013). The Coalition was particularly important in supporting the mobilisation around the provincial changes to labour laws that affected live-in caregivers, known as Bill 210 (MWAC member, interview 70 by author, Canada, 22 August 2013). According to one activist, the Ruby Dhalla affair also provided the ideal timing for the Coalition to bring to the Ontario government the 'package of changes on recruitment' they had developed 'for years' (MWAC member, interview 63 by author, Canada, 13 August 2013).

MWAC provided a context for autonomous conscious-raising by temporary foreign workers themselves. As an example, in 2010, members of the organisation arranged a pilgrimage across Canada on Thanksgiving that followed the path of black slaves entering Canada many decades earlier (Goutor and Ramsaroop 2009). The Coalition formed alliances within trade union groups, such as the Alberta Federation of Labour and the United Food and Commercial Workers Union. Nonetheless, in contrast to trade union groups in Australia, grass-roots organisations such as MWAC also took a more proactive stance in bringing a critical gender and race lens to their activities.

How, if at all, was the activity of these groups supported by institutional venues? In this chapter, I consider the role of sympathetic bureaucrats, legislative committees, federalist structures and judicial regimes. In previous chapters, I have shown that the GBA unit within CIC played a role in ensuring that the gender dimension of skilled immigration reforms was brought to the policy table in Canada. In this last case study, the GBA function was unimportant. No GBA was undertaken of the reforms to the TFWP in 2009, although a gendered analysis did subsequently accompany Treasury Board submissions (Ahmad 2013). CIC's Annual Reports to Parliament do identify the higher representation of women in the Low-Skilled Pilot but do not interrogate what the lack of portability opportunities for low-skilled visa holders might mean from a gender perspective (CIC 2010a, 2011b, 2012c). This is despite this issue being raised by a variety of activists in parliamentary hearings (Brickner and Straehle 2010; Standing Committee 2009b). In Australia, there was no evidence that gender was considered as an important policy lens within the general drive to increase the 457 visa programme, or as a dimension within the significant debates around labour protections from 2009 onwards.

Parliamentary committees and indeed extra-parliamentary committees did provide a forum for debates around temporary economic immigration in both countries. In Australia, several government inquiries precipitated changes to the 457 visa in 2007 and 2008 and created opportunities for engagement by interest groups in the process. For instance, a large number of groups proposed reforms to the 457 visa in the 2008 Deegan Inquiry. A separate inquiry within the parliamentary Joint Standing Committee on Migration occurred in the Australian federal parliament in 2007 with hearings held in most major cities (JSCM 2007: xxvi). In addition, the Skilled Migration Consultative Panel brought attention to temporary skilled immigration issues across industry, trade unions and state and territory governments (DIAC 2008a). Yet, despite the broad range of parties involved in these inquiries, neither gender nor race was raised and diversity-seeking groups were not involved in the policy process.

The Standing Committee on Citizenship and Immigration hearings across Canada in 2009 into the Low-Skilled Pilot provided an important venue for groups to raise concerns about that visa and the LCP. Caregivers participated in the hearings and brought attention to the precarious and gendered nature of the TFWP more broadly. Most importantly, the cross-examination of Ruby Dhalla herself during the committee hearings brought significant national media attention to the plight of caregivers and created the context for legislative reforms at both federal and provincial levels. While activists did not achieve their broader goal of immediate permanent status for caregivers, they were successful in changing provincial labour laws in Ontario to ensure recruiters were penalised.

Related to this last point, federalism was important in Canada in permitting a multi-level field for engagement over temporary foreign workers. In Canada, the national level is largely responsible for the selection of immigrants, while the provincial level is responsible for labour laws. When activists failed to bring around major changes at the national level, they concentrated their efforts on the labour rights of temporary workers already present in Canada. There have been successful campaigns in Quebec, Ontario and Manitoba to change labour laws to benefit temporary immigrants, with activists taking inspiration from successes in other provinces (Flecker 2011: 16–17). The difficulty of executing campaigns at the federal level in Canada also motivated activists to focus on provincial claims. According to one activist 'we wage on a provincial basis, and try to carve out those kinds of changes we can win provincially to build confidence' (MWAC member, interview 68 by author, Canada, 22 August 2013). In Australia, by contrast, the amendments to labour standards for 457 visa-holders were brought by the federal government which holds exclusive immigration and labour law-making powers.

In neither country have the courts been used to challenge the growth in temporary economic immigration. In Canada, a variety of legal and quasi-legal institutions have also been used to protect the industrial rights of temporary workers already present, or to raise attention to prior rights violations (Flecker 2011: 13–14). Some of the diversity-seeking groups and coalition members interviewed for this book also acted as interveners in key court cases (MWAC member, interview 70 by author, Canada, 22 August 2013) or initiated cases on behalf of low-skilled temporary workers before the Ontario Human Rights Tribunal or to various workplace safety boards (MWAC member, interview 63 by author, Canada, 13 August 2013). One MWAC member commented that the Tribunal was useful 'around things like discrimination … so on gender, and sexuality and racism. So whenever we can provide a ground we can go and … turn to the provincial government and say the Human Rights Tribunal is pointing out what is actually a structural flaw'. As such, legal challenges were viewed as an important first step to initiate broader policy change in Canada. These cases did not in themselves create law reform but they have had the benefit of drawing attention to the plight of temporary low-skilled workers.

Conclusion

Gender stratification is clearly present in the area of temporary economic immigration policy, with distinctive 'his' and 'her' modes of selection. These differing, gendered pathways to entry carry with them varied rights, privileges and burdens. Temporary skilled immigration is more likely to exclude women than permanent skilled immigration. On the other hand, women have significant capacity to enter as temporary low- or semi-skilled immigrants, given that they predominate in related occupational areas. Chief among these areas of work is care.

This situation creates a paradox from a feminist perspective. On the one hand, temporary skilled immigration often excludes female principal applicants. Yet skilled channels offer more long-term rights for those immigrants who are successful than unskilled streams, the latter of which often restrict portability to permanent residency. As such, I argue that in the temporary arena there is a gendered and racialised 'rights versus numbers' trade-off at play, with higher rates of temporary unskilled immigration offering greater mobility rights for women, but with fewer other rights. Further evidence of this trade-off is evident in the LCP in Canada. Since the introduction of regulatory improvements in 2009, entrant numbers have also dropped significantly (CIC 2012a). As Martin Ruhs (2013) persuasively argued, there is no simple solution to the rights versus numbers trade-off. Increasing the selectivity of temporary labour will reduce mobility rights but deregulation and movement into the low- and semi-skilled space generally correlates with fewer rights. To this I would add that it is often women and racialised minorities who experience this rights reduction, given their disproportionate representation as low- and semi-skilled temporary migrants.

Aside from assessing this complex intersectional gender issue, this chapter also demonstrates different patterns of engagement by diversity-seeking groups in the two countries in the temporary economic policy space. In Australia, diversity-seeking groups other than trade unions were absent from the temporary skilled immigration policy arena, while in Canada there was a great deal of diversity-seeking activism around the same issue. Some of this difference relates to differences in availability of viable venues for raising concerns, in particular, a greater capacity for venue shopping across different provinces in Canada. However, there is also a supply-side issue that must be interrogated; in short diversity-seeking activists simply appear more present and numerous in Canada than in Australia over the same time period. This is consistent with previous case studies in this book where I have demonstrated that diversity-seeking groups in Australia are weak and largely inactive in the skilled immigration policy arena. In the final chapter of this book, I interrogate the reasons for this difference from a supply-side perspective, which focuses on the organizational nature of diversity-seeking groups both historically and in the present day.

Notes

1 Migration Amendment Regulations (2009) (No 5) Amendment Regulations 2009 (No 2) inserting regulation 2.72 (10(cc)).
2 Audrey Macklin (1992: 692) documents the history of live-in caregivers in Canada noting that the programme became temporary in 1973. Canada had a longer history of bringing Eastern European women in on a permanent basis to provide care work under the previous Foreign Domestic Movement that preceded this temporary scheme.
3 Monica Boyd (2014: 10–11) points out that LMOs are not always required for skilled labour and that, increasingly, many temporary employment migrants have been entering through intra-company transfers and other categories that do not demand LMOs.
4 The veracity of the claims was never confirmed in a court case. Ruby Dhalla did ultimately lose her federal seat as a result of the scandal (Grewal 2011).
5 This chapter does not consider in detail the immigration status rights of temporary visa holders on maternity leave. Although it would appear that temporary immigrants are entitled to maternity leave in both Australia and Canada, a recent case in Australia demonstrates possible discrimination on this basis and the forfeiture of a pregnant 457 visa-holder's visa. The employer in question was later banned from 457 sponsorship, although at the same time, permitting unpaid maternity leave would have rendered the immigrant in breach of the wage threshold requirement (Walker 2008). The suggestion by Oliver (2009) is that the lack of stability presented by temporary work visas might limit the mobility of skilled migrant women of child bearing and rearing age.
6 Temporary low-skilled foreign workers are denied a variety of rights conferred on high-skilled workers including rights to renew visas while present in Canada, rights to enter without a confirmed job opportunity, rights to bring family

members (given assistance requirements that are hard for low-skilled migrants to meet), travel costs of spouses and children which are not covered for the low-skilled and the fact that high-skilled temporary foreign workers can apply for open permits, whereas low-skilled workers are tied to a particular employer. Further, the spouses of high-skilled temporary workers can enjoy an open permit whereas those on low-skilled visas must have an employer sponsor of their own and cannot access an open permit (Fudge and MacPhail 2009: 15–22; Marsden 2010; Nakache and D'Aoust 2012: 163). Note that since 2007, the children of live-in caregivers may accompany their parents but the parent must first prove that they have sufficient funds to support them (Bakan and Stasiulis 2012: 205). The array of differential rights are not the focus of the current chapter, as they provide little comparison to Australia; however, they are important to acknowledge as additional indicators of the relevance of skill classification for the subsequent position of the immigrant.

7 Caregivers Action Centre, Migrante, Workers Action Centre, Parkdale Community Legal Clinic, Canadian Auto Workers, United Food and Commercial Workers Union, Asian Community AIDS Service, The Alliance for South Asian AIDS Prevention and No One is Illegal (Toronto).

8

Activist mobilising, state sponsorship and venue shopping capabilities

Introduction

Governments in Australia and Canada have over the last quarter century pushed towards a more economically selective immigration programme. Initially, Australian policy-makers were better able to realise this goal, although there has been a convergence in policy achievements and processes around both temporary and permanent skilled immigration policies in the two countries since the mid-2000s. In both countries, governments now exercise high levels of bureaucratic control over the policy processes. Yet, important differences remain – in particular, an enduring capacity for extra-parliamentary and legal intervention by diversity-seeking activists in Canada when compared with Australia. Throughout this book, I have argued that these differences in policy processes contributed to differences in the policies that emerged from a gender-aware perspective. However, the capacity of diversity-seeking groups to engage in institutional venues also depends upon key supply-side factors considered in this chapter; in particular the existence of strong diversity-seeking groups and networks in the immigration arena. In this chapter, I argue that the strength of these groups and networks is in turn informed by the internal structure of such organisations.

In this book thus far, I have demonstrated that institutional venue matters for the gender awareness of economic immigration policies. Yet, even if the venue for policy-making were different in Australia, the outcome may have been the same due to the lack of critical voices in the Australian policy landscape. In short, diversity-seeking activists were in most respects absent in the Australian debates over permanent and temporary skilled immigration, while they remain vibrant in Canada. What could be the reason for differences in presence and strength across the two countries? I argue here that these differences are themselves a product of differing historical state strategies towards women's and ethnocultural interests that stem from organizational and policy decisions made by government and activists during the advent of multiculturalism in both countries from the early 1970s onwards. This chapter draws upon empirical data and theoretical scholarship to consider the implications of these historical decisions for current day practice. Briefly, I argue that three factors matter for diversity-seeking presence and strength: i) the sources of funding of these organisations; ii) their internal organisation; and iii) the extent of coalition building across these organisations. These three factors, when executed correctly, bolster diversity-seeking organisations even when functioning in hostile political environments.

The next part of this chapter assesses the historical scholarship on ethnic and feminist engagement in Canada and Australia. It then sets out the three-tiered argument for differences across organisations, employing elite interview material. This part of the chapter analyses budget reports of various diversity-seeking organisations to demonstrate the importance of the particular departmental origins of the funding mix. The following part of the chapter returns to the venue shopping argument and compares the theory's application across the four case studies. I conclude the book with a discussion of its theoretical and practical public policy implications for skilled immigration policy-making both in Australia, Canada and globally.

Understanding diversity-seeking strength: historical legacies of state funding

This book argues that diversity-seeking engagement matters for the production of gender-aware policies in the skilled immigration field, at least in traditional settler states. The involvement of immigrants (first and second generation) in immigration policy-making in settler states is a key difference from continental European immigration countries, where patterns of integration are less effective and the political enfranchisement of those of immigrant background, less common (Guiraudon 1997). Comprising significant sections of the populations and the electorate, immigrants and their offspring in Australia and Canada are potentially vital players in immigration policy-making in settler states. Immigrant groups and immigrant women's groups, in particular, may not be sidelined politically in settler states to the same extent that they can be in less open immigration countries. They also may not necessarily rely upon bureaucracies to achieve progressive policies on their behalf (cf. Guiraudon 1997: 69, 277). In fact, the interviews undertaken for this book do not locate a distinctive 'pro-diversity' or 'pro-gender' cultural attitude within immigration bureaucracies. Instead, bureaucratic views on diversity concerns appear mixed and there is no clear evidence to suggest that bureaucrats in the Australian and Canadian setting can be relied upon to always act as vanguards of feminist and racial equality issues. Indeed, this book finds that diversity-seeking groups are most successful at achieving gender-aware policies when they participate through more open institutional venues, such as through parliamentary committees or the courts and, generally, when they act in coalition with other interest groups.

This book has found that generally diversity-seeking groups were less active in Australia than in Canada. There, diversity-seeking groups were often involved at the agenda-setting stage of policy development. They were successful in galvanising large-scale opposition to mandatory English testing under the IRPA points test (Chapter 5). They also played a proactive role in calling for and achieving a gender analysis of the new immigration act and seeking the establishment of the GBA Unit within CIC (Chapter 5). They continue to mobilise at both federal and provincial level around the Low-Skilled Pilot and the Live-in Caregiver Program (LCP) (Chapter 7). Yet, institutional venue, while constraining or facilitating the action of these groups and the possibilities for agenda-setting behaviour, does not explain the original emergence of these groups. Even in cases where diversity-seeking groups in Australia had access to public venues (such as around the 457 reforms under the Rudd–Gillard government), such groups were neither present, active, nor determinative in policy processes. To understand the reasons for the much lower levels of diversity-seeking mobilisation in Australia compared with Canada from the late 1980s to the early 2000s, especially around gender issues, it is necessary to consider the three supply-side factors historically rooted in the social organisations of both countries.

The sources and mix of funding for diversity-seeking groups

Resources matter for social mobilisation. The advocacy scholarship has long established a link between the availability of liquid assets and the use of insider engagement strategies in lobbying (Mahoney 2008, citing Schlozman and Tierney 1986 and Smith 1984). In the United States, much of this funding is from private sources, which marks a key difference to Australia and Canada, where government is often a central provider (Bloemraad 2005). There are differing views within the interest group scholarship on the likely effect of government funding of organisations upon levels of mobilisation. Some scholars in the US context find no relationship between government funding and the suppression of advocacy (e.g. Chaves and Galaskiewicz 2004). In contrast, the 'crowding-out' thesis proposes that state support will 'crowd out' grassroots mobilisation and undermine associational life. According to this formulation 'if financial stability rests on public funds, organisations might be reluctant to bite the hand that feeds them' (Bloemraad 2006: 171, 162 citing de Tocqueville [1835] 1945; Habermas 1989; Joyce and Schambra 1996; Olasky 1992).

Scholars in both Australia and Canada have similarly argued that government funding pacifies advocacy. Ellie Vasta (1992), for instance, suggests that government funding of the peak Australian ethnocultural body, the Federation of Ethnic Communities' Councils of Australia (FECCA) 'allowed the government to use the ethnic welfare agencies for direct political patronage and it meant that multiculturalism became a means of controlling migrants' (Vasta 1992: 18, citing Jakubowicz 1981: 8; see also Agnew 1996: 166 for Canada). In Canada, Sunera Thobani (cited in Khan 2007) argues that state funding of feminist associations is a 'double-edged sword'. On the one hand, Thobani suggests that funding can assist those (such as women) who 'are not participating equally in the political structures of the society'.

On the other it can 'contain the movement's radicalism and disempower the militants'. Marian Sawer, writing on the Australian experience, argues that peak organisations have historically been an important source of support and representation for otherwise marginalised minorities 'which are electorally unpopular' (Sawer 2002: 39). Yet, on the specific issue of whether government funding weakens advocacy in Australia, the findings are mixed with some scholars identifying an inconclusive effect for state funding (Casey and Dalton 2006; Dalton and Lyons 2005) while for others, state funding stifles advocacy (Maddison and Denniss 2005).

I do not contest the general finding that some support is better than no support for diversity-seeking groups. It is clear from the empirical analysis undertaken for this book that state funding of diversity-seeking organisations in Canada and Australia did assist in their mobilisation in the area of skilled immigration policy-making. When state support dries up, so often too does political activity. Instead, I counter that the nature of state funding and the funding mix is crucial for the level of and critical nature of diversity-seeking advocacy.

Both Canada and Australia share a legacy of large-scale state funding of ethnocultural and feminist organisations. Historically, the funding model adopted in both countries could be characterised as the 'citizenship financing model' whereby government funds 'recognize[ed] the right of every individual to enjoy more or less the same benefits as do other citizens' (Phillips *et al.* 2010: 193). The equalisation of groups across society through the provision of state funds was a central principle of the citizenship-financing model. The 1970s in Canada saw a new politics of government support for social groups. Jane Jenson and Susan Phillips (1996: 119) argue that a central rationale of this funding was to 'bring these groups onto a more equal footing with other social actors and thereby encourage participation'. The funding of ethnic groups in particular was a key legacy of Prime Minister Pierre Trudeau's multicultural policy of the time (Acheson 2012: 236). Ongoing programme or core funding, which was originally available through the Canadian Citizenship Branch of the Secretary of State, but later through a range of government agencies, was viewed as vital for the mobilisation of ethnocultural and women's groups in Canada (Bloemraad 2005: 869–70; EIC 1987: 19–21; Kobayashi 2008: 131; Pal 1993: Chapter 6). Importantly with regard to ethnocultural groups, no one peak national body was established. Instead, a range of ethnocultural organisations, many ethnically based, emerged, and sought funding from the state.

From the late 1980s onwards, cuts to the core funding of both ethnocultural and women's organisations began in Canada and accelerated under the Chrétien Liberal government (Jenson and Phillips 1996: 124; Kobayashi 2008: 149–50). Interestingly, under the Conservative Harper government from 2006 onwards, there has been an expansion of funding for ethnocultural service providers (Alboim and Cohl 2013: 15). However, some commentators argue that these funds have become both more conditional and more tightly focused on service provision for 'adaptation and labour market readiness', to the exclusion of other important issues affecting immigrant communities, in particular those involving advocacy and political work (e.g. Acheson 2012: 238; Diversity-seeking activist, interview 64 by author, Canada, 13 August 2013). Ontario, which is the home to many of the diversity-seeking groups interviewed for the purposes of this book, did receive funding cuts to its settlement services in 2011 through to 2013, although other parts of Canada, including Alberta, actually saw net increases in such funding over the same period (Alboim and Cohl 2013: 15; Senior immigration official, interview 57 by author, Canada, 6 August 2013). In the area of women's affairs, cuts have been more obvious under the Conservative Harper government from 2006 onwards, including a CS5 million cut to the Women's Program and the Policy Research Fund in 2008 (Holly 2009: 120). Yet, despite these budgetary cuts, the current sources of funding in Canada differ across diversity-seeking organisations and remain varied in their institutional origins. As I argue in detail below, this variation in funding sources strengthens rather than weakens diversity-seeking activism in Canada.

In Australia, the position is very different. Following the establishment of the Ethnic Communities Council in Victoria in 1974 and NSW in 1975, core federal funding was provided for immigrants themselves to coordinate their units into one national peak body: the Federation of Ethnic Communities' Councils of Australia (FECCA) (Vasta 1992:18). FECCA was established following the Galbally Report in 1979, which recommended state funding to enable autonomous immigrant representation (Hinz 2009: 29–31). The funding of women's organisations began in the 1970s under the Whitlam Labor government and continued over the 1980s and 1990s (Chappell 2002: 32–3), while the Association of Non-English Background Speaking Women of Australia (ANEBSWA) was created in 1986 to give independent representation for women of immigrant background. However, by the late 1990s, organisations, including FECCA, were losing core funding and were required to rely upon grants for particular projects to continue their work (Representative, ethnocultural organisation, interview 50 by author, Australia, 25 October 2013). Some scholars argue that this move away from core funding of advocacy groups towards a more 'consumer-based' model of funding for individual projects began as early as the Hawke–Keating Labor governments and accelerated subsequently under the Coalition government (Maddison and Denniss 2005: 41; Sawer 2002: 43).

There were also significant cuts to funding for women's organisations in Australia from 1996 onwards. In 1999, operational funding for women's organisations was abolished and while secretariats were established to represent women's interests, there was no separate body for immigrant women (Sawer 2008: 28–9, 37). ANESBWA lost its funding in 1997. Over this period, the FECCA also had its funding made more contingent, with reapplications required on an annual basis. While the state-based units of FECCA enjoyed continued access to state funding, they were inactive in the debates over skilled immigration selection, focusing instead on integration issues that occur post settlement. Funding to a range of women's groups did increase under the Rudd–Gillard government in 2007 (Sawer

Table 8.1: Relevant diversity-seeking groups in Australia, 1988–2013, organisation type and sources of funding over time

Organisation	Type of organisation	Source of funding	Ceased funding?
Association of Non-English Speaking Background Women of Australia (ANESBWA)	Women's and ethnocultural: advocacy	1983–97: Government (Federal: largely Department of Immigration; as well as the Office of the Status of Women; Office of Multicultural Affairs; State: NSW Department of Industrial Relations, Employment, Training and Further Education)	1997. Thereafter subsumed within FECCA.
Ethnic Communities' Council of New South Wales (ECC NSW)	Ethnocultural: advocacy and service provision	NSW Community Relations Commission	n/a
Federation of Ethnic Communities' Council of Australia (FECCA)	Ethnocultural: advocacy	Government (largely Department of Immigration) and, since 2009, the Department of Ageing and Office of the Status of Women	n/a

Sources: Table compiled by author. ANESBWA (1995, 1997); FECCA (2002); Interviews with members of various organisations.

2012: 21).[1] Yet none of these funded organisations have been active in debates over skilled immigration since 2007. These changes in Australia over the late 1990s to the present day were matched by a cultural shift away from government presenting peak bodies as vanguards of marginalised interests towards casting such groups as 'special interests' distinctive from 'mainstream culture' (Sawer 2002: 43).

Despite cuts and increased grant conditionality in both Canada and Australia, many of the diversity-seeking groups interviewed for the purposes of this book continue to receive some form of state funding. This is clear from Tables 8.1 and 8.2 below that set out the diversity-seeking organisations in existence in 2013 in both countries and their key sources of funding based upon the annual reports of these organisations. As such, the issue is more nuanced than whether or not funding exists. Instead, I argue that funding mix across government departments and between public and private sources holds implications for diversity-seeking presence and strength in the area of skilled immigration policy.

Table 8.2: Relevant diversity-seeking groups in Canada, 1988–2013, organisation type and sources of funding over time

Organisation	Type of organisation	Source of funding	Funding ceased
African Canadian Legal Centre (ACLC)	Ethnocultural and other: advocacy and advice	Government (mixed agencies)	n/a
Canadian Bar Association (CBA)	Legal: advice, representation	Private organisation	n/a
Canadian Council for Refugees (CCR)	Other: advocacy and advice	Non-government, philanthropic; membership dues	n/a
Canadian Ethnocultural Council (CEC)	Ethnocultural: advocacy and advice	Government (Department of Multi-culturalism; Department of Heritage; mix of departments after 1993)	Core funding: up to 1993; project funding thereafter from a range of departments
Canadian Labour Congress	Trade union	Union membership fees	n/a
Caregivers Action Centre	Activist organisation and service advice to caregivers	Volunteer based	n/a
Chinese Canadian National Council (CCNC)	Ethnocultural: advocacy	Government (mixed agencies at the federal level and provincial level), volunteer, membership	Core funding: up to 1998; project funding thereafter
Income Security Advocacy Centre	Legal: advice, representation.	Government (Ontario Legal Aid.	n/a
Intercede	Other: advocacy and advice	Mixed	n/a
Metro Chinese Canadian Legal Centre	Ethnocultural: Advocacy and advice	Government (Toronto, community legal).	n/a
Metropolitan Action Committee on Violence Against Women and Children (METRAC)	Other: advocacy and advice; women's focus	Government (Ontario and City of Toronto); private sponsorship; membership	n/a
National Action Committee on the Status of Women (NAC)	Women's advocacy	Government (prior to 1995: federal Human Resources Development Canada. After 1995, Status of Women Canada)	Core funding: up until 1998. No funding: 2001–4. Project-based funding: 2004 onwards
National Association of Women and the Law (NAWL)	Women's advocacy	Government (prior to 1995: Human Resources Development Canada. After 1995, Status of Women Canada)	Core funding: up until 1998. Project-based funding: 1998–2006. End of funding:2006

Organisation	Type of organisation	Source of funding	Funding ceased
National Organization of Immigrant Visible Minority Women Canada (NOIVMWC)	Women's: advocacy and advice	Government (prior to 1995: Human Resources Development Canada. After 1995, Status of Women Canada)	Core funding: up until 1998. Project-based funding thereafter
Ontario Council of Agencies Serving Immigrants (OCASI)	Ethnocultural: advocacy and advice	Government (mixed agencies); volunteer; membership	n/a
Parkdale Legal Centre Toronto	Legal centre, advocacy coalition (see below)	Province of Ontario	n/a
United Food and Commercial Workers Union	Trade union	Union membership fees	n/a
West Coast Domestic Workers' Association	Women's: advocacy and advice	Government (British Columbia) and philanthropic	n/a
Workers Action Centre	Advocacy and advice on labour rights	Foundations and left-wing think tanks; volunteers	n/a
Coalitional members			
Coalition for a Just Immigration and Refugee Policy	ACLC; CCR; CCNC; Metro; OCASI		
Ad Hoc Committee on Gender Analysis of the Immigration Act	Disabled Women's Awareness Network; FREDA Centre for Research on Violence Against Women and Children; Lesbian and Gay Immigration Services Organization (OCISO); NOIVMWC; NAWL; WCDWA		
Migrant Workers Alliance for Change	Caregivers Action Centre, Migrante, Workers Action Centre, Parkdale Community Legal Clinic, Canadian Auto Workers, United Food and Commercial Workers Union, Asian Community AIDS Service, The Alliance for South Asian AIDS Prevention and No One is Illegal (Toronto)		

Sources: Table compiled by author using: ACLC (2005); CCR (2010); Kobayashi (2000: 242ff); OCASI (1999: 3); OCASI (2006: 4); WCDWA (2010); Interviews and correspondences with various organisations.

As noted, under the Coalition government in Australia, FECCA did not lose its funding. Instead, funding was made more contingent and the period of grant allocations truncated. Rather than receiving three-year guarantees of funding, the organisation was required to reapply on an annual basis (Former member, ethnocultural organisation, interview 38 by author, Australia, 6 March 2010). In addition, while the organisation has made efforts to seek external support and has more recently received funding from the Departments of Ageing and Office of the Status of Women, the bulk of the funding continues to come from the Department of Immigration and Border Protection, the very department the organisation is most likely to criticise (Member, ethnocultural organisation, interview 50 by author, Australia, 25 October 2013). The reliance by FECCA on that department is intrinsic to the funding arrangement. As a former senior immigration official put it succinctly: 'We look after [ethnocultural groups] "cradle to grave" almost' (Interview 32 by author, Australia, 11 November 2009). Or as formulated by a former ANESBWA member: '[T]he difficulty ... they have been facing at FECCA is the fact that core funding comes from Immigration, and Immigration is the key department that FECCA has arguments with. That puts you in a really difficult situation because you have to be very strategic in how you tackle those issues without losing your funding' (Interview 3 by author, Australia, 16 September 2009). This raises the question of whether the direct, departmental funding arrangement between diversity-seeking groups in Australia and the Department of Immigration has had a quieting effect on related activism. Some informants suggested that it did (Ethnocultural leader and government opposition member, interviews 1 and 23 by author, Australia, 8 September 2009 and 21 October 2009). Others contested this claim (Ethnocultural leaders, interviews 13 and 38 by author, Australia, 9 October 2009 and 6 March 2010), but the empirical analysis of reports and submissions made to government in the area of skilled immigration reform from 1988 through to 2013 indicates that FECCA was virtually absent from debates over the period of analysis. ANEBSWA was the only organisation in Australia to advocate squarely on women's diversity issues in the immigration field. Several former members argued that ANESBWA's defunding in 1997 followed outspoken public criticism by organisation members of Immigration Minister Philip Ruddock (Interviews 3, 6 and 36 by author, 16 September 2009; 20 September 2009; 24 November 2009). Philip Ruddock justified the defunding on financial grounds (Ruddock 1997). Whatever the reason for defunding, the almost total reliance of ANESBWA on immigration department funding meant that there was no separate financial backing for the organisation once this funding was pulled, and the organisation fell apart shortly thereafter. It is important to acknowledge that while social justice and refugee groups were present in Australian immigration debates in the asylum field, they were not active in the skilled immigration area. As I demonstrate below, this is a marked difference to Canada, where there was more cross-over between different areas of immigration policy-making where a broader range of diversity-seeking actors drew upon a more varied mix of funding sources. Generally, the Australian

case provides evidence for the argument developed by Jenny Onyx and collaborators (2008: 634) that 'funding from line management departments is more often
used to constrain advocacy than funding from other sources'.

Canada also experienced significant cuts to funding of women's groups from a
high of C$12.5 million in 1985 to C$8.5 by 1999–2000 (SWC 2000, in Newman
and White 2006: 141). These cuts saw an end to core funding and a move towards
'project funding', whereby groups were offered financial support for particular
projects with achievement of project deliverables a condition of future funding.
This shift from core to project-based funding was particularly detrimental for
the more radical women's organisations, such as the National Action Committee
on the Status of Women (NAC), which had focused on ongoing advocacy rather
than delivery of particular projects or services, and was therefore less suited to the
'project-based' model. As the former President of the Committee, Sunera Thobani
noted, '[a]s soon as state funding was cut, many organisations did not survive'
(cited in Khan 2007). A former member of the Canadian Ethnocultural Council
(CEC) also argued that '[n]othing had a stronger impact ....on the ability of public
groups, and especially ethnocultural groups to function' than 'the switch across
the board from sustained funding to project based funding' ... 'CEC just became
a shell of its former self' (Interview 17 by author, Canada, 2 September 2008).
Nicholas Acheson (2012: 237) argues that these changes in funding were consistent with a trend within Canada both to remove 'symbolic support' for migrant
organisations, and to shift responsibility for service delivery to the provincial
model, through a series of federal-provincial agreements.[2]

Yet, despite this negative funding context, many diversity-seeking groups
in Canada have developed new and innovative ways to navigate these allocation rule changes and to continue to engage in the area of skilled immigration
policy-making. First, many of the key organisations considered in this book, in
contrast to those in Australia, do not rely solely upon government funding, but
rather draw upon funding from a range of government, philanthropic and private sources. Table 8.2 above documents the financial position of the range of
diversity-seeking groups active in the skilled immigration area. A few key points
arise: first, unlike FECCA, Canadian groups were never solely reliant on CIC for
funding. Second, legal centres such as Metro Toronto Chinese and South East
Asian Legal Centre, Parkdale Legal Centre and the African Canadian Legal Centre,
which provide legal advice to new immigrants but also partake in advocacy work
in the area of skilled immigration and have initiated legal cases against various
aspects of government policy, have been successful in retaining funding, which
they receive from the provincial Legal Aid Ontario (Parkdale representative, interview 68 by author, Canada, 22 August 2013). It is arguably more difficult for government to defund those organisations that provide crucial legal services, in turn
allowing these groups to be more fearless in the criticisms that they pursue. Other
groups, such as lawyers and barristers, are funded privately through legal fees and
are not beholden to government at all. Further, in the area of temporary economic

immigration in Canada, trade unions have played an increasing role in financially backing diversity-seeking organisations. According to one activist involved in this area in Ontario, unions were important because they 'bring money to a lot of progressive spaces and resources because they have paid staff and actual resources to do the work' (Interview 70 by author, Canada, 22 August 2013). Another activist commented that increasingly, mobilisation in the temporary economic immigration space is funded by foundations and left-wing think tanks and noted that '[n]ot too many people that I know of that do [TFWP] organising get federal funding' (Interview 68 by author, Canada, 22 August 2013). Even those organisations that were reliant on government funding often sought support from a range of government agencies, at both the provincial and federal level, rather than at only one level or from one or two federal departments, as was the case in Australia. It is important to note that in both countries, access to core funding was unavailable for diversity-seeking organisations; however, variation of funding sources, including through provincial pools, was much more commonly undertaken in Canada than in Australia. This finding resonates with Peter Elson's analysis (2011: 143) of the growing importance in Canada of provincial support of the non-governmental sector in a period of budgetary cuts at the federal level. As a result, many organisations in Canada have seen a net increase in funding over the 2000s (Ethnocultural leader, interview 26 by author, Canada, 18 September 2008) and have remained politically engaged.

Further, even when funding cuts were introduced in Canada in the mid-to-late 1990s, the capacity of groups to successfully attract project funding and redirect this to advocacy work was an essential component of ongoing mobilisation. Irene Bloemraad (2006: 182) refers to this activity as 'program slippage', which involves 'liberal understandings of program goals to pursue empowerment and advocacy work'. This slippage between core and project-based work was raised by a number of interviewees in Canada. For instance, a former activist from the National Association of Women and the Law (NAWL) argued that:

> Groups were receiving project funding and you had to deliver on that project, so it is clear that if you had money for a, b, c and d and x was happening politically, groups would still stretch their resources and act on it but it was very hard. ... NAWL was very skilled ... at rolling up our stuff and presenting it as a project. We were very good at it. (Interview 10 by author, Canada, 12 August 2008)

The series of federal-provincial agreements negotiated for service delivery to immigrant communities also became a new source of funding for some migrant groups in Canada. For instance, the Canada Ontario Immigration Agreement (COIA) allocated C$920 million to Ontario in 2005 over a five-year period (Acheson 2012: 237). This agreement saw a net increase in funding for some migrant-focused organisations in Ontario. The benefits of devolved funding do not remove entirely the broad negative ramifications of the shift towards project-based funding that has occurred in Canada since the mid-1990s. One ethnocultural leader argued that the need to attract project funding 'drives a lot of organisations ... We have to submit a lot of funding applications to justify minimal funding from the government ... but that takes up a lot of time from the original advocacy work.' Further, she noted that because funding was largely for service work, advocacy 'has to be operated on a very, very lean budget and the majority of our work has been done on a voluntary basis' (Interview 25 by author, Canada, 17 September 2008). Generally, however, the sources of funding were more diverse in Canada than in Australia, and groups in Canada were skilled in their negotiation and utilisation of new funding arrangements. This allowed for a concomitant diversification of the associated risks of activism, which was not the case in Australia where activists often did have to bite (directly) the hand that fed them.

The internal structure of diversity-seeking organisations

Differences in the funding structures available to diversity-seeking groups in the two countries do not alone explain the differences in their decision to focus on particular dimensions of equality claims, such as gender and racial equality. In order to understand these differences, it is necessary to consider the position of racialised women internally within mainstream women's and ethnocultural organisations across the two countries. In Canada, racialised women, after significant struggles, were successful in entering and in some cases leading key feminist organisations (Agnew 1996: 84–7). In addition to forming autonomous organisations (such as the National Action Committee on the Status of Women (NAC) and the National Organization of Immigrant and Visible Minority Women of Canada) immigrant women in Canada also reached powerful positions within the 'mainstream' women's movement and shaped its direction in important ways over the 1990s. For instance, Sunera Thobani, former President of NAC, presented the entrance of 'women of colour' into 'mainstream' women's organisations as the principal change in feminist organising in Canada over this period. It is no surprise that immigration issues became a central area of concern for these activists, many of whom were of immigrant background (Khan 2007). Further, the position of immigrant women within the broader diversity-seeking movement in Canada was also important. Even once women's groups were defunded in Canada, there were other organisations that consistently raised gender issues. The Canadian Council for Refugees and the Metro Toronto Chinese and Southeast Asian Legal Clinic were particularly instrumental in calling for a gender-based analysis of the IRPA. Individuals with feminist principles have a strong presence within these organisations and gender equality was treated as one of several important social justice issues that should be addressed (Key diversity-seeking activists and CIC GBA officers, interviews 1, 2, 3, 6 and 8 by author, Canada, 7 July 2008; 15 July 2008; 16 July 2008; 25 July 2008; 29 July 2008).

In contrast, in Australia, there was a strong perception by female, Non-English Speaking Background activists that mainstream ethnocultural and women's organisations did not take immigrant women's issues seriously (Interviews 3, 6 and 36 by author, Australia, 16 September 2009; 20 September 2009; 24 November 2009; see also Vasta 1992: 13). The following quotation from a former member of ANESW of Australia makes this point powerfully:

> [O]ur criticism of the women's sector was, that ... [there was] the primacy of gender and that's all it was, our criticism of the 'ethnic sector' so to speak was that, they couldn't see gender if it whacked them in the head. So, you know, here was the sort of organisation that was trying to not only raise the question of intersectionality but almost defend it, because it was like, well, you can't have that. (Interview 36 by author, Australia, 24 November 2009)

As Marian Sawer (1990) documents in her study of the Australian women's movement, there was considerable tension between the 'mainstream' women's and Non-English Speaking women's movements over the 1980s. Similarly, according to feminist activists of migrant background interviewed for the purposes of this book, there was a clear lack of attention by FECCA in these early years of activism to all but the most obvious of gender issues – domestic violence. This paucity of support for women's and gender issues within FECCA has a historical basis and was seen as one of the central reasons for the emergence of ANESBWA as an autonomous organisation in 1986 (Vasta 1992: 20). This focus on autonomous organisation building by visible minority women in Australia contributed to a lack of networks when ANESBWA was defunded in 1997 (Interview 36 by author, Australia, 24 November 2009). In addition, the hierarchical structure of the ethnocultural movement in Australia based on a peak body (FECCA) with state and territory affiliates, did not assist the ascendancy of women leaders, a point which Jean Martin has made (1991: 124): 'For females [the structured model of FECCA] means that the claims of women are always secondary to, or a sub-clause of, the ethnic claims; there is no mention of an equivalent female community.' The devaluation of the position of women within the broader ethnocultural movement was particularly problematic as women were not able to reach powerful positions within FECCA during much of the period of analysis of this book, although there have been some improvements in recent years with some second generation women taking over the helm of the organisation (Ethnocultural leader, interview 50 by author, Australia, 25 October 2013).

The hierarchical ethnocultural structure in Australia can be contrasted with the looser conglomeration of ethnocultural organisations in Canada, where no one clear peak body exists. Leslie Pal (1993: 203) has argued historically that this conglomeration fragmented ethnic groups in Canada. However, the empirical evidence presented in this book suggests the opposite. The diffuse arrangement of ethnocultural groups in Canada appears to have minimised the organisational and funding risks associated with a hierarchical model, such as those faced by FECCA from 1996 onwards. It has also provided women diversity-seeking activists with a broader range of engagement opportunities.

Coalition building across diversity-seeking groups and beyond

A third factor that differentiates Australia and Canada is the extent of coalition building within and across diversity-seeking groups. Interest group scholarship highlights the importance of coalition building for successful activist mobilisation (e.g. Mahoney 2008; Tattersall 2010). This literature notes the economies-of-scale in resource allocation that can be achieved through coalition building (Hojnacki 1998) and the utility of coalitions, especially when policy proposals are politically salient (Mahoney 2008: 170). In Canada, in the skilled immigration policy domain, coalition building happened within and across the diversity-seeking community, whereas in Australia, it occurred, as I discuss below, through the party system. Several key coalitions emerged in Canada in the immigration setting from the 1970s onwards. According to Jane Ku (2011: 273) these coalitions originally formed to 'resist the representation of racialised immigrants as foreigners and racial discrimination'; however, from the 1980s onwards, these coalitions also mobilised around broader immigration reforms. One of the earliest of these groups, the Coalition for a Just and Fair Refugee and Immigration Policy, made interventions in the parliamentary Standing Committee on Citizenship and Immigration in 2002 around the newly developed points test for permanent skilled immigration. According to one key ethnocultural leader: 'I think that it is better to have [a coalition]. Because when you work with the media you want to ... present to the media that there are a lot of people who are for or against certain positions' (Interview 21 by author, Canada, 12 September 2008). Coalitions also provided a supportive basis for gender issues to be raised within social justice issues of 'the most disadvantaged' and gender analysis subsequently 'integrated into the discussion' (Ethnocultural leader, interview 1 by author, Canada, 7 July 2008).

Coalition building was important in the Temporary Foreign Worker Program (TFWP) case study. In particular, the Migrant Workers Alliance for Change (MWAC) was instrumental both in calling attention to the precarious position of low-skilled temporary foreign workers in Canada, but also in assisting the Caregivers Action Centre of Toronto in realising progressive changes to provincial industrial laws. One caregiver activist noted that she believed in 'strong, solid networking' and 'not just a monopoly of one organisation' (Interview 66 by author, Canada, 19 August 2013). As was the case with some of the earlier coalitions, MWAC emerged organically from existing networks across Toronto. According to one MWAC activist: 'We had had relationships for many years with Parkdale Legal. Justicia and the Caregivers Action Centre have a longstanding relationship. So, we were already in alliance' (Interview 70 by author, Canada, 22 August 2013). Interestingly, Jane Ku (2011: 282–3) also suggests that government and other funders may have inadvertently assisted in coalition building by requiring partnership grant applications on efficiency grounds. This requirement, in turn, created a context for inter-organisational alliances to form. Further, Nicholas Acheson (2012: 248) finds in his study of diversity-seeking activism in Ottawa that coalitions provide protection against government targeting of individual organisations, insofar that government is far less likely to defund a large coalition of organisations than a small singular group.

Coalition building across ethnocultural, legal and feminist groups was not evident in Australia. Many elite interview informants in Australia raised a perceived lack of solidarity across ethnic groups, across temporal waves of immigration to Australia and across generations of migrants, as the source of this absence of coalition building. Central to the establishment of peak organisations in Australia such as FECCA was a rationale that such groups could be based on shared experience (here migrant experience) rather than ethnic specificity. As Marian Sawer (2002: 41) notes, 'it was Australian government policy not to support ethnic-specific advocacy groups, but rather cross-cultural advocacy on behalf of those with special needs arising from language background, migration, refugee status or minority culture'.

However, many of the elite interviewees consulted for this research argued that this attempt at the establishment of a pan-ethnic identity by early administrations had failed in Australia. For instance, one ethnocultural leader noted that FECCA faced the challenge of creating a coherent voice across a large number of different organisations. He asked rhetorically: 'What makes FECCA work? You're not unifying on religion, on culture, on language, you're actually unifying on the fact that they [migrants] are perceived as ethnicities or minorities. So what aspect of that minority status can you actually represent?' This leader noted that older waves of immigration had very different concerns in terms of their minority status than the newer migrant flows (Interview 50 by author, Australia, 25 October 2013). An informant within government argued that the concentration in the leadership of FECCA of older European migrant waves meant that the organisation was interested in 'things like ageing policy for ethnic seniors, cultural maintenance, ethnic festivals' rather than recent trends in immigration selection. He continued: '[T]hey've sort of taken their eye totally off the main game of migration policy and migration planning levels' (Interview 51 by author, Australia, 11 November 2013). These views correspond with Bronwyn Hinz's (2010: 13) analysis of the challenges facing the Ethnic Communities Council of Victoria in recent years, where she notes that '[t]he enormous proportion of first and second-generation migrants [in the Australian population] has meant that many of their needs are now too diverse and too complex to be met by a single, broad umbrella-body'.

Further, quite a few informants in Australia complained of weak political leadership and infighting within key ethnocultural organisations, including over the dominance (perceived or actual) of certain ethnic groups, which did not assist coalition building or government perceptions of a strong cohesive 'ethnic voice'

(Interviews 10, 13, 30 and 35 by author, Australia, 2 October 2009; 9 October 2009; 10 November 2009; 13 November 2009). In terms of coalition building with other social groups, diversity-seeking groups saw the now defunct minor party, the Democrats, as the most effective means to raise equality concerns in Parliament in Australia (Interviews 1 and 38 by author, Australia, 8 September 2009 and 6 March 2010). This is consistent with the finding of Australian political scientists that interest groups in Australia often act in the 'shadow' of strong political parties (Matthews 1997: 282; Matthews and Warhurst 1993: 83). However, in Australia, diversity-seeking groups could not garner the political support of the major parties as well as minority parties, who generally did not have the political strength to halt regulatory reform in the area of skilled immigration policy.

Partisan explanations for differences in diversity-seeking mobilisation

Related to this last point, it is important to ask whether partisan politics informs funding decisions that in turn affect coalitional capabilities in the skilled immigration field. In Australia, informants argued that there was a partisan dimension to the defunding of women's and ethnocultural organisations from 1996 under the Howard Coalition government (Interviews 1, 2, 3, 6 and 36 by author, Australia, 8 September 2009; 14 September 2009; 16 September 2009; 20 September 2009; 24 November 2009). It is true that these groups were generously funded under some previous Labor governments. Under Labor Immigration Minister Gerry Hand, for instance, ANESBWA received a 29 per cent increase in grant funding from 1991 to 1992 (Hand 1992). That said, by 1994, when the ALP was still in power, the organisation was already suffering funding cuts (ANESBWA 1994). Similar patterns of defunding are observable for women's groups more broadly in Australia from the early 1990s onwards under Labor. Yet, the most significant defunding did occur under the Coalition government (e.g. Chappell 2002; Sawer 2006). This suggests that partisan politics may have played into funding decisions and subsequently the strength of diversity-seeking groups. However, other factors, including the pre-existing structure of the ethnocultural and women's movement and a concentration of funding sources within federal government, also appear to have been important. Adding further support to this argument is the fact that despite the election of the Harper Conservative government in 2006 and some cuts to funding mentioned earlier, diversity-seeking activity remains robust and active in Canada.

Comparing the cases: the importance of venue to minimise bureaucratic control

The previous section identified a variety of reasons for differences in the emergence and strength of diversity-seeking groups in Australia and Canada from the late 1980s up to 2013. Yet diversity-seeking group engagement in the policy process alone is an insufficient explanation of gender-aware immigration policies. As Table 8.3 below indicates, while diversity-seeking groups were concerned about changes in the mix in Canada (Chapter 4), the concentration of policy-making processes within the core executive and immigration bureaucracy meant that these groups had little capacity to affect change. Diversity-seeking groups in Canada raised gender issues during the first, IRPA, iteration of the Federal Skilled Worker points test (Chapter 5); however, they were also assisted in these efforts by an open parliamentary venue. In the second case study on permanent skilled immigration (Chapter 6) by contrast, policy-making was centralised within the immigration bureaucracy and the engagement of diversity-seeking groups in the policy process was weakened. In the temporary field in Canada (Chapter 7) diversity-seeking groups were heavily engaged in consultations over the TFWP and the LCP. However, they were also facilitated in this regard by access to an array of institutional venues, including parliamentary committees, federalist structures and, to a lesser extent, the judiciary. In Australia, by contrast, decision-making was generally centralised within the immigration bureaucracy and the minister's office. Even when there was opportunity for engagement in more open policy processes – such as committee hearings in the case of reforms to the 457 visa (Chapter 7) – this avenue was not utilised by diversity-seeking groups, who were largely absent from the policy landscape.

This book has argued that there is a tendency in Westminster-inspired systems of government for immigration policy-making to be centralised in the bureaucracy and the minister's office, given the fusion of the executive and legislative functions that typifies such systems. I refer to this phenomenon in Chapter 3 as 'bureaucratic control'. Such control empowers policy-makers with considerable choice over whether to introduce policy reforms through legislation or regulation, or through regulatory instruments. This choice in turn informs the policy-making process and, at least in part, the possible engagement of groups in that process. To follow Baumgartner and Jones (1993: 240), the choice of venue can open up a greater number of venues for policy-making, which in turn allows actors to disrupt existing policy monopolies and to punctuate the policy equilibrium. Alternatively, governments may foreclose venues and allow monopolies to perpetuate, or create new monopolies. Following these insights from the public agenda literature, the institutional venue for policy-making has been identified as a necessary factor for gender-aware skilled immigration policies.

The choice of venue is a dynamic process in which government and groups engage and at times compete, albeit with highly unequal bargaining power. As Leslie Pal and Kent Weaver (2003: 27) explain, opponents of policy reform will try to shift the venue for decision-making to an open one in order to 'maximize accountability by making sure that unpopular actions are taken openly and separately and by threatening to publicise the relevant votes'. Similarly, in this book, we have seen how diversity-seeking groups pressured government to consider policies in the parliamentary sphere in order to increase participatory opportunities and

Table 8.3: Gender awareness of immigration selection policies in Australia and Canada, 1988–2013

	Australia			Canada		
	Gender aware	Venue	Diversity-seeking groups	Gender aware	Venue	Diversity-seeking groups
Mix policy (1988–2003) (Chapter 4)	No	Executive and immigration department	Some limited activism by FECCA	No	Executive and immigration department	Some activism
Points test policy (1999–2003) (Chapter 5)	No	Executive and immigration department	Inactive	Yes	Parliamentary committees; Executive and immigration department; judiciary	Active
Points test policy (2006–13) (Chapter 6)	No	Executive and immigration department	Inactive	No	Executive and immigration department; judiciary	Some activism
Temporary skilled immigration policies (2007–13) (Chapter 7)	No	Some engagement of external parliamentary committees but largely Executive and immigration department	Inactive	Mixed	Executive and immigration department; judiciary; provinces; parliamentary committees	Active

to draw attention to gender concerns. This was the case in Canada with demands by diversity-seeking activists to have the regulations to the IRPA amended by the Standing Committee of Citizenship and Immigration (Chapter 5). Where these legislative strategies failed, diversity-seeking groups exploited legal avenues to raise attention to policies, in some cases resulting in judicial amendment and delays in implementation. Similarly, although Immigration Minister Jason Kenney in Canada was successful in containing much of the activism around changes to the points test between 2008 through to 2013 (Chapter 6), the decision to retrospectively cull previous applications was appealed before the Federal Court.

Multiple interviews with immigration bureaucrats conducted for this book provided support for the bureaucratic control thesis. In both countries, officials viewed the parliamentary and judicial venues as more open and more politicised than the executive and were well aware of the implications of venue choice for subsequent policies. A former senior immigration official in Canada commented:

> [B]ecause the legislative process is a slow one, what you have is disproportionate influence by the lobby groups because typically the platform that is presented is fairly balanced, and generally with immigration it tended to glean a lot of mainstream support. Six months down the road while you're still trying to work through the legislative process … the interest groups are still interested, it's the only thing they're interested in and so further compromises are usually wrung out of the Department. (Interview 35 by author, Canada, 4 March 2009)

Similarly, Australian immigration officials, when asked about drafting a new immigration act similar to the IRPA in Canada, noted that the legislative process was a political one, not simply a technical legal exercise. On this basis, choice of instrument by policy-makers was often decisive and deliberate. According to a senior legal official in the Australian Department of Immigration and Citizenship, consideration of these issues is common:

> We work very closely with our policy colleagues, on, looking at, well, what is the policy outcome you want to change, and what are the mechanisms that may be available to you to get to that policy outcome. And, you have to weigh out … all of those different potential implications, depending on whether it's principal legislation, whether it's regulatory change, whether it's simply a change in the way in which you process applications, or use the existing requirements that are there. Because there are … risks and costs associated with each of the different approaches to things. It's much slower, and generally speaking more expensive to change principal legislation, than to issue regulations and things. (Interview 18 by author, Australia, 15 October 2009)

Notwithstanding this uneven terrain in which the minister and the bureaucracy clearly enjoy the upper hand – both in terms of choice of venue and policy instrument – there are several avenues available to diversity-seeking groups to impact upon policy-making in Westminster systems. The existence of women's political machinery, the role of parliamentary committees, strong bicameralism, horizontal federalism and a powerful judiciary were identified in Chapter 3 as potential features in the Australian and Canadian political systems that could militate against the centralising effects of Westminster-inspired systems. These factors and their application across and within the various case studies are compared across the chapters in the following section.

The existence of women's policy machinery

The theoretical feminist literature proposes that given the fusion of the executive and legislative function in Westminster systems, feminist activists may be most successful if they target the state from within and establish themselves as 'femocrats' in the bureaucracy (Chappell 2002; Eisenstein 1996: xvii; Mazur 2002: 4–5; Sawer 1990; Stetson 2001: 271). Differences in women's political machinery in Australia and Canada do appear to have played a role – although not a decisive role – in informing differences in the gender awareness of some of the policies considered in this book. The empirical material certainly suggests differing levels of activity by women's political machinery in the two countries. In Australia, such machinery was unimportant. Although a Women's Desk in the Department of Immigration and Multicultural Affairs was not formally abolished until 1996, several key informants argued that the Women's Desk function was at its greatest under the Hawke government, and was weakened from 1993 onwards (Interviews 2, 3 and 6 by author, Australia, 14 September 2009; 16 September 2009; 20 September 2009). During the period in which the Women's Desk was in operation, according to one former immigration official, it did 'not look at the programme in depth [from a gender perspective]' (Interview 55 by author, Australia, 14 November 2013; DILGEA 1991).

Generally, elite interviews conducted in Australia revealed that senior officials within the Department were either unaware of the previous existence of a Women's Desk or saw it as having been a theme of the 1980s. One senior official in the Department stated '[w]e did not need somebody in the corner to say "this is a women's issue". We all understood women's issues' (Interview 19 by author, Australia, 15 October 2009). Another saw the Women's Desk as 'a trend at the time' commenting that it did not 'achieve much'. Further, he noted that as new departmental heads entered the job, the Desk 'just dissipated' (Interview 32 by author, Australia, 11 November 2009). These quotations from former senior immigration officials suggest that women's political machinery was not viewed as particularly important in the immigration bureaucracy in Australia; at least not at the upper echelons of the Department.

In contrast, in Canada, the GBA Unit, while relatively new and radical for its time, was also seen to play an important role in changing immigration department culture around gender issues (Interviews 4, 9, 13 and 46 by author, Canada, 19 July 2008; 8 August 2008; 19 August 2008; 1 October 2009). The location of the GBA Unit within the Strategic Policy Section of CIC was seen as important in impacting upon the general policy direction of immigration reform over the period of analysis (Former GBA officer, interview 46 by author, Canada, 1 October 2009). This was because the Strategic Policy Section of CIC was responsible for the overall policy direction of the Department (see Boucher 2010).

Analysis in this book indicates a mixed role for women's machinery in Canada in bringing attention to gender issues within skilled immigration policy design in particular. During the early years of its existence, the GBA Unit did provide a gender assessment of the new Federal Skilled Worker Program (FSWP) (Chapter 5), and this assessment contributed to the acknowledgement of part-time and non-continuous work patterns in the new points test. However, the GBA Unit was less involved in assessing broader gender implications of these changes, such as the key issue of skill definition or the mix of the immigration programme (Chapter 4). Since 2005, the GBA Unit has been mainstreamed within CIC. While ongoing gender analyses have been included in the Minister's Annual Report to Parliament and in all Treasury Board submissions, the enduring effects of these GBAs upon policy design are less apparent. As argued in Chapter 6, the diffusion of the GBA function within CIC has diminished its importance in immigration policy-making. Commenting on the importance of an institutional home for gender policy analysis, one officer for Status of Women Canada argued '[i]t is one thing to have a network but with the way people come and go as they do in the government of Canada ... you need to have continuity and the only way you can do that is if there is anchored somewhere in the system of the department, an entity that has a handle on these issues' (Interview 6 by author, Canada, 25 July 2008). Perhaps as a product of this mainstreaming process, analysis in Chapters 6 and 7 suggests that the critical edge of the GBAs has weakened over time. Other policy concerns, in particular the economic rationale of the programme, appear to have grown in relative importance. Further, policy officials interviewed around the new points test and the TFWP were less able to communicate key details about the relevance and importance of GBA to the author than in interviews conducted over earlier case studies.

Parliamentary committees and bicameralism

Parliamentary committees can provide important spaces for intervention by diversity-seeking groups in the policy process. Engagement in these venues offers groups opportunities to shape the gender awareness of policies in ways that might not otherwise be possible in Westminster-inspired political systems. In particular, committees in bicameral upper houses – as in the Australian Senate – could also offer venues for engagement by interest groups, as these chambers are not always dominated by the government of the day (Matthews and Warhurst 1993: 83; Pross 1993: 69).

In Canada, informants viewed the bipartisan nature of the Standing Committee of Citizenship and Immigration as important in providing a venue for engagement. One ethnocultural leader active in the first IRPA reforms, when asked why she had found that Committee responsive, noted:

> Well, I guess in general the committee is a ... all party kind of committee so you tend to have a more receptive kind of audience than you would if it's just with the government. So, I find that the committee usually do come up with statements or policy or recommendation that [are] more progressive ... whichever is the party in house. (Interview 21 by author, Canada, 12 September 2008)

Another senior figure in the non-governmental sector stated that key groups worked with Judy Waslylycia-Leis, the minority National Democratic Party leader in the Standing Committee, to develop clause-by-clause amendments to the IRPA legislation. These amendments were subsequently proposed to the entire committee (Interview 23 by author, Canada, 16 September 2008). This informant claimed 'that's where you feel like you actually may be making a difference', suggesting what issues are really core'. The decision to subject the IRPA regulations to such detailed analysis was itself a product of Standing Committee intervention (Interviews 2, 5 and 13 by author, Canada, 15 July 2008; 20 July 2008; 19 August 2008). This process effectively brought administrative law making, which is usually undertaken in the bureaucracy, into the legislative venue. As we saw in Chapter 5, changes to the cut-off for age, the pass mark, points for languages and the introduction of GBA, all followed engagement by diversity-seeking groups in the Standing Committee regulation-making process.

However, legislative committees were not always a decisive policy venue for intervention by diversity-seeking groups either in Australia or Canada. In Australia, government was able to circumvent the Senate in all case studies presented in this book. This occurred either through use of ministerial discretion, resource allocation decisions, or through the tabling of regulations that did not attract parliamentary debate. One clear example was the reclassification of the concessional class into the skilled stream in Australia (Chapter 4). This reclassification contributed to a change in the mix of the immigration programme, yet involved no parliamentary approval. The prioritisation of processing of temporary 457 visas, similarly, radically shifted the immigration programme towards a temporary focus, however was achieved through ministerial direction and funding allocation (Evans 2009b).

Since Bill C-50 in Canada, many aspects of the FSWP that might previously have been the subject of Standing Committee analysis are now achieved primarily through ministerial instruction. This concentration of power in the immigration ministry has in turn narrowed the scope for engagement by diversity-seeking groups in the policy process in Canada. Reflecting on differences between the IRPA and Bill C-50 reforms, one diversity-seeking leader in Toronto noted: 'We had the formal processes, through parliamentary committees, the standing committees, through open consultation, but interestingly C-50, what they've done is limited the opportunities by either cutting down the consultation time [or] the number of people who can appear' (Interview 27 by author, Canada, 18 September 2008). Further, several diversity-seeking groups noted that since Bill C-50 there had been a shift in consultation methods undertaken by the Harper government with fewer public inquiries, more invitation-only events and an increased use of online submissions and surveys (e.g. Interviews 53 and 64 by author, Canada, 23 July 2013 and 13 August 2013). Questioned on the use of online surveys, one senior immigration official noted: '[I]t's effective, it allows you broad reach and it's very cost effective. So to be able to get the message out and to solicit views, that's been something we've relied on more and more' (Interview 47 by author, Canada, 11 July 2013). However, groups also raised concerns about how the various perspectives raised in these surveys were ultimately balanced in the policy formulation stage, especially as the full results of online surveys were not publicly available (Interviews 53 and 64 by author, Canada, 23 July 2013 and 13 August 2013).

Federalism

The literature on the effects of federalism on participation of diversity-seeking groups is inconclusive. While federalist structures multiply the venues for political participation for outside groups, they can at the same time contribute to strained alliances and dispersed resources for activists (Pralle 2007: 21; cf. Dobrowolsky 2000: 24; McRoberts 1993: 161, 171). Federalism also encourages intergovernmentalism, which can lead to increased executive decision-making, and reduced opportunities for legislative engagement (Guiraudon 1997: 265–6; Simeon 1972; Smith 2005: 122–3).

Despite these concerns, federalist structures also open opportunities for diversity-seeking engagement. Federalism most strongly played out in the temporary economic immigration case study (Chapter 7) where diversity-seeking groups in Canada, faced with a hostile political environment at the national level, were able to seek important legislative reforms to labour law codes in the provinces. The fact that immigration is both a federal and provincial power in Canada, while labour law is a provincial power, provided an important political space for engagement by the provinces over this issue. In Australia, where the federal level controls both labour laws and immigration laws (and where the national government itself introduced key labour law reforms in 2009 following the Deegan Inquiry), this was not the case. Generally, however, federalism plays a smaller role than anticipated in the case studies in this book.

Strong judicial regimes

The courts are a key venue for engagement by diversity-seeking groups. However, the capacity to use legal rules to challenge executive decision-making varies across judicial regimes. In Chapter 3, I considered how both constitutional rights protections and public law procedures minimise the centralising effects of Westminster. The literature often identifies the role of bills of rights in providing an alternate judicial venue for the disenfranchised when engagement through the legislature or the executive fails (Dobrowolsky 2000; Guiraudon 1997: 260; Pal and Weaver 2003: 325). In Canada, the Ontario Human Rights Tribunal has been used to bring human rights-based claims for temporary foreign workers. In Australia, where there is no bill of rights at the federal level, groups have not made similar human rights-based claims.

Aside from the presence or absence of human rights provisions, another key difference between Australia and Canada lies with legal standing rules. In Canada, class action powers have been used to bring large-scale public law suits against the retroactive application of the points test for skilled immigration and, more recently, attempts to cull the backlog of Federal Skilled Worker immigration applications. Further, the scope for legal engagement in Canada and the increased complexity of immigration policy has contributed to the growing engagement of legal actors such as solicitors, barristers and large immigration law firms in the skilled immigration field (Interviews 13, 16 and 17 by author, Canada, 19 August 2008; 27 August 2008; 2 September 2008). The increased role for lawyers in the immigration policy space in Canada is important when we recall the importance of financial autonomy from the state in order to undertake fearless activism.

Australia's legal system operates according to similar common law principles as in Canada. However, the lack of class action opportunities in the immigration field and narrow standing rules have seen less active engagement by immigration lawyers outside of the refugee area. One senior immigration official in Australia noted: '[t]here's not many doors people can come through anyway. Even if they wanted to take us to court, it would be highly unlikely to succeed' (Interview 53 by author, Australia, 12 November 2013). The movement towards SkillSelect further reduces appeal rights by rendering an Expression of Interest a 'non-decision' for the purposes of administrative law, and therefore outside the remit of judicial review. Legal standing to bring an action in Australia is narrowly limited to those who are party to a visa grant (Migration Act, s486C(2)). Further, applicants outside of Australia who do not have Australian sponsors to litigate on their behalf, do not have standing to bring a legal challenge to immigration decisions, other than in the High Court. These restrictions on litigation in Australia have no doubt contributed to a smaller role for the judiciary in the skilled immigration policy space in Australia than in Canada. However, it is also apparent that legal activists in Australia have focused on refugee issues with far less attention to other diversity concerns across the immigration portfolio. Indeed, one analyst referred to the immigration field as a 'bifurcated profession' divided between refugee and other practitioners (Interview 18 by author, Australia, 15 October 2009). As such, an analysis of refugee policy, focusing on a different range of actors, might reach different conclusions than those in this book regarding skilled immigration.

Conclusion

This book has found that institutional venue matters for immigration policy outcomes. Diversity-seeking groups, employer and trade union organisations and government all use institutional venues strategically to aid and abet policy change in the immigration setting. It is clear that government and diversity-seeking groups often select institutional venues deliberately. The legislative and judicial venues were frequently chosen by diversity-seeking groups in Canada to broaden political debate and to raise new issues and perspectives. Conversely, in Australia where government often deliberately chose executive policy tools to achieve efficient and seamless policy development there are also limited interventions by outsider groups. As existing powers were broad, these policies did not require new laws. In recent years, Canadian policy-makers, increasingly aware of the relevance of venue for policy-making, have employed Budget Bill C-50 powers to centralise many aspects of skilled immigration selection within the minister's office. Increases in temporary economic immigration in both countries have also privatised much of the decision-making around immigration policy and placed it in the hands of employers. Further, the growth of temporary economic immigration has been achieved through visa processing prioritisation decisions that are budgetary, not legislative, in nature. In short, in Australia and Canada over the last quarter century, we have seen an approach to immigration policy that has become increasingly centralised within the bureaucracy and within the immigration ministry and, at the same time, outsourced some important selection powers to individual employers.

Against this centralising trend, there are nonetheless clear differences between the two countries. The most important is that Canadian economic immigration policy remains more attuned to gender equality issues than Australian policy. This is largely a product of ongoing attention to such concerns by diversity-seeking groups in Canada, in particular in the major immigrant-rich cities of Vancouver, Montreal and Toronto. In Australia, there is a virtual absence of such critical voices around permanent skilled immigration. While trade unions have contested some 457-visa issues, these are primarily related to competition between domestic and foreign workers. This chapter has provided a number of reasons for the much greater presence and engagement of diversity-seeking groups in the Canadian than the Australian context. Resource diversification, internal dynamics and coalition building were identified as central and provide important lessons for social justice activists in future campaigns.

This book also contributes to our understanding of gender bias within skilled immigration policies globally. No single country in the twelve examined demonstrates exemplary 'best standard' from a gender perspective. While Canada ranks highly on the GenderImmi Index, qualitative analysis through the four case studies in this book demonstrates that the meaning of 'gender awareness' and the quality of GBAs conducted in Canada have been diluted over time.

What policy solutions flow from the analysis in this book? The first relates to the relevance of robust women's political machinery for achieving gender-aware policies. While it is clear from the substantial scholarship on the topic that such machinery is important for achieving feminist goals within government, it is also apparent that the presence of such machinery alone is insufficient. Unless such machinery is well resourced and located within the upper echelons of the relevant government departments, and unless it has the support of the relevant minister, it is unlikely to have a substantial effect upon policy design. As such, while it is clear from the discussion in Chapter 5 that the GBA Unit served an important function within CIC under the supportive ministership of Eleanor Caplan, by the later case studies (explored in Chapters 6 and 7) GBA only operated at the periphery of the reforms.

Publication of gender-disaggregated data is a necessary first step in this regard, and is currently only undertaken by a small number of countries. However, as I argue elsewhere (Boucher 2010), data alone do not amount to gender analysis. Data can be presented without any background context, or the key patterns can be overlooked. While states take an important step forward by publishing gender, source country and intersectional data (both gender and source country together), they do a greater service in reflecting upon what these patterns mean for policy design. This requires the inclusion of gender and source country controls within statistical analysis of skilled immigration outcomes, which is rare within the numerous immigration reports analysed for this book.

The structure of skilled immigration policy, with its continued division between principal and secondary applicants, is antiquated and stems from a now entirely outdated male breadwinner/female trailing spouse model. As discussed in Chapter 4, this distinction has real implications for the skills accreditation, labour market performance and economic independence of secondary applicants who are disproportionately women. In a global context where women are not only increasingly balancing work and family life, but are also working in the growth areas of service and care, there is a strong argument for the skills of these individuals to be equally acknowledged within skilled immigration points tests. This could be easily achieved through allowing couples to apply jointly under points tests, rather than restricting secondary applicant contribution to a small number of 'bonus' points for the principal applicant's application. Single applicants could continue to apply under a modified 'singles' points test. Given that economic analysts point to the importance of family networks for immigration flows (e.g. Beine *et al.* 2012), supporting all family members to maximise economic performance might also improve the retention of sought-after skilled immigrants over the longer term. This would also go some way to improving the underemployment of secondary applicants in both Australia and Canada that has been documented in several studies (e.g. Banerjee and Phan 2014; Elrick and Lightman 2014; Richardson *et al.* 2004). In general, government should also assess the economic outcomes of both principal and secondary applicants in their longitudinal analysis, rather than focusing narrowly upon only the 'breadwinners', who comprise the minority of the migrating family unit.

Selection criteria within points tests could also be easily adjusted to better accommodate the different life courses of men and women. For instance, a failure to acknowledge part-time work experience necessarily excludes many women who may engage in this form of work on a temporary basis during child rearing years. Yet, if the goal of skilled immigration policies is to invest in human capital over the long term, a short period of reduced labour force engagement of women would seem less important than enduring human capital credentials. Similarly, including regulatory provision for non-continuous work is important in order to accommodate career breaks that are a common feature of the life course of parents, both female and increasingly male. The issue of age limits is a more complex one because the economic evidence in favour of younger applicants is clearly demonstrated by available studies. However, immigration departments could potentially operate on a principle similar to that applied in academic research circles where an applicant is assessed 'relative to opportunity' in order to acknowledge the effect that career breaks may have had on attainment at certain age brackets, rather than taking birth age as a crude measure of career years and potential.

There is a real need for government to engage with the question of how and whether care work should be accommodated within existing skilled immigration channels. It is apparent that domestic labour forces alone will be ill equipped to meet the burgeoning care needs of the next century. Just as government has responded to increased demand in the mining sector with particular immigration programmes, so too must greater attention be granted to significant skills shortages within the child and aged care sectors. The costs of meeting this demand may be considerable but so are the costs of a bulging care gap, as is already evident in those nations with the fastest ageing populations such as Italy and Japan. The proposition here is distinct from that made in some business settings that care workers could be brought in through unskilled or semi-skilled immigration pathways on a temporary guest worker basis. Especially in light of growing demand for care workers globally, governments must begin to develop policies to accommodate care workers within skilled immigration schemes that are both non-exploitative and which maintain high standards of care for consumers.

Finally, looking at the trend towards employer selection, especially within temporary immigration policy, there is a need for government to undertake detailed, ongoing monitoring of this approach for gender and ethnicity diversity outcomes. While commenters have drawn attention to the risks of devolving selection to employers in terms of labour market training of both immigrants and domestic workers (e.g. Alboim and Cohl 2013: 19), we must also consider the implications of such policies for the enduring adherence to multicultural, non-discriminatory selection policies. As this book has demonstrated, employers select different immigrants than states both in terms of gender and source country and they select these immigrants from different skill levels. To maintain commitment to non-discriminatory immigration policies, government must carefully evaluate the dynamics of changing country and gender flows as they increasingly adopted employer-driven models.

Notes

1 These were: the Australian Immigrant and Refugee Women's Alliance, the National Rural Women's Coalition and Network, the Australian Women's Health Network and to peak organisations representing sole parents and women with disabilities (Sawer 2012: 21).
2 Australia has not seen the same degree of devolution of service provision for migrant organisations as Canada. This may relate in part to the prevailing peak body structure under FECCA that has been in place for several decades, but also due to the exclusive constitutional authority over immigration selection at the federal level in Australia. In Canada, in contrast, both immigration selection and social assistance are joint federal-provincial responsibilities providing institutional scope for more engagement by the provinces in immigration policy-making (see generally Carney and Boucher 2009).

Elite interviews conducted with relevant Australians

* Please note, where location of the interview or phone interview or the name of organisation would disclose the person, these details have been retained.

1. Former member of ethnocultural organisation (Sydney, 8 September 2009).
2. Academic, Australian National University (Canberra, 14 September 2009).
3. Former member of the Association of National English Speaking Background Women of Australia (Phone interview, 16 September 2009).
4. Senior policy officer, Department of Immigration and Citizenship (Canberra, 18 September 2009).
5. Policy officer, Department of Immigration and Citizenship (Canberra, 18 September 2009).
6. Former member of the Association of National English Speaking Background Women of Australia (Sydney, 20 September 2009).
7. Former member of the Australian Chamber of Commerce and Industry (Canberra, 23 September 2009).
8. Senior policy officer, Department of Immigration and Citizenship (Canberra, 24 September 2009).
9. Former senior Labor Member of Parliament and government, 1991–93 (Sydney, 1 October 2009).
10. Former member of ethnocultural organisation (Sydney, 2 October 2009).
11. Former policy officer, Welfare Rights Centre NSW (Sydney, 2 October 2009).
12. Academic (Phone interview between Canberra and Sydney, 8 October 2009).
13. Former member of ethnocultural organisation (Canberra, 9 October 2009).
14. Senior policy officer, Department of Families, Housing, Community Services and Indigenous Affairs (Canberra, 13 October 2009).
15. Senior policy officer, Department of Families, Housing, Community Services and Indigenous Affairs (Canberra, 13 October 2009).
16. Academic, University of Sydney (Phone interview between Canberra and Sydney, 13 October 2009).
17. Former member, Housing Industry Association Ltd (Canberra, 14 October 2009)

18. Senior lawyer, Department of Immigration and Citizenship (Canberra, 15 October 2009).
19. Senior policy officer, Department of Immigration and Citizenship (Canberra, 15 October 2009).
20. Senior policy officer, Department of Immigration and Citizenship (Canberra, 15 October 2009).
21. Former senior Liberal-National Member of Parliament and government (Canberra, 19 October 2009).
22. Labor Member of Parliament and Labor Opposition, 1996–97 (Canberra, 20 October 2009).
23. Former Democrats Senator (Canberra, 21 October 2009).
24. Former senior policy officer, Department of Immigration and Ethnic Affairs; Department of Immigration and Multicultural Affairs (Canberra, 23 October 2009).
25. Former senior policy officer, Department of Immigration and Ethnic Affairs; Department of Immigration and Multicultural Affairs; Department of Immigration and Multicultural and Indigenous Affairs (Canberra, 30 October 2009).
26. Senior policy officer, Department of Immigration and Citizenship (Canberra, 30 October 2009)
27. Senior policy officer, Department of Immigration and Citizenship (Canberra, 30 October 2009).
28. Academic, University of Melbourne (Melbourne, 9 November 2009).
29. Former senior Labor Member of Parliament and government (Melbourne, 9 November 2009).
30. Academic, Monash University (Melbourne, 10 November 2009).
31. Academic, Monash University (Melbourne, 10 November 2009).
32. Former senior policy officer, Department of Immigration and Citizenship (Melbourne, 11 November 2009).
33. Former member of the Association of National English Speaking Background Women of Australia (Melbourne, 11 November 2009).
34. Industrial officer, Australian Council of Trade Unions (Melbourne, 11 November 2009).
35. Academic, Swinburne University (Melbourne, 13 November 2009).
36. Former member of the Association of National English Speaking Background Women of Australia (Phone interview between Melbourne and Sydney, 24 November 2009).
37. Former Democrats Senator (Sydney, 9 December 2009).
38. Former member of ethnocultural organisation (Adelaide, 6 March 2010).
39. Industry representative, Aged and Community Services Australia (Canberra, 7 October 2013).
40. Industry representative, Australian Council of Chamber and Industry (Canberra, 9 October 2013).

41. Senior policy officer, Department of Employment (Canberra, 9 October 2013).
42. Senior policy officer, Department of Employment (Canberra, 9 October 2013).
43. Former senior policy officer, Department of Immigration and Citizenship (Canberra, 11 October 2013).
44. Member, Australian Workplace Productivity Agency Board (Canberra, 16 October 2013).
45. Former immigration ministerial adviser (Canberra, 16 October 2013).
46. Industry representative, Business Council of Australia (Canberra, 17 October 2013).
47. Former senior immigration officer, Department of Immigration and Citizenship (Canberra, 18 October 2013).
48. Senior policy officer, Australian Workplace Productivity Agency (Canberra, 24 October 2013).
49. Former immigration ministerial adviser (Canberra, 24 October 2013).
50. Representative, ethnocultural organisation (Sydney, 25 October 2013).
51. Senior immigration officer, Department of Immigration and Citizenship (Canberra, 11 November 2013).
52. Senior immigration officer, Department of Immigration and Citizenship (Canberra, 12 November 2013).
53. Senior immigration officer, Department of Immigration and Citizenship (Canberra, 12 November 2013).
54. Senior immigration officer, Department of Immigration and Citizenship (Canberra, 12 November 2013).
55. Former immigration officer, Department of Immigration and Citizenship (Canberra, 14 November 2013).
56. Senior immigration officer, Department of Immigration and Citizenship (Canberra, 29 November 2013).

Appendix 2

Elite interviews conducted with relevant Canadians

* Please note, where location of the interview or phone interview or the organisation would disclose the person, these details have been retained.

1. Former member, ethnocultural organisation (Ottawa, 7 July 2008).
2. Non-government member of the Standing Committee on Citizenship and Immigration, Canada, 2000–2 (Ottawa, 15 July 2008).
3. Gender-Based Analysis Officer, Citizenship and Immigration Canada (Ottawa, 16 July 2008).
4. Member, ethnocultural organisation (Montreal, 19 July 2008).
5. Non-government member of the Standing Committee on Citizenship and Immigration, Canada, 2002–3 (Montreal, 20 July 2008).
6. Gender-Based Analysis Officer, Status of Women Canada, 2008–present (Ottawa, 25 July 2008).
7. Officer, Policy Directorate, Status of Women Canada (Ottawa, 25 July 2008).
8. Executive member, National Action Committee Status of Women (Phone interview from Ottawa, 29 July 2008).
9. Departmental officer, Citizenship Immigration Canada (Ottawa, 8 August 2008).
10. Former member of the former National Association of Women and the Law (NAWL) (Ottawa, 12 August 2008).
11. Non-government member of the Standing Committee on Citizenship and Immigration, Canada, 2002–3 (Phone interview from Ottawa, 13 August 2008).
12. Former member of the former National Association of Women and the Law (NAWL) (Ottawa, 14 August 2008).
13. Senior departmental official, Citizenship and Immigration Canada (Ottawa, 19 August 2008).
14. Senior departmental official, Citizenship and Immigration Canada (Ottawa, 21 August 2008).
15. Former government member of the Standing Committee on Citizenship and Immigration, Canada (Ottawa, 26 August 2008).

16. Former senior departmental official, Citizenship Immigration Canada (Ottawa, 27 August 2008).
17. Former member, Canadian Ethnocultural Council (Phone interview from Ottawa, 2 September 2008).
18. Former Executive Member, National Action Committee on the Status of Women (Phone interview from Ottawa, 3 September 2008).
19. Senior member, Canadian Labour Congress (Ottawa, 5 September 2008).
20. Member, Canadian Bar Association, Immigration Section and immigration lawyer (Toronto, 11 September 2008).
21. Member, ethnocultural organisation (Toronto, 12 September 2008).
22. Member, National Organisation of Immigrant and Visible Minority Women of Canada (Toronto, 15 September 2008).
23. Former member of the Maytree Foundation (Toronto, 16 September 2008).
24. Former member, ethnocultural organisation (Toronto, 17 September 2008).
25. Former member, ethnocultural organisation (Toronto, 17 September 2008).
26. Senior policy officer, ethnocultural organisation (Toronto, 18 September 2008).
27. Senior policy officer, ethnocultural organisation (Toronto, 18 September 2008).
28. Senior member, Ukrainian Canadian Congress (UCC) (Toronto, 18 September 2008).
29. Former senior member, Ukrainian Canadian Congress (UCC) (Toronto, 18 September 2008).
30. Former senior policy officer, ethnocultural organisation (Toronto 19 September 2008).
31. Senior member, Canadian Chamber of Commerce (Toronto, 22 September 2008).
32. Former policy adviser to Minister Caplan, Minister for Citizenship and Immigration (Toronto, 22 September 2008).
33. Former executive member of the Canadian Ethnocultural Council (Toronto, 25 September 2008).
34. Member, Canadian Bar Association, Immigration Section and immigration lawyer (Toronto, 25 September 2008).
35. Former senior departmental official, Citizenship Immigration Canada (Phone interview from London, UK, 4 March 2009).
36. Senior policy officer of the Ontario Council of Agencies Serving Immigrants (OCASI) (Phone interview between London, UK and Toronto, 4 May 2009).
37. Former senior Liberal Member of Parliament and Liberal government member (Phone interview between London, UK and Toronto, 19 May 2009).
38. Senior policy officer, Citizenship Immigration Canada (Phone interview from London, UK, 20 May 2009).
39. Academic, Simon Fraser University (Phone interview between London, UK and Vancouver, 19 July 2009).
40. Senior officer, Region of Peel (Phone interview between Sydney and Peel, Ontario, 12 August 2008).

41. Senior officer, Region of Peel (Phone interview between Sydney and Peel, Ontario, 12 August 2008).
42. Policy officer, Region of Peel (Phone interview between Sydney and Peel, Ontario, 12 August 2008).
43. Policy officer, Region of Peel (Phone interview between Sydney and Peel, Ontario, 12 August 2008).
44. Former senior Liberal Member of Parliament and government member (Phone interview from Sydney, 19 August 2009).
45. Former senior officer, Province of Ontario (Phone interview between Canberra and Ontario, 25 September 2009).
46. Former Gender-Based Analysis Officer, Citizenship Immigration Canada (Phone interview between Sydney and Ottawa, 1 October 2009).
47. Senior immigration official, Policy Unit, Citizenship Immigration Canada (Ottawa, 11 July 2013).
48. Senior immigration official, Economic Analysis Branch, Citizenship Immigration Canada (Ottawa, 15 July 2013).
49. Former Conservative Party government member (Phone interview from Ottawa, 18 July 2013).
50. Senior immigration official, Economic Analysis Branch, Citizenship Immigration Canada (Ottawa, 19 July 2013).
51. Industry representative, Canadian Construction Association (Ottawa, 23 July 2013).
52. Industry representative, Canadian Construction Association (Ottawa, 23 July 2013).
53. Representative, Canadian Labour Congress (Ottawa, 23 July 2013).
54. Senior immigration official, Research and Evaluation Branch, Citizenship Immigration Canada (Ottawa, 25 July 2013).
55. Activist, Immigrant Workers Centre (Montreal, 29 July 2013).
56. Member, ethnocultural organisation (Montreal, 31 July 2013).
57. Senior immigration official, Settlement Services, Citizenship Immigration Canada (Ottawa, 6 August 2013).
58. Senior immigration official, Research Section, Citizenship Immigration Canada (Ottawa, 6 August 2013).
59. Immigration official, Strategic Policy Branch, Citizenship Immigration Canada (Ottawa, 7 August 2013).
60. Immigration official, Strategic Policy Branch, Citizenship Immigration Canada (Ottawa, 7 August 2013).
61. Senior immigration official, Citizenship Immigration Canada (Ottawa, 7 August 2013).
62. Activist, PINAY Association for domestic women (Phone interview between Toronto and Montreal, 13 August 2013).
63. Activist, Migrant Workers Alliance for Change (Toronto, 13 August 2013).
64. Activist, peak migrant organization (Toronto, 13 August 2013).

65. Senior policy official, Immigration Branch, Citizenship Immigration Canada (Toronto, 14 August 2013).
66. Activist, Migrante BC (Phone interview between Toronto and Vancouver, 19 August 2013).
67. Activist, Thorncliffe Community Centre (Toronto, 21 August 2013).
68. Migrant Workers Alliance for Change Organiser, Parkdale Legal Centre (Toronto, 22 August 2013).
69. Lawyer, Parkdale Legal Centre (Toronto, 22 August 2013).
70. Migrant Workers Alliance for Change Organiser, Parkdale Legal Centre (Toronto, 22 August 2013).
71. Activist, Migrante Canada/International Migrants Alliance/Philippine Solidarity Movement (Toronto, 22 August 2013).
72. Activist, Justicia Ontario (Toronto, 22 August 2013).
73. Policy officer, Canadian Chamber of Commerce (Phone interview between Ottawa and Toronto, 23 August 2013).

Appendix 3

Methodological appendix

This appendix sets out the key methodologies adopted in Part II of this book, which incorporated media analysis, archival research, elite interviews and legal analysis. First, I carried out a qualitative media analysis of two major dailies from each country (the *Australian* and the *Sydney Morning Herald* in Australia and the *Globe and Mail* and the *Toronto Star* in Canada) over the twenty-five-year period to accurately trace the key policy events in the skilled immigration field. This amounted to around 800 newspaper articles. The media analysis was complemented by desk analysis of all major immigration reports published by immigration departments and external committees over this period, as well as a comprehensive analysis of archival material held in the Canadian National Archives on the passage of the new Immigration Refugee Protection Act between 2001 and 2003 and a later inquiry into temporary skilled immigration (Standing Committee 2009b). Gender-disaggregated immigration statistics were also requested from immigration departments.

Given the centrality of bureaucracies in immigration policy-making in both countries, elite interviews provided a key method to supplement this text-based analysis of publicly available information. I interviewed 128 key actors who were central players in the immigration field in Australia and Canada over the last twenty-five years. Informants ranged from senior bureaucrats to former members of Cabinet to captains of industry and trade union officials, to the leaders of women's and immigrant organisations, all of whom fitted broadly into a definition of 'political elites'. Richards (1996: 199) defines an 'elite' as 'a group of individuals, who hold, or have held, a privileged position in society and, as such, as far as a political scientist is concerned, are likely to have had more influence on political outcomes than general members of the public'. This definition of elites, with its focus on 'privileged positions' easily includes senior bureaucrats, former members of Cabinet and leaders in the fields of business and law, all of whom were interviewed. However, it presents less of a justification for interviewing leaders of immigrant associations and women's groups, who do not generally enjoy positions of privilege or power. Yet, notwithstanding their relative disadvantage compared with 'conventional' elites, such groups may have an impact upon recognition of gender awareness in policy outputs, under certain conditions. Indeed, to ignore these groups would be to define the term 'elite' too narrowly and could lead to a form of interview selection bias on gender and ethnicity grounds, which I explicitly aim to avoid. Given the high profile nature of many of the interview subjects and the sensitive subject matter, confidentiality was assured. Appendices 1 and 2 list the relevant interview subjects according to general position and city, as well as the date of the interview, but do not reveal the identity of the subjects.

A purposive approach to the selection of interviewees was adopted. This meant that the aim was not to gain a representative sample of the population but rather to select those elites most relevant to the case examined (Tansey 2007: 770). Interviews are used in this book to reconstruct the policy-making process in both countries, to draw light upon activities within bureaucracies and other organisations and to process trace policies. An open-ended approach to interviewing was adopted, with a list of existing questions adapted throughout the interview process, depending upon the revealed focus and knowledge of the interviewee. An example of the interview schedule is provided below. Most interviews lasted for one hour, and many up to two hours. All interviews were professionally transcribed and analysed in detail in order to evaluate policy events.

Research for the book also involved detailed legal analysis. This book states the law as of July 2013 in both countries. In the area of immigration, policy is a complex web of acts of parliament, secondary legislation (regulations), other regulatory instruments such as ministerial directives and guidelines, resource allocation decisions and the outputs that flow from legal interpretation of legislation, regulations and administrative policies by courts. This book adopted an expansive definition of 'policies' that considers overlaps and interactions between these different instruments. This approach is important from a venue shopping perspective insofar that some forms of policy reforms require legislative intervention, whereas others can be achieved simply through policy or resource allocation decisions.

It is necessary to briefly explain the overarching structure of immigration law regimes in Australia and Canada. In both countries, there are immigration acts: Australia's Migration Act (1958) (Cth) and Canada's Immigration and Refugee Protection Act (2002) (Cdn) provide the organising framework for the immigration regimes in place. However, it is the regulations to these acts, not the primary legislation itself, that provide much of the policy detail (Migration Regulations (1994) (Cth) (Aust) and the Immigration Refugee Protection Regulations (2002) (IRPR)). Policy Advice Manuals, known as PAMS in Australia and, since 2008, ministerial instruments in Canada, augment the regulations and assist the decision-makers of individual immigration applications. Given the importance of these guides and instruments to everyday immigration decision-making, they are also considered and listed in a separate section in the bibliography below.

A second important point to make is that these legal regimes divide immigration selection into a variety of categories. At its most crude, there is the division between economic immigration (largely comprising skilled immigration and referred to interchangeably in this book as the 'skilled stream' or the 'economic stream'), family reunification and humanitarian migration. Despite these important distinctions, there are overlaps between these entrance streams. Some family migrants have economic skills. There are entrants in the skilled stream who receive entry dispensations due to their family connections. Further, skilled immigrants sometimes bring family members as 'dependents' or 'secondary applicants' but these immigrants are categorised as skilled entrants, even if they do not work or contribute to the accumulation of points under the points test (for a longer discussion see Inglis *et al.* 1994: 21 and Li 2003: 43–4). To ignore this overlap is to ignore the complexity of immigration regulation, which is a recurrent theme in this book.

Example of elite interview

The interviews for this book took an open-ended approach and the interview schedule was customised for each interview. The following provides an example of the questions asked to a senior policy official in Australia for the temporary skilled immigration case study (Chapter 7).

***

EMAs

Can you explain the genesis of the EMA to me? I understand that the National Resources Sector Employment Taskforce was important in informing its establishment, but what were the other factors?

To what extent were the EMAs also a means to appease the resources sector over the mining tax?

Has there been discussion of use of similar agreements in other areas with strong labour shortages? E.g. in the care sector (aged and child care as well as personal carers for the disabled)?

How was government able to overcome potential objections of trade unions around the EMAs in the original development of the policy?

Much of the detail of the EMAs will not be made publically available. What were the key reasons for this? Will this also be the case for RMAs?

RMAs

What was the impetus behind the decision to create RMAs? Why was this visa viewed as necessary in addition to the Regional Skilled Migration Scheme that currently brings in some semi-skilled labour?

Why has movement in this area been slow?

How long will RMA visas last for and which sectors will they focus on?

What will be the interaction of RMAs and EMAs?

Was there any discussion of lowering the skill level for the RMAs below ANZSCO Level 4 (specialised semi-skilled occupations)?

Bibliography

Legal sources (Australia and Canada)

Constitutions

Australia

Commonwealth of Australia Constitution Act (1900) [Australian Constitution]

Canada

Canadian Charter of Rights and Freedoms, Part 1 of the Constitution Act, (1982) [Charter]
Constitution Act (1867) (Cdn)

Legislation and bills of Parliament

Australia

Legislation

Administrative Decisions (Judicial Review) Act (1977) (Cth)
Australian Citizenship Act (2007) (Cth)
Legislative Instruments Act (2003) (Cth)
Migration Act (1958) (Cth) (various consolidations)

Canada

Legislation

Citizenship Act (1985) (Cdn)
Federal Courts Act, R.S.C. (1985) (Cdn)
Immigration Refugee Protection Act (2002) (IRPA) (Cdn)

Bills

Bill C-31 (2000) An Act respecting immigration to Canada and the granting of refugee protection to persons who are displaced, persecuted or in danger

Bill C-50. Budget Implementation Act (2008) (Cdn)

Regulations, guides and policy instruments

Australia

Migration Regulations (1994) (Cth) (Regulations) (consolidated on 1 July 1999; 10 December 1998)
Migration Regulations (Amendment) SR 1991, No.60
PAM [Policy Advice Manual] (for immigration), various consolidations

Canada

Immigration Regulations (1978) (Cdn) (now superseded)
Immigration Refugee Protection Regulations (2002) (IRPR)
Cabinet Directive on Streamlining Regulations 2007. www.tbs-sct.gc.ca/ri-qr/direct-ive/directive01-eng.asp#_Toc162687224, accessed 28 May 2010
Regulations Amending the Immigration and Refugee Protection Regulations (Temporary Foreign Workers) SOR/2010–172

Case law

Canada

Borisova v. *Canada* FC [2003] 4 FC 408
Chesters v. *Canada (Minister of Citizenship and Immigration)* [2003] 1 FC 361, TD
Dragan v. *Canada* [2003] 4 FC 189; [2003] FCJ No 260 (TB) (QL)
Friends of the Oldman River Society v. *Association of Professional Engineers, Geologists and Geophysicists of Alberta* [1997] 5. W.W.R. 179 (Alta. Q.B.)
Tabingo v. *Canada (Minister for Citizenship and Immigration)* [2013] FCL No 410

Legal and policy sources for other countries

Austria

Bundesministerium des Innernes (2013), 'Other Key Workers.' Vienna: Bundes-ministerium des Innernes. www.migration.gv.at/en/types-of-immigration/permanent-immigration-red-white-red-card/other-key-workers.html, accessed 14 February 2013.
Bundesministerium des Innernes (2013), 'Skilled Workers in Shortage Occupations.' Bundesministerium des Innernes: Vienna. www.migration.gv.at/en/types-of-immigration/permanent-immigration-red-white-red-card/skilled-workers-in-shortage-occupations.html, accessed 14 February 2013.

Belgium

Mussche, N., Corluy, V., and Marx, I. 2010. 'Satisfying Labour Demand Through Migration in Belgium: Study of the Belgian Contact Point of the European Migration Network.' Brussels: Immigration Office/Commissioner General for

Refugees and Stateless Persons/Centre for Equal Opportunities and Opposition
to Racism. [includes discussion of laws].

Denmark

Danish Immigration Service. 2013. 'The Greencard Scheme.' Copenhagen: Danish
Immigration Services. https://www.nyidanmark.dk/en-us/coming_to_dk/work/
greencard-scheme/greencard-scheme.htm, accessed 14 February 2013.
Danish Immigration Service. 2013. 'The Positive List.' Copenhagen: Danish
Immigration Services. https://www.nyidanmark.dk/en-us/coming_to_dk/work/
positivelist/, accessed 13 August 2013.

Finland

Finnish Immigration Service [Maahanmuutoovirasto]. 'The EU Blue Card for Work
that Requires High Level Competence.' Helsinki: Maahanmuutoovirasto. www.
migri.fi/working_in_finland/an_employee_and_work/eu_blue_card, accessed
14 February 2013.

France

French Office of Immigration and Integration. 2013. 'For the Promotion of Economic
Migration.' Paris. www.immigration-professionnelle.gouv.fr/en/new-provisions/
sheet/skills-and-talents, accessed 18 July 2013.

Germany

Aufenthaltsgesetz (2005).
Bundesministeriums, Bundesministeriums für Arbeit und Soziales und des and des
Innern. 2013. 'Verordnung zur Änderung des Ausländerbeschäftigungsrechts.'
Bonn: Bundesministeriums für Arbeit und Soziales und des Bundesministeriums
des Innern.

Ireland

Department of Jobs, Enterprise and Innovation [Ireland]. 2011. 'Employment Permits
Arrangements: Guide to Green Card Permits.' Dublin.
Department of Jobs, Enterprise and Innovation. 2013. Highly Skilled Occupations List.
Dublin: DJEI. www.djei.ie/labour/workpermits/highlyskilledoccupationslist.htm,
accessed 18 August 2013.

New Zealand

INZ [Immigration New Zealand]. 2012a. 'Immigration New Zealand Operational
Manual: Temporary Entry.' Immigration New Zealand.
INZ. 2012b. 'Immigration New Zealand Operational Manual: Residence.' Immigration
New Zealand.

INZ. 2013. 'Immigration New Zealand Operational Manual.' Appendix 4 – Long Term Skill Shortage List. www.immigration.govt.nz/opsmanual/46052.htm, accessed 18 August 2013.

Norway

Utlendingsdirektoratet, Norwegian Directorate of Immigration. 2013. 'Entry Visa for Skilled Worker.' Oslo: UDI. www.udi.no/Norwegian-Directorate-of-Immigration/Central-topics/Work-and-residence/Apply-for-a-residence-permit/Skilled-workers/Entry-visa-for-skilled-workers/, accessed 14 February 2013.

United Kingdom

Home Office UK Border Agency. 2012. 'Tier 2 of the Points Based System – Policy Guidance.' 12/12 edn.; London: Home Office UK Border Agency.
Home Office UK Border Agency. 2013. 'Tier 2 of the Points Based System – Policy Guidance.' 07/13 edn.; London: Home Office UK Border Agency.
United Kingdom Border Agency. 2013. 'Tier 2 Shortage Occupation List.' London: UKBA. www.ukba.homeoffice.gov.uk/sitecontent/documents/workingintheuk/shortageoccupationlistnov11.pdf, accessed 18 August 2013.

United States

Immigration and Nationality Act 1952
Code of Federal Regulations

All other sources

Abbott, M. G., and C. M. Beach. 1993. 'Immigrant Earnings Differentials and Birth-Year Effects for Men in Canada: Post-War-1972.' *Canadian Journal of Economics* 26 (3): 505–24.
ABS [Australian Bureau of Statistics]. 2002. 'Employment Type: Employed Persons on Sex, Full-time/Part-time and Occupation, August 1996–August 2007.' Report 6105.0. Canberra: ABS.
Abu-Laban, Y. and C. Gabriel. 2002. *Selling Diversity: Immigration, Multiculturalism, Employment Equity and Globalization.* Peterborough: Broadview Press.
ACCI (Australian Council of Chamber and Industry). 2013. *Inquiry into the Current Framework and Operation of Subclass 457 Visa, Enterprise Migration Agreements and Regional Migration Agreements.* Canberra: ACCI.
Acheson, N. 2012. 'From Group Recognition to Labour Market Insertion: Civil Society and Canada's Changing Immigrant Settlement Regime.' *British Journal of Canadian Studies* 25 (2): 231–51.
Acker, J. 1992. 'From Sex Roles to Gendered Institutions.' *Contemporary Sociology* 21 (5): 565–9.
ACLC (African Canadian Legal Clinic). 2005. *Annual Report 2005.* For presentation at the 2005/6 Annual General Meeting, Toronto, Canada. Available at www.aclc.net/, last accessed 20 April 2010.

ACSA (Aged and Community Services Australia). 2010. ACSA's Submission to the Productivity Commission Inquiry into Caring for Older Australians. Canberra: ACSA.

ACTU (Australian Council of Trade Unions). 2007. Submission to Joint Standing Committee on Migration Inquiry into Temporary Business Visas, February. Melbourne: ACTU. www.actu.asn.au/Images/Dynamic/attachments/5163/ACTU-Submission-Jo int-Standing-Cttee-Feb2007.doc, accessed December 2014.

AEAC (Adult Entertainment Association of Canada). 2009. *Study of Undocumented and Temporary Foreign Workers Submission.* Ottawa: Standing Committee on Citizenship and Immigration, Parliament of Canada.

Agnew, V. 1996. *Resisting Discrimination.* Toronto: University of Toronto Press.

Ahmad, S. 2013. Email regarding GBA assessments undertaken in CIC, between GBA officer, CIC and A. Boucher. Ottawa to Sydney email correspondence, 24 October 2013.

Aigner, D., and G. Cain. 1977. 'Statistical Theories of Discrimination in Labor Markets.' *Industrial and Labor Relations Review* 30 (2): 175–87.

Albaek, E., C. Green-Pedersen, and L. B. Nielsen. 2007. 'Making Tobacco Consumption a Political Issue in the United States and Denmark: The Dynamics of Issue Expansion in Comparative Perspective.' *Journal of Comparative Policy Analysis: Research and Practice* 9 (1): 1–20.

Alboim, N., and K. Cohl. 2013. *Shaping the Future: Canada's Rapidly Changing Immigration Policies.* Ottawa: Maytree Foundation.

Alexander, C., D. Burleton, and F. Fong. 2012. 'Knocking Down Barriers Faced by New Immigrants to Canada: Fitting the Pieces Together.' Special Report. TD Economics.

Aliweiwi, J., and R. Laforest. 2009. 'Citizenship, Immigration and the Conservative Agenda.' In *The New Federal Policy Agenda and the Voluntary Sector,* edited by R. Laforest, 137–53. Kingston: Queen's University Press.

Alphonso, C. 2009. 'Dhalla Paints Herself "the Victim" in Nanny Scandal: Liberal MP Comes Out Swinging, Calling Allegations She Mistreated Foreign Caregivers an Organized Attack on Her Reputation.' *The Globe and Mail,* 9 May 2009.

ALRC (Australian Law Reform Commission). 1994. Equality Before the Law: Women's Equality. Commonwealth of Australia.

ANESBWA (Association of Non English Speaking Background Women of Australia). 1992. ANESBWA Newsletter, January 1992, Sydney. Stored in the ANESBWA files 1985–2000, State Library of NSW, MLMSS 7883, Box 4/31.

ANESBWA (Association of Non English Speaking Background Women of Australia). 1994. Notes from meeting with the Minister for Immigration and Ethnic Affairs, Senator Nick Bolkus, 15 July 1994.

ANESBWA (Association of Non English Speaking Background Women of Australia). 1995. Association of Non English Speaking Background Women of Australia, *Fourth Annual Report 1994–95,* Sydney: New South Wales Printing Service.

ANESBWA (Association of Non English Speaking Background Women of Australia). 1997. Letter from Minister for Immigration and Multicultural Affairs, Philip Ruddock to Sevgi Kilic, Chair of the Association of Non-English Background

Women of Australia, Canberra to Sydney, dated 19 May 1997, provided to author by former member of ANESBWA.

Anthias, F., and N. Yuval-Davis. 1992. 'Connecting Race and Gender.' In *Racialized Borders, Race, Nation, Gender, Colour and Class and the Anti-Racist Struggle*, edited by F. Anthias and N. Yuval-Davis, 96–131. London/New York: Routledge.

Appelbaum, E., and M. Gatta. 2005. 'Managing for the Future: 21st Century Skills and High School Education Workers.' Centre for Women and Work.

Arat-Koc, S. 1999a. 'Gender and Race in "Non-Discriminatory Immigration Policies in Canada: 1960s to the Present." ' In *Scratching the Surface: Canadian Anti-Racist Feminist Thought*, edited by D. Enakshi and A. Robertson, 207–33. Toronto: Women's Press.

—— 1999b. 'NAC's Response to the Immigration Legislative Review Report.' *Canadian Women's Studies* 19 (3): 18–23.

Arat-Koc, S., and F. Villasin. 1990. *Report and Recommendations on the Foreign Domestic Movement Program*. Toronto: Intercede.

Arkoudis, S., L. Hawthorne, C. Baik, G. Hawthorne, K. O'Loughlin, K. Bexley, and D. Leach. 2009. 'Analysis of Interviews with Recent Offshore Graduates.' In *The Impact of English Language Proficiency and Workplace Readiness on the Employment Outcomes of Tertiary International Students*, edited by S. Arkoudis, L. Hawthorne, C. Baik, G. Hawthorne, K. O'Loughlin, K. Bexley and D. Leach, 104–9. Canberra: Department of Employment, Education and Workplace Relations.

Aronson, M., B. Dyer, and M. Groves. 2009. *Judicial Review of Administrative Action*. Pyrmont: Thomson Reuters Australia.

Australian Productivity Commission. 2011. *Caring for Older Australians*. Melbourne: Australian Productivity Commission. www.pc.gov.au/inquiries/completed/aged-care/report, accessed 29 June 2015.AWPA (Australian Workplace Productivity Agency). 2012. *Future Focus Australia's Skills and Workforce Development Needs*. Canberra: Australian Workplace Productivity Agency.

Australian Productivity Commission. 2013. 'About Us'. www.awpa.gov.au/about-us/Pages/default.aspx, accessed 22 December 2013.

Babcock, L., and S. Laschever. 2008. *Ask For It: How Women Can Use Negotiation to Get What They Really Want*. Sydney: Random House Publishing Group.

Bacchi, C., and E. Eveline. 2003. 'Mainstreaming and Neoliberalism: A Contested Relationship.' *Policy and Society: Journal of Public, Foreign and Global Policy* 22 (2): 98–118.

Badkar, J., P. Callister, V. Krishnan, R. Didham, and R. Bedford. 2006. *Patterns of Gendered Skilled and Temporary Migration in New Zealand*. Wellington, New Zealand: Department of Labour.

—— 2007. 'Gender, Mobility and Migration in New Zealand: A Case Study of Asian Migration.' *Social Policy Journal of New Zealand* 32 (November): 126–54.

Bakan, A. B., and D. Stasiulis. 2012. *The Political Economy of Migrant Live-in Caregivers: A Case of Unfree Labour? Legislated Inequality: Temporary Labour Migration in Canada*. Montreal: McGill Queens University Press.

Baldez, L. 2011. 'The UN Convention to Eliminate All Forms of Discrimination Against Women (CEDAW): A New Way to Measure Women's Interests.' *Politics and Gender* 7 (3): 419–23.

Banerjee, R. and M. Phan. 2014. 'Do "Tied-Movers" Get Tied Down? The Labour Market Adjustment of Immigrant Women in Canada.' *Journal of International Migration and Integration.* DOI 10.1007/s12134-014-0341-9.

Bardasi, E., and J. C. Gornick. 2003. 'Women and Part-Time Employment: Workers' "Choices" and Wage Penalties in Five Industrialised Countries.' In *Women in the Labour Market in Changing Economies: Demographic Issues,* edited by B. Garcia, R. Anker and A. Pinnelli, 209–43. Oxford: Oxford University Press.

Barker, D., and S. F. Feiner. 2004. *Liberating Economics: Feminist Perspectives on Families, Work, and Globalization.* Ann Arbor: University of Michigan Press.

Baumgartner, F. R., C. Green-Pedersen, and B. D. Jones. 2006. 'Comparative Studies of Policy Agendas.' *Journal of European Public Policy* 13 (7): 959–74.

Baumgartner, F. R., and B. D. Jones. 1993. *Agenda and Instability in American Politics.* Chicago: University of Chicago Press.

Baumgartner, F. R., B. R. Jones, and J. Wilkerson. 2011. 'Comparative Studies of Policy Dynamics.' *Comparative Political Science* 44 (8): 947–72.

Beach, C. M., and C. Worswick. 1993. 'Is There a Double-Negative Effect on the Earnings of Immigrant Women?.' *Canadian Public Policy* 19: 36–53.

Beach, C. W., A. G. Green, and C. Worswick. 2007. 'Impacts of the Point System and Immigration Policy Levers on Skill Characteristics of Canadian Immigrants.' *Research in Labor Economics* 27: 349–401.

Beaverstock, J. 1994. 'Rethinking Skilled International Labor Migration World Cities and Banking Organizations.' *Geoforum* 25: 323–38.

——— 1996. 'Lending Jobs to Global Cities: Skilled International Labor Migration, Investment Banking and the City of London.' *Urban Studies* 33: 1377–94.

Becker, G. 1964. *Human Capital: A Theoretical and Empirical Analysis with Special Reference to Education.* Chicago: University of Chicago Press.

——— 1993. 'Investment in Human Capital: Effects on Earnings.' In *Human Capital: A Theoretical and Empirical Analysis with Special Reference to Education,* edited by G. Becker, 29–54. Chicago: University of Chicago Press.

Beckwith, K. 2000. 'Beyond Compare? Women's Movements in Comparative Perspective.' *European Journal of Political Research* 37 (4): 31–68.

——— 2010. 'Introduction: Comparative Politics and the Logics of a Comparative Politics of Gender.' *Perspectives on Politics* 8 (1): 159–68.

Bedford, R. 2012. 'By Invitation Only? Selecting Skilled Migrants Down Under.' Presentation for the National Institute of Demographic and Economic Analysis, University of Waikato, 23 August 2012.

Beem, B. 2009. 'Leaders in Thinking, Laggards in Attention? Bureaucratic Engagement in International Arenas.' *The Policy Studies Journal* 37 (3): 497–518.

Beine, M., F. Docquier, and C. Ozden. 2012. 'Dissecting Network Externalities in International Migration.' Working Paper, University of Luxembourg.

Beiser, M., and F. Hou. 2000. 'Gender Differences in Language Acquisition and Employment Consequences among Southeast Asian Refugees in Canada.' *Canadian Public Policy* 26 (3): 311–30.

Bellante, D., and C. A. Kogut. 1998. 'Language Ability, US Labor Market Experience and the Earnings of Immigrants.' *International Journal of Manpower* 19 (5): 319–30.

Bendel, P., A. Ette, R. Parkes, and M. Haase. 2011. *The Europeanization of Control: Venues and Outcomes of EU Justice and Home Affairs Cooperation*. Berlin: Lit Verlag.

Benería, L., C. D. Deere, and N. Kabeer. 2012. 'Gender and International Migration: Globalization, Development, and Governance.' *Feminist Economics* 18 (2): 1–33.

Benoit, K., and M. Laver. 2006. 'Party Policy in Modern Democracies: Expert Survey Results from 47 Countries, 2003–2004.' www.tcd.ie/Political_Science/ppmd/, accessed 27 January 2010.

Betts, K. 1999. *The Great Divide: Immigration Politics in Australia*. Sydney: Duffy and Snellgrove.

Bevas, J. 2013. 'Government Defends Slow Take-up of Low-paid Seasonal Workers Visa.' *ABC News*, 21 August 2013.

Beyers, J., and B. Kerremans. 2012. 'Domestic Embeddedness and the Dynamics of Multilevel Venue Shopping in Four EU Member States.' *Governance: An International Journal of Policy, Administration, and Institutions* 25 (2): 263–90.

BIR (Bureau of Immigration Research). 1993. *Immigration Updates: Eligibility Category of Settler Arrivals*. Melbourne: BIR.

Birrell, B. 1984. 'A New Era in Australian Migration Policy.' *International Migration Review* 18 (1): 65–84.

—— 1996. 'The Scale and Consequence of Professional Migration Movement to Australia since 1983.' In *Population Shift*, edited by M. Bell and P. Newton. Canberra: Australian Government Publishing Service.

—— 1997. *Immigration Reform in Australia: Coalition Government Proposals and Outcomes since March 1996*. Melbourne: Centre for Population and Urban Research, Monash University.

—— 1998. 'Skilled Migration under the Coalition.' *People and Place* 6 (4): 16–29.

Birrell, B., and T. Birrell. 1981. *An Issue of People: Population and Australian Society*. Melbourne: Longman Chesire.

Birrell, B., and L. Hawthorne. 1997. *Immigrants and the Professions in Australia*. Melbourne: Centre for Population and Urban Studies, Monash University.

—— 1999. *Skilled Migration Outcomes as of 1996: A Contribution to the Review of the Independent and Skilled-Australian Linked Categories being Conducted by the Department of Immigration and Multicultural Affairs*. Canberra: DIMA.

Birrell, B., L. Hawthorne, and S. Richardson. 2006. *Evaluation of the General Skilled Migration Categories Report*. Canberra: Department of Immigration and Citizenship.

Birrell, B., and E. Healy. 2008. 'How Are Skilled Migrants Doing?' *People and Place* 16 (1): 1–19 (supplement). Melbourne: Centre for Population and Urban Research, Monash University.

—— 2012. *Immigration Overshoot*. Melbourne: Centre for Population and Urban Research, Monash University.

Birrell, R., T. F. Smith, and E. Healy. 1992. *Migration Selection During the Recession*. Canberra: Department of the Parliamentary Library, Parliament House of Australia.

Black, D. 2013a. 'Federal Skilled Worker Program Will Reopen with Improvements.' *The Toronto Star*, 3 May 2013.

——— 2013b 'Immigration Minister Jason Kenney Announces Tighter Regulations for Family Reunification Program.' *The Toronto Star*, 19 June 2013.

Blackburn, R. M., K. Browne, B. Brooks, and J. Jarman. 2002. 'Explaining Gender Segregation.' *British Journal of Sociology* 53 (4): 513–36.

Blackshield, T. and G. Williams. 2002. *Australian Constitutional Law and Theory*. Leichardt, Sydney: The Federation Press.

Blank, R. M. 1989. 'The Role of Part-Time Work in Women's Labor Market Choices Over Time.' *The American Economic Review: Papers and Proceedings of the Hundred and First Annual Meeting of the American Economic Association* 79 (2): 295–9.

Blau, F., and L. Kahn. 1997. 'Swimming Upstream: Trends in the Gender Wage Differential in the 1980s.' *Journal of Labour Economics* 15(1): 1–42.

Bloemraad, I. 2005. 'The Limits of de Tocqueville: How Government Facilitates Organizational Capacity in Newcomer Communities.' *Journal of Ethnic and Migration Studies* 31 (5): 865–87.

——— 2006. *Becoming a Citizen: Incorporating Immigrants and Refugees in United States and Canada*. London/Berkeley: University of California Press.

——— 2013. 'Accessing the Corridors of Power: Puzzles and Pathways to Understanding Minority Representation.' *West European Politics* 36 (3): 652–70.

Bloom, D. E., G. Greiner, and M. Gunderson. 1995. 'The Changing Labour Market Position of Canadian Immigrants.' *Canadian Journal of Economics* 46 (28): 987–1005.

Boeri, T., H. Brüker, F. Docquier, and H. Rapoport. 2012. *Brain Drain and Brain Gain: The Global Competition to Attract Highly-Skilled Migrants*. Oxford: Oxford University Press.

Bolkus, N. 1996. Migration Regulations, Disallowance Motion, Australian Senate Hansard, Parliament of Australia, Canberra, 7 November 1996.

Boothe, K., and K. Harrison. 2009. 'The Influence of Institutions on Issue Definition: Children's Environmental Health Policy in the United States and Canada.' *Journal of Comparative Policy Analysis: Research and Practice* 11 (3): 287–307.

Borjas, G. 1987. 'Self Selection and the Earnings of Immigrants.' *American Economic Review* 77: 531–53.

——— 1989. 'Economic Theory and International Migration.' *International Migration Review* 23 (3): 457–85.

——— 1990. *Friends or Strangers*. New York: Basic Books.

——— 1996. 'Human Capital: Education and Earnings.' In *Labor Economics*, edited by G. J. Borjas, 220–48. Singapore: McGraw Hill.

——— 1999. *Heaven's Door: Immigration Policy and the American Economy*. Princeton: Princeton University Press.

Boswell, C. 2007. 'Theorizing Migration Policy: Is There a Third Way?' *International Migration Review* 41 (1): 75–100.

Boucher, A. 2007. 'Skill, Migration and Gender in Australia and Canada: The Case of Gender-Based Analysis.' *Australian Journal of Political Science* 42 (3): 383–401.

—— 2010. 'Gender Mainstreaming in Skilled Immigration Policy: From Beijing 1995 to the Canadian Immigration and Refugee Protection Act (2002).' In *Human Rights and Social Policy: A Comparative Analysis of Values and Citizenship in OECD Countries*, edited by A. Neville, 174–200. Cheltenham, UK: Edward Elgar.

—— 2013a. 'Bureaucratic Control and Policy Change: A Comparative Venue Shopping Approach to Skilled Immigration Policies in Australia and Canada.' *Journal of Comparative Policy Analysis* 15 (4): 349–67.

—— 2013b. 'Familialism and Migrant Welfare Policy: Restrictions on Social Security Provision for Newly-Arrived Immigrants.' *Policy and Politics*, published online 17 April 2013.

Boucher, A., and L. Cerna. 2014. 'Current Policy Trends in Skilled Immigration Policy.' *International Migration* 52 (3): 21–5.

Boudjenane, M. 2008. *Submission of the Canadian Arab Federation to the Standing Committee on Finance Inquiry into Bill C-50*. Ottawa: Parliament of Canada, Standing Committee on Finance, 12 May 2008: 1530.

Bourette, S. 2007. 'Welcome to Canada.' *Globe and Mail*, 28 September 2007.

Boushey, G., and A. Luedtke. 2006. 'Fiscal Federalism and the Politics of Immigration: Centralized and Decentralized Immigration Policies in Canada and the United States.' *Journal of Comparative Policy Analysis* 8 (3): 207–24.

Bowles, S., and H. Ginitis. 2002. 'Schooling in Capitalist America Revisited.' *Sociology of Education* 75 (1): 1–18.

Boyd, M. 1991. 'Migrating Discrimination: Feminist Issues in Canadian Immigration Policies and Practices.' *Working Paper 6*. London, Ontario: The Centre for Women's Studies and Feminist Research, University of Western Ontario.

—— 1995. 'Migration Regulations and Sex Selective Outcomes in Developed Countries.' In *International Migration Policies and the Status of Female Migrants*. New York: United Nations, United Nations Department for Economic and Social Information and Policy Analysis.

—— 1997. 'Migration Policy, Female Dependency, and Family Membership: Canada and Germany.' In *Women and the Canadian Welfare State*, edited by P. Evans and G. Werkle, 142–69. Toronto: Toronto University Press.

—— 2006. 'Push Factors Resulting in the Decision for Women to Migrate.' In *Female Migrants: Bridging the Gaps Throughout the Life Cycle, Selected Papers of the UNFPA-IOM Expert Group Meeting, 2–3 May 2006*, 29–39. New York.

—— 2014. 'Recruiting High Skill Labour in North America Policies, Outcomes and Futures.' *International Migration* 52 (3): 40–54.

Boyd, M., and X. Cao. 2009. 'Immigrant Language Proficiency, Earnings, and Language Policies.' *Canadian Studies in Population* 36 (1–2): 63–86.

Bratton, K. 2005. 'Critical Mass Theory Revisited: The Behavior and Success of Token Women in State Legislatures.' *Politics and Gender* 1 (March): 97–125.

Bräuninger, T., and M. Debus. 2009. 'Legislative Agenda-Setting in Parliamentary Democracies.' *European Consortium for Political Research* 48: 804–39.

Brazao, D. 2009. 'Report Calls for "Nannygate" Probe.' *The Toronto Star*, 7 June 2009.

Brazao, D., and R. J. Brennan. 2011. 'Nannies Win Work Freedom; Following Star Investigation, Caregivers Waiting for Residency Can Leave Employer, Seek New Job.' *The Toronto Star*, 16 December 2011, A1.

Breeman, G., D. Lowery, C. Poppelaars, L. Resodihardjo, A. Timmermans, and J. de Vries. 2009. 'Political Attention in a Coalition System: Analysing Queen's Speeches in the Netherlands 1945–2007.' *Acta Politica* 44 (1): 1–27.

Breitenbach, E., and Y. Galligan. 2006. 'Measuring Gender Equality: Reflecting on Experiences and Challenges in the UK and Ireland.' *Policy & Politics* 34 (4): 597–614.

Breunig, C., and A. Luedtke. 2008. 'What Motivates the Gatekeepers? Explaining Government Party Preference on Immigration.' *Governance: An International Journal of Policy and Administration* 21 (1): 123–46.

Brickner, R. K., and C. Straehle. 2010. 'The Missing Link: Gender, Immigration Policy and the Live-in Caregiver Program in Canada.' *Policy and Society* 29: 309–20.

Brouard, S., F. R. Baumgartner, and J. Wilkerson. 2008. 'Legislative Productivity in Comparative Perspective: An Introduction to the Comparative Agenda Project.' Paper presented at ECPR Joint Sessions, Rennes, 11–16 April 2008.

Brown, P., and A. Hesketh. 2004. *The Mismanagement of Talent: Employability and Jobs in the Knowledge Economy*. Oxford: Oxford University Press.

Brücker, H., C. Stella, and A. Marfouk. 2013. 'A New Panel Data Set on International Migration by Gender and Educational Attainment.' In *Migration: New Developments, Spring 2013*, NORFACE, 31–2.

Bruning, G., and J. Platenga. 1999. 'Parental Leave and Equal Opportunities: Experiences in Eight European Countries.' *Journal of European Social Policy* 9 (3): 195–209.

Bucken-Knapp, G. 2007. 'Varieties of Capitalism and Labour Migration Policy.' Working Paper, University West.

Bukodi, E., S. Dex, and H. Joshi. 2012. 'Changing Career Trajectories of Women and Men Across Time.' In *Gendered Lives: Gender Inequalities in Production and Reproduction*, edited by J. Scott, S. Dex and A. C. Plagnol, 48–73. Cheltenham, UK: Edward Elgar.

Bulmer, S. 2011. 'Shop Till You Drop? The German Executive as Venue-Shopper in Justice and Home Affairs.' In *The Europeanization of Control: Venues and Outcomes of EU Justice and Home Affairs Cooperation*, edited by P. Bendel, A. Ette and P. Parkes, 41–76. Berlin: Lit Verlag.

CAAIP (Committee to Advise on Australia's Immigration Policy). 1988. *Immigration: A Commitment to Australia: The Report to the Committee to Advise on Australia's Immigration Policy*. Canberra: Australian Government Publishing Service.

CAMC (Canadian Association of Management Consultants). 2002. *Submission to the Regulations to the Immigration and Refugee Protection Act*. Ottawa: Standing Committee on Citizenship and Immigration, Parliament of Canada, filed in the National Archives of Canada, Ottawa, RB14, BAN 2007-00060-1, Box 17, Wallet 4.

Campbell, I., and J. Tham. 2013. 'Labour Market Deregulation and Temporary Migrant Labour Schemes: An Analysis of the 457 Visa Program.' *Australian Journal of Labour Law* 26.

Campion Smith, B. 2008. 'Immigration Reform Passes in Commons.' *The Toronto Star*, 3 June 2008.

Canadian Press. 2012. 'Canada's Skilled Immigrants Backlog To Be Eliminated Soon.' 2 November 2012. www.cbc.ca/news/politics/canada-s-skilled-immigrants-backlog-to-be-eliminated-soon-1.1290847, accessed 29 June 2015.

Cangiano, A., I. Shutes, S. Spencer, and G. Leeson. 2009. *Migrant Care Workers in Ageing Societies: Research Findings in the United Kingdom*. Oxford: COMPAS.

Carasco, E., S. J. Aiken, D. Galloway, and A. Macklin. 2007. *Immigration and Refugee Law: Cases, Material and Commentary*. Toronto: Edmond Montgomery.

Carney, T. and A. Boucher. 2009. 'Social Security and Immigration: An Agenda for Future Research.' *Zeitschrift für ausländisches und internationales Arbeits-und Sozialrecht* 23 (ii): 36–57.

Carroll, S. J. 1994. *Women as Candidates in American Politics*, 2nd ed. Bloomington: Indiana University Press.

Carruthers, F. and R. McGregor. 1998. 'Skilled Émigrés Pay Dividends.' *The Australian*, 27 May 1998, 5.

Casey, J., and B. Dalton. 2006. 'The Best of Times, the Worst of Times: Community Sector Advocacy in the Age of Compacts.' *Australian Journal of Political Science* 41 (1): 23–38.

Castles, S. 2006. 'Guestworkers in Europe: A Resurrection?' *International Migration Review* 40 (4): 741–66.

CBA (Canadian Bar Association National Citizenship and Immigration Section). 2008. Letter from Alex Stojicevic, Chair of the National Citizenship and Immigration Section to Mr. Rob Merrifield, Chair, Standing Committee on Finance, 30 April 2008.

CBI (Confederation of British Industry). 2007. *Shaping up the Future – The Business Vision for Education and Skills*. London: CBI.

CCC (Canadian Chamber of Commerce). 2012. *Canada's Skill Crisis: What We Heard*, a CCC report on cross-country consultations in 2012. Toronto: CCC.

CCR (Canadian Council of Refugees). 2008. *Questions and Answers on Bill C-50*. Montreal: CCR.

CCR (Canadian Council of Refugees). 2009. *From Permanent to Temporary Migration: Canada's Dramatic Policy Shift*. Montreal: CCR.

CCR (Canadian Council of Refugees). 2010a. About the Canadian Council for Refugees (CCR), Supporting the CCR through Donations. Available at www.ccrweb.ca, accessed 19 April 2010.

CCR (Canadian Council of Refugees). 2013. *Key Refugee and Immigration Issues for Women and Girls*. Montreal: CCR.

CDPDJ (Commission des droits de la personne et des droits de la jeunesse du Québec). 2008. *Background Notes for the Submission at the Canada-wide Hearings of the House of Commons Standing Committee on Citizenship and Immigration*. Quebec City: Standing Committee on Citizenship and Immigration, Parliament of Canada.

Cerna, L. 2007. 'The Varieties of High-Skilled Immigration Policies: Sectoral Coalition and Outcomes in Advanced Industrial Countries.' European Union Studies Association Conference, Montreal, 17–19 May 2007.

―――― 2008. *Towards an EU Blue Card? The Delegation of National High-Skilled Immigration Policies in the EU Level.* Oxford: COMPAS.

―――― 2009. 'The Varieties of High-Skilled Immigration Policies: Coalitions and Policy Outputs in Advanced Industrial Countries.' *Journal of European Public Policy* 16 (1): 144–61.

―――― 2010. 'The EU Blue Card: A Bridge Too Far?' Fifth Pan-Europe Conference on EU Politics, Porto, Portugal 23–26 June 2010.

―――― 2014. 'The EU Blue Card: Preferences, Policies and Negotiations Between Member States.' *Migration Studies* 2 (1): 73–96.

Chaloff, J., and G. Lemaitre. 2009. 'Managing Highly-Skilled Labour Migration: A Comparative Analysis of Migration Policies and Challenges in OECD Countries.' *OECD Social, Employment and Migration Working Paper* (29).

Chappell, L. 2002. *Gendering Government: Feminist Engagement with the State in Australia and Canada.* Vancouver: University of British Columbia Press.

Charles, M. 2003. 'Deciphering Sex Segregation: Vertical and Horizontal Inequalities in Ten National Labour Markets.' *Acta Sociologica* 46(4): 267–87.

Chase, S. 2013. 'Ottawa to Play Matchmaker for Foreign Workers: New System Will Be "Like a Dating Site" for Top Global Talent, Immigration Minister Jason Kenny Tells The Globe.' *The Globe and Mail*, 2 January 2013, A1.

Chaves, M. L., and J. Galaskiewicz. 2004. 'Does Government Funding Suppress Nonprofits' Political Activity?' *American Sociological Review* 69 (April): 292–316.

Childs, S., and M. L. Krook. 2006. 'Gender and Politics: The State of the Art.' *Politics* 26 (1): 18–28.

Chiswick, B. R. 1978. 'The Effect of Americanization on the Earnings of Foreign-Born Men.' *Journal of Political Economy* 86: 897–921.

Chiswick, B. R., and P. W. Miller. 1992. 'Language in the Immigrant Labor Market.' In *Immigration, Language and Ethnicity: Canada and the United States*, edited by B. R. Chiswick, 229–96. Washington, D.C.: The AEI Press.

―――― 1995. 'The Endogeneity Between Language and Earnings: International Analyses.' *Journal of Labor Economics* 13: 246–88.

―――― 2002. 'Immigrant Earnings: Language Skills, Linguistic Concentrations and the Business Cycle.' *Journal of Population Economics* 15 (1): 31–57.

―――― 2007. 'Modeling Immigrants' Language Skills.' Bonn: IZA Discussion Paper Series, 2974.

Chiswick, V. 2013. 'Record Births, but Wave of Migrants Push Nation Past 23m.' *The Sydney Morning Herald*, 23 April 2013, 7.

Choudry, A., J. Hanley, S. Jordan, E. Shragge, and M. Stiegman. 2009. *Fight Back: Work Place Justice for Immigrants.* Halifax: Fernwood Publishing.

Chow, O. 2009. *Submission before the Standing Committee on Citizenship and Immigration Investigation into the Live-in Caregiver Program.* Ottawa: Standing Committee on Citizenship and Immigration, 26 May 2009, 0930.

Christensen, R., J. Szmer, and J. M. Stritch. 2012. 'Race and Gender Bias in Three Administrative Contexts: Impact on Work Assignments in State Supreme Courts.' *Journal of Public Administration, Research and Theory* 22 (4): 625–48.

CIC (Citizenship and Immigration Canada). 1994a. *A Broader Vision: Immigration and Citizenship Plan 1995–2000, Annual Report to Parliament.* Supply and Services Canada.

CIC (Citizenship and Immigration Canada). 1994b. Immigration Consultations 1994: The Report of Working of Group Number 2: 'What Criteria Should We Set to Achieve Our Social and Economic Objectives in Determining Who Will Come to Canada?' Ottawa: CIC.

CIC (Citizenship and Immigration Canada). 1994c. *The Relative Performance of Selected Independents and Family Class Immigrants in the Labour Market.* Ottawa: CIC.

CIC (Citizenship and Immigration Canada). 1994d. *The Social Welfare Implications of Immigrant Family Sponsorship Default: Phase 1, Progress Report,* edited by Policy Sector Strategic Research and Analysis Branch, CIC. Ottawa: CIC.

CIC (Citizenship and Immigration Canada). 1995. *A Broader Vision, 1996 Report to Parliament.* Ottawa: CIC.

CIC (Citizenship and Immigration Canada). 1996. *Staying the Course: Annual Immigration Plan 1997.* Ottawa: CIC.

CIC (Citizenship and Immigration Canada). 1997. *A Stronger Canada: Annual Immigration Plan 1997.* Ottawa: CIC.

CIC (Citizenship and Immigration Canada). 1998a. 'Towards a New Selection Model: Current Selection Criteria: Indicators of Successful Establishment?' Research Paper. Ottawa: Economic Policy and Programs Division, Selection Branch, CIC.

CIC (Citizenship and Immigration Canada). 1998b. *Canada – A Welcoming Land – 1999 Annual Immigration Plan.* Ottawa: CIC.

CIC (Citizenship and Immigration Canada). 1999a. *The Economic Performance of Immigrants Education Perspective, IMDB Profile Series.* Ottawa: CIC.

CIC (Citizenship and Immigration Canada). 1999b. *Skilled Worker Selection Model, Federal-Provincial Working Group.* Ottawa: CIC.

CIC (Citizenship and Immigration Canada). 1999c. *Canada – The Place to Be, Annual Immigration Plan for the Year 2000.* Ottawa: CIC.

CIC (Citizenship and Immigration Canada). 2000. 'Skilled Worker Immigration: Three Models for Discussion.' Consultation Paper. Ottawa: CIC.

CIC (Citizenship and Immigration Canada). 2001a. *Draft Gender-Based Analysis of Bill C-31/C-11.* Ottawa: CIC.

CIC (Citizenship and Immigration Canada). 2001b. 'Regulatory Impact Statement to the Immigration and Refugee Protection Act.' *Canadian Gazette* 1 (December 15): 4477–4576.

CIC (Citizenship and Immigration Canada). 2001c. *Planning Now for Canada's Future. Introducing a Multi-Year Planning Process and the Immigration Plan for 2001 and 2002.* Ottawa: CIC.

CIC (Citizenship and Immigration Canada). 2002a. *Immigration and Refugee Protection Act, Gender-based Analysis Chart, Regulatory Impact Assessment Statement.* Ottawa: CIC.

CIC (Citizenship and Immigration Canada). 2002b. *Response to Information Request from the Standing Committee on Citizenship and Immigration.* Ottawa: Standing Committee on Citizenship and Immigration, Parliament of Canada.

CIC (Citizenship and Immigration Canada). 2002c. *Annual Report to Parliament on Immigration.* Ottawa: CIC.

CIC (Citizenship and Immigration Canada). 2005. *Facts and Figures: Immigration Overview, Permanent and Temporary Residents, Permanent Residents by Category.* Ottawa: CIC.

CIC (Citizenship and Immigration Canada). 2007. *Annual Report to Parliament on Immigration 2007: Conclusion.* Ottawa: CIC.

CIC (Citizenship and Immigration Canada). 2008a. *Annual Report to Parliament on Immigration 2008: Section 7, Gender-Based Analysis of the Impact of the Immigration and Refugee Protection Act.* Ottawa: CIC.

CIC (Citizenship and Immigration Canada). 2008b. *Backgrounder: Action Plan for Faster Immigration: Ministerial Instructions.* Ottawa: CIC.

CIC (Citizenship and Immigration Canada). 2008c. 'Ministerial Instruction, 29 November 2008.' *Government Notices, Department of Citizenship and Immigration, Immigration and Refugee Protection Act* 142 (48).

CIC (Citizenship and Immigration Canada). 2009a. 'Regulatory Impact Assessment Statement: Regulations Amending the Immigration and Refugee Protection Regulations (Temporary Foreign Worker Program).' *Canada Gazette* 143 (41), 10 October 2009.

CIC (Citizenship and Immigration Canada). 2009b. 'Regulatory Impact Assessment Statement: Regulations Amending the Immigration and Refugee Protection Regulations (Live-in Caregiver Program).' *Canada Gazette* 143 (41), 19 December 2009.

CIC (Citizenship and Immigration Canada). 2010a. *Gender-Based Analysis of the Impact of the Immigration and Refugee Protection Act in Annual Report to Parliament on Immigration.* Ottawa: CIC.

CIC (Citizenship and Immigration Canada). 2010b. *Evaluation of the Federal Skilled Worker Program: Evaluation Division.* Ottawa: CIC, Research and Evaluation Division.

CIC (Citizenship and Immigration Canada). 2010c. 'Ministerial Instruction.' *Canadian Gazette* 144 (26), 26 June 2010.

CIC (Citizenship and Immigration Canada). 2011a. *Facts and Figures 2011: Immigration Overview – Permanent and Temporary Residents 15 Years of Age or Older by Age and Category.* Ottawa: CIC.

CIC (Citizenship and Immigration Canada). 2011b. 'Gender-Based Analysis of the Impact of the *Immigration and Refugee Protection Act.*' In *Annual Report to Parliament on Immigration.* Ottawa: CIC.

CIC (Citizenship and Immigration Canada). 2011c. 'Ministerial Instruction: (MI3) Federal Skilled Workers, Immigrant Investor Program, Entrepreneurs.' *Canadian Gazette* 145 (26).

CIC (Citizenship and Immigration Canada). 2012a. *Annual Report to Parliament on Immigration.* Ottawa: CIC.

CIC (Citizenship and Immigration Canada). 2012b. 'Canada – Permanent Residents by Category, 2008–2012.' In *Preliminary Tables – Permanent and Temporary Migration.* Ottawa: CIC.

CIC (Citizenship and Immigration Canada). 2012c. 'Gender-Based Analysis of the Impact of the *Immigration and Refugee Protection Act.*' In *Annual Report to Parliament on Immigration.* Ottawa: CIC.

CIC (Citizenship and Immigration Canada). 2012d. 'Regulations Amending the Immigration and Refugee Protection Regulations.' In *146/33.* Department of Citizenship and Immigration Ottawa.

CIC (Citizenship and Immigration Canada). 2013a. *Facts and Figures 2012 – Immigration Overview: Permanent and Temporary Residents.* Ottawa: CIC.

CIC (Citizenship and Immigration Canada). 2013b. *FW1: Foreign Worker Manual.* Ottawa: CIC.

CIC (Citizenship and Immigration Canada). 2013c. *Ministerial Instructions 9 (MI8).* Ottawa: CIC.

CIC (Citizenship and Immigration Canada). 2013d. *Specific Eligibility Criteria – Federal Skilled Workers.* Ottawa: CIC.

CIC (Citizenship and Immigration Canada). 2013e. 'Temporary Residents Present on December 1st by Gender and Yearly Status, 1988 to 2012.' In *Facts and Figures 2012: Immigration Overview: Permanent and Temporary Residents.* Ottawa: CIC.

CIC (Citizenship and Immigration Canada). 2013f. 'Temporary Residents: Total Entries of Foreign Workers by Gender and Occupational Skill Level.' In *Facts and Figures 2012: Immigration Overview: Permanent and Temporary Residents.* Ottawa: CIC.

CIC (Citizenship and Immigration Canada). 2013g. 'Total Entries of Foreign Workers by Yearly Sub-status.' In *Total Entries of Foreign Workers by Yearly Sub-status.* Ottawa: CIC.

CIC (Citizenship and Immigration Canada). 2013h. Unpublished data request to CIC by author, RDM, August 2013. Extract, RE-12-0806.

CJIRP (Coalition for a Just Immigration and Refugee Policy). 2000. *Position Paper on Bill C-31 by the Coalition for a Just Immigration and Refugee Policy).* Ottawa: Standing Committee on Citizenship and Immigration, Parliament of Canada.

CJIRP (Coalition for a Just Immigration and Refugee Policy). 2002. *Submission to the Standing Committee on Citizenship and Immigration on the Regulations to the Immigration and Refugee Protection Act.* In Ottawa: Standing Committee on Citizenship and Immigration, Parliament of Canada.

Clark, C. 2002. 'Would-be Immigrants Caught in Switch of Rules Could Get Fee Refunds.' *The Globe and Mail,* 30 June 2002, A8.

CLC (Canadian Labour Congress). 2011. *Canada's Temporary Foreign Worker Program (TFWP) Model Program – or Mistake?* Ottawa: CLC.

CLC (Canadian Labour Congress). 2012. *Department of Citizenship and Immigration Canada in August 2012 Proposed Changes to the Immigration Refugee Protection Act (IRPA) Regulations.* Ottawa: CLC.

CME (Canadian Manufacturers and Exporters). 2001. 'Comments on the Proposed Protection Regulations, Part 1–17.' Ottawa: Standing Committee on Citizenship and Immigration, Parliament of Canada.

Coalition (Coalition for a Just Refugee and Immigration Policy). 1988. The Coalition for a Just Refugee and Immigration Policy Newsletter. Filed in the papers of the National Action Committee on the Status of Women, Canadian Women's Movement Archives, University of Ottawa.

Coderre, D. 2002. Government Response to the Report of the Standing Committee on Citizenship and Immigration, Building a Nation: The Regulations under the Immigration and Refugee Protection Act. CIC.

Collier, D., H. Brady, and J. Seawright. 2004. 'Critiques, Responses, and Trade-Offs: Drawing Together the Debate.' In *Rethinking Social Inquiry: Diverse Tools, Share Standards*, edited by H. Brady and D. Collier, 195–227. Lanham, MD: Rowman & Littlefield.

Community Coalition (Community Coalition on Immigration). 1987. Letter from Ed Graca, C.T.L.C. to members of the Coalition, Toronto, Canada, 12 May 1987. Filed in the papers of the National Action Committee on the Status of Women, Canadian Women's Movement Archives, University of Ottawa.

Cook-Martin, D. 2013. *The Scramble for Citizens: Dual Nationality and State Competition for Immigrants*. Stanford, CA: Stanford University Press.

Cook-Martin, D., and D. FitzGerald. 2010. 'Liberalism and the Limits of Inclusion: Race and Immigration Law in the Americas, 1850–2000.' *Journal of Interdisciplinary History* 41: 7–25.

Copenhagen Post (2010). 'Foreigners Need Points to Get Permit.' 16 March 2010. Available at www.cphpost.dk, accessed 25 March 2010.

Corbett, D. 1957. *Canada's Immigration Policy*. Toronto: University of Toronto Press.

Cornelius, W., T. Tsuda, P. L. Martin, and J. F. Hollifield. 2004. *Controlling Immigration: A Global Perspective*. Stanford, CA: Stanford University Press.

Cox, E. 1992. 'Policy Stocktake.' The Politics of Speaking Out: Immigrant Women Ten Years On conference, Granville, NSW.

Crépeau, F. 2008. Presentation before the Standing Committee on Citizenship and Immigration. Ottawa: Parliament of Canada, Standing Committee on Citizenship and Immigration, 12 May 2008: 1055.

Crock, M. 1998. *Immigration and Refugee Law in Australia*. Leichardt, Sydney: The Federation Press.

——2006. 'Judging Refugees: The Clash of Power and Institutions in the Development of Australian Refugee Law.' *Sydney Law Review* 26: 51–73.

Crock, M., and L. Berg. 2011. *Immigration and Refugee Law in Australia*. Leichardt, Sydney: The Federation Press.

Dalton, B. M., and M. Lyons. 2005. 'Advocacy Organisations in Australian Politics: Governance and Democratic Effects.' *Third Sector Review* 11 (2): 59–78.

Daugbjerg, C., and J. Studsgaard. 2005. 'Issue Redefinition, Venue Change and Radical Agricultural Policy Reforms in Sweden and New Zealand.' *Scandinavian Political Studies* 28 (2): 103–24.

Dauvergne, C. 2000. 'Gendering Permanent Residency Statistics.' *Melbourne University Law Review* 24: 280–309.

—— 2005. *Humanitarianism, Identity, and Nation: Migration Laws in Canada and Australia*. Vancouver: UBC Press.

—— 2009. 'Globalizing Fragmentation – New Pressures on the Women Caught in the Immigration Law – Citizenship Law Dichotomy.' In *Migrations and*

Mobilities: Citizenship, Borders and Gender, edited by S. Benhabib and J. Resnick, 333–55. New York/London: New York University Press.

Dauvergne, C., L. C. Angeles, and A. Huang. 2006. *Gendering Canada's Refugee Process.* Ottawa: Status of Women Canada.

Deegan, B. 2008. *Visa Subclass 457: Integrity Review.* Canberra: Department of Immigration and Citizenship.

Delacourt, S. 2009. 'Dhalla vs. Nannies Dispute to Begin New Round Today; Discussions Continuing on Whether MP's Brother, Mother Will Also Be Called to Testify at Committee.' *Toronto Star*, 14 May 2009, A08.

DeLaet, D. 1999. 'Introduction: The Invisibility of Women in Scholarship on International Migration.' In *Gender and Migration*, edited by G. A. Kelson and D. L. DeLaet, 1–17. New York: New York University Press.

Dench, J. 2008. *Submission of the Canadian Council of Refugees to the Standing Committee on Citizenship and Immigration Hearing on Bill C-50.* Ottawa: Parliament of Canada, Standing Committee on Citizenship and Immigration, 12 May 2008: 1550.

Department of Employment Australia. 2013. Historical list of occupations on the gazetted Migration Occupations in Demand List (MODL) – to 17 May 2008. Canberra: Department of Employment Australia, unpublished excel spreadsheet provided to author by Jane Press, Director of Population and Migration Section, 24 October 2013.

DeVoretz, D. J. 1995. 'New Issues, New Evidence, and New Immigration Policies for the Twenty-First Century.' In *Diminishing Returns: The Economics of Canada's Recent Immigration Policy*, edited by D. J. DeVoretz, 1–30. Toronto: C.D. Howe Institute/ The Laurier Institute.

DIAC (Department of Immigration and Citizenship). 2006. *Population Flows: Immigration Aspects 2005–6.* Canberra: DIAC.

DIAC (Department of Immigration and Citizenship). 2007a. *Fact Sheet 1: Background 3.* Canberra: DIAC.

DIAC (Department of Immigration and Citizenship). 2007b. *Migration Program Outcome – Skill Stream – 1996/1997 to 2006-7*, gender disaggregated, unpublished data provided to author by Statistics Unit, DIAC, Canberra.

DIAC (Department of Immigration and Citizenship). 2008a. *Media Release: Panel of Experts to Advise on Changes to 457 Visa Program.* Canberra: DIAC.

DIAC (Department of Immigration and Citizenship). 2008b. *Skilled Occupation List (SOL) and Employer Nomination Scheme Occupation List (ENSOL), Form 1121i.* Canberra: DIAC.

DIAC (Department of Immigration and Citizenship). 2009a. *Fact Sheet 1 – Immigration: the Background Part One.* Canberra: DIAC.

DIAC (Department of Immigration and Citizenship). 2009b. Migration Program Outcome – Skill and Family Stream – 1996/1997 to 2007-08, unpublished data provided by Professor Mary Crock to author. Canberra: DIAC.

DIAC (Department of Immigration and Citizenship). 2010a. *Australia Reforms Migration Rules to Deliver Australia's Skills Needs.* Canberra: DIAC, 8 February 2010.

DIAC (Department of Immigration and Citizenship). 2010b. *Changes to Priority Processing.* Canberra: DIAC.

DIAC (Department of Immigration and Citizenship). 2010c. *Changes to the General Skilled Migration Program.* Canberra: DIAC, 8 February 2010.

DIAC (Department of Immigration and Citizenship). 2010d. *How New Migrants Fare: Analysis of the Continuous Survey of Australia's Migrants.* Canberra: DIAC.

DIAC (Department of Immigration and Citizenship). 2010e. *New List of Skilled Occupations Intended to Replace the Current Skilled Occupation List.* Canberra: DIAC.

DIAC (Department of Immigration and Citizenship). 2010f. *Discussion Paper: Review of the General Skilled Migration Points Test.* Canberra: DIAC.

DIAC (Department of Immigration and Citizenship). 2011a. *Discussion Paper: Review of the Permanent Employer Sponsored Visa Categories.* Canberra: DIAC.

DIAC (Department of Immigration and Citizenship). 2011b. *Employer Sponsored Workers – Additional Funding for 457 Visa Processing.* Canberra: DIAC.

DIAC (Department of Immigration and Citizenship). 2011c. *Points Test for Certain Skilled Migration Visas.* Canberra: DIAC.

DIAC (Department of Immigration and Citizenship). 2012a. *Changes to Points Tested Skilled Migration Visas* Canberra: DIAC.

DIAC (Department of Immigration and Citizenship). 2012b. *Fact Sheet 24a – Priority Processing for Skilled Migration Visas.* Canberra: DIAC.

DIAC (Department of Immigration and Citizenship). 2012c. *General Skilled Migration Points Test under SkillSelect.* Canberra: DIAC.

DIAC (Department of Immigration and Citizenship). 2012d. *SkillSelect.* Canberra: DIAC.

DIAC (Department of Immigration and Citizenship). 2013a. *Australia's Migration Trends 2011–12.* Canberra: DIAC.

DIAC (Department of Immigration and Citizenship). 2013b. *Migration Program Data, Gender Disaggregated.* Canberra: Economics Analysis Unit, DIAC.

DIAC (Department of Immigration and Citizenship). 2013c. *Skilled Occupation List.* Canberra: DIAC.

DIAC (Department of Immigration and Citizenship). 2013d. Subclass 457 Principal Applicant Grants: Gender by Nominated Occupation. Unpublished data provided to author by Economics Analysis Unit, DIAC, Canberra.

DIBP (Department of Immigration and Border Protection). 2013a. *Fact Sheet 48c – Regional Migration Agreement.* Canberra: DIBP.

DIBP (Department of Immigration and Border Protection). 2013b. *Increase to the Temporary Skilled Migration Income Threshold.* Canberra: DIBP.

DIEA (Department of Immigration and Ethnic Affairs). 1986. *About Migrant Women: Statistical Profile 1986.* Canberra: Women's and Advising Section.

DILGEA (Department of Immigration, Local Government and Ethnic Affairs). 1987. *Australia's Population Trends and Prospects 1987.* Canberra: Australian Government Publishing Service.

DILGEA (Department of Immigration, Local Government and Ethnic Affairs). 1988. Table 1.4 Eligibility Category of Settler Arrivals. Canberra: DILGEA.

DILGEA (Department of Immigration, Local Government and Ethnic Affairs). 1989. *Australia's Population Trends and Prospects 1989*. Canberra: DILGEA, Australian Government Publishing Service.

DILGEA (Department of Immigration, Local Government and Ethnic Affairs). 1990. Table 1.4 Eligibility Category of Settlement Arrivals. Canberra: DILGEA.

DILGEA (Department of Immigration, Local Government and Ethnic Affairs). 1991. *Women's Issue Plan.* Canberra: Canberra Printing Services.

DILGEA (Department of Immigration, Local Government and Ethnic Affairs). 1992. Table 2.7 Settler Arrivals by Eligibility Category, 1990–91 to 1999–00; Australian Immigration Consolidated Statistics Number 21. Canberra: DILGEA.

DILGEA (Department of Immigration, Local Government and Ethnic Affairs). 1993. Table 2.7 Settler Arrivals by Eligibility Category, 1990–91 to 1999–00; Australian Immigration Consolidated Statistics Number 21. Canberra: DILGEA.

DILGEA (Department of Immigration, Local Government and Ethnic Affairs). 1994. Table 2.7 Settler Arrivals by Eligibility Category, 1990–91 to 1999–00; Australian Immigration Consolidated Statistics Number 21. Canberra: DILGEA.

DILGEA (Department of Immigration, Local Government and Ethnic Affairs). 1995. Table 2.7 Settler Arrivals by Eligibility Category, 1990–91 to 1999–00; Australian Immigration Consolidated Statistics Number 21. Canberra: DILGEA.

DIMA (Department of Immigration and Multicultural Affairs). 1996. Table 2.7 Settler Arrivals by Eligibility Category, 1990–91 to 1999–00: Australian Immigration Consolidated Statistics Number 21. Canberra: DIMA.

DIMA (Department of Immigration and Multicultural Affairs). 1997. Table 2.7 Settler Arrivals by Eligibility Category, 1990–91 to 1999–00; Australian Immigration Consolidated Statistics Number 21. Canberra: DIMA.

DIMA (Department of Immigration and Multicultural Affairs). 1998. Table 2.7 Settler Arrivals by Eligibility Category, 1990–91 to 1999–00; Australian Immigration Consolidated Statistics Number 21. Canberra: DIMA.

DIMA (Department of Immigration and Multicultural Affairs). 1999. *Review of the Independent and Skilled-Australian Linked Categories.* Canberra: Commonwealth of Australia.

DIMA (Department of Immigration and Multicultural Affairs). 2000a. *DIMA Gender Equity Statement: Detailed Priorities Plan 2000–2002.* Canberra: DIMA.

DIMA (Department of Immigration and Multicultural Affairs). 2000b. 'Managing the Migration Program.' DIMA Fact Sheet 21. www.immi.gov.au/facts/21manage.htm, accessed 26 June 2000.

DIMA (Department of Immigration and Multicultural Affairs). 2000c. Table 2.7 Settler Arrivals by Eligibility Category, 1990–91 to 1999–00; Australian Immigration Consolidation Statistics Number 21. Canberra: DIMA.

DIMA (Department of Immigration and Multicultural Affairs). 2001. Table 1.1 Settler Arrivals by Selected Characteristics; Immigration Update, July–December 2001. Canberra: DIMA.

DIMA (Department of Immigration and Multicultural Affairs). 2003. Table 1.1 Settler Arrivals by Selected Characteristics; Immigration Update, July–December 2003. Canberra: DIMA, 8.

DIMIA (Department of Immigration and Multicultural and Indigenous Affairs). 2001. *Population Flows: Immigration Aspects 2000–1.* Canberra: DIMIA.

DIMIA (Department of Immigration and Multicultural and Indigenous Affairs). 2002. Table 1.1 Settler Arrivals by Selected Characteristics; Immigration Update, July–December 2002. Canberra: DIMIA.

DIMIA (Department of Immigration and Multicultural and Indigenous Affairs). 2002b. *Population Flows: Immigration Aspects 2003–4.* Canberra: DIMIA.

DIMIA (Department of Immigration and Multicultural and Indigenous Affairs). 2003. Table 1.1 Settler Arrivals by Selected Characteristics; Immigration Update, July–December 2003. Canberra: DIMIA.

Dobrowolsky, A. 2000. *The Politics of Pragmatism: Women, Representation and Constitutionalism in Canada.* Oxford: Oxford University Press.

Dobrowolsky, A., and E. Tastsoglou. 2006. 'Crossing Boundaries and Making Connections.' In *Women, Migration and Citizenship: Making Local, National and Transnational Connections,* edited by A. Dobrowolsky and E. Tastsoglou, 1–35. Aldershot: Palgrave.

Dobson, B., and J. Crush. 2004. 'A Report on Gender Discrimination in South Africa's 2002 Immigration Act: Masculinizing the Migrant.' *Feminist Review* 77: 96–119.

Dobson, D. L., and S. J. Carroll. 1991. *Reshaping the Agenda: Women in State Legislatures.* New Brunswick: Centre for the American Woman and Politics, Rutgers, The State University of New Jersey.

Docquier, F., and A. Marfouk. 2005. 'Measuring the International Mobility of Skilled Workers (1990–2000).' Release 1.0 Policy Research Working Papers. World Bank.

Docquier, F., A. Marfouk, C. Özden, and C. Parsons. 2011. *Geographic, Gender and Skill Structure of International Migration.* Washington, D.C.: World Bank.

Dore, C. 1997. 'PM Cuts Family Reunion Migrants.' *The Australian,* 22 May 1997, 1.

Drobnic, S., H. P. Blossfeld, and G. Rohwer. 1999. 'Dynamics of Women's Employment Patterns Over the Family Life Course: A Comparison of the United States and Germany.' *Journal of Marriage and Family* 61 (1): 133–46.

Dumont, J., J. Martin, and G. Spielvogel. 2007. 'Women on the Move: The Neglected Gender Dimension of the Brain Drain.' Discussion Paper, IZA, Hamburg.

Duncan, C., and W. Loretto. 2004. 'Never the Right Age? Gender and Age-Based Discrimination in Employment.' *Gender, Work & Organization* 11 (1): 95–115.

Dür, A., and D. D. Bièvre. 2007. 'Inclusion without Influence? NGOs in European Trade Policy.' *Journal of Public Policy* 27 (1): 79–101.

Durbin, S. 2011. 'Creating Knowledge through Networks: A Gender Perspective.' *Gender, Work and Organisation* 18 (1): 90–112.

ECC NSW (Ethnic Communities Council NSW). 1998. Dr Tony Pun, Chairperson, Ethnic Communities Council of NSW Inc., Submission to the External Reference Group on the Skilled and Australian-Linked Categories. Canberra, Department of Immigration and Multicultural and Indigenous Affairs, Australia.

Ehrenreich, B., and A. Russell. 2002. *Global Woman: Nannies, Maids and Sex Workers in the New Economy.* London: Granta Books.

EIC (Employment and Immigration Canada). 1987. *Annual Report to Parliament on Future Immigration Levels.* Ottawa: EIC.

EIC (Employment and Immigration Canada). 1989. *Annual Report to Parliament on Future Immigration Levels.* Ottawa: EIC.

EIC (Employment and Immigration Canada). 1990. *Annual Report to Parliament: Immigration Plan for 1991-1995.* Ottawa: Supply and Services.

Eichhorst, W., and J. Leschke. 2012. *Understanding Women's Reasons for Working Part-Time: A Multi-Country Study.* Edinburgh: EPSAnet.

Eisenstein, H. 1996. *Inside Agitators: Australian Femocrats and the State.* Sydney: Allen & Unwin.

Elazar, D. 1987. *Exploring Federalism.* Tuscaloosa, AB: University of Alabama Press.

Elrick, J., and N. Lightman. 2014. 'Sorting or Shaping? The Gendered Economic Outcomes of Immigration Policy in Canada.' *International Migration Review.* Published online 15 August 2014.

Elson, P. 2011. 'The Emergence of Structured Subnational Voluntary Sector-Government Relationships in Canada: A Historical Institutional Analysis.' *Voluntary Sector Review* 2 (2): 133-55.

England, P. 1982. 'The Failure of Human Capital Theory to Explain Occupational Sex Segregation.' *Journal of Human Resources* 17 (3): 358-70.

England, P., M. J. Budig, and N. Folbre. 2002. 'Wage of Virtue: The Relative Pay of Care Work.' *Social Problems* 49 (4): 455-73.

England, P., M. S. Herbert, B. Stanek Kilbourne, L. L. Reid, and L. McCreary Megdal. 1994. 'The Gendered Valuation of Occupations and Skills: Earnings in 1980 Census Occupations.' *Social Forces* 73 (1): 65-100.

Estevez-Abe, M. 2005. 'Gender Bias in Skills and Social Policies: The Varieties of Capitalism Perspective on Sex Segregation.' *Social Politics: International Studies in Gender, State and Society* 12 (2): 180-215.

———2012. 'Gendered Consequences of Vocational Training.' In *The Political Economy of Collective Skill Formation,* edited by M. R. Busemeyer and C. Trampusch, 259-83. Oxford: Oxford University Press.

European Commission. 2005. Policy Plan on Legal Migration. 21 December 2005, SEC: 1680.

European Commission. 2013. France: What Do I Need Before Leaving? Highly Qualified Worker. EU Immigration Portal.

Evans, C. 2009a. 'Big Drop in Temporary Overseas Workers.' Media release. Canberra: Department of Immigration and Citizenship.

———2009b. 'Government Announces Changes to 457 Visa Program.' Media release. Canberra: Department of Immigration and Citizenship.

——— 2010. 'Changes to Australia's Skilled Migration Program.' Speech by Senator Chris Evans, Australian Minister for Immigration and Citizenship. Australian National University.

Evans, S. 1994. 'Welfare Dependency Amongst Recently Arrived Aged Migrant Parents.' *People and Place* 2 (2): 35-9.

EWL (European Women's Lobby). 2010. Immigration, Integration and Asylum Policies from a Gender Perspective. www.womenlobby.org/our-work/Immigration-Integration-and-Asylum/?lang=en, accessed 29 June 2015.

EWLA (European Women Lawyers Association). 2003. *Resolution on European Immigration, Asylum and Refugee Legislation and Gender Mainstreaming.* Helsinki: General Assembly of EWLA.

External Reference Group (Visa Subclass 457 External Reference Group). 2008. *Final Report to the Minister for Immigration and Citizenship.* Canberra: Commonwealth of Australia.

Facchini, G., A. M. Mayda, and P. Mischra. 2007. 'Do Interest Groups Affect Immigration?' Riga: Marie-Curie Research Network Transnationality of Migration.

Favell, A., M. Feldblum, and M. P. Smith. 2006. 'The Human Face of Global Mobility: A Research Agenda.' In *The Human Face of Global Mobility: International Highly Skilled Migration in Europe, North America and the Asia-Pacific,* edited by M. P. Smith and A. Favell, 1–25. New Brunswick/London: Transaction Publishers.

FECCA (Federation of Ethnic Communities' Councils of Australia). 1988. Ethnic Spotlight, Newsletter of the Federation of Ethnic Communities' Councils of Australia, 14 July 1988. Canberra.

FECCA (Federation of Ethnic Communities' Councils of Australia). 1998. Mr Randolph Alwis, Chairperson, Federation of Ethnic Communities' Councils of Australia, Submissions to the External Reference Group on the Skilled and Australian-Linked Categories, 1998. Canberra: DIMIA.

FECCA (Federation of Ethnic Communities' Councils of Australia). 2002. Annual Report, Profit and Loss Statement, FECCA 07/02/2001 through 06/30/2002, Canberra. Available at www.fecca.org.au, accessed 20 April 2010.

FECCA (Federation of Ethnic Communities' Councils of Australia). 2006. *Submission to the Parliamentary Inquiry into Eligibility Requirements and Monitoring, Enforcement and Reporting Arrangements for Temporary Business Visas.* Canberra: FECCA. Provided to author by Chris Wright.

FECCA (Federation of Ethnic Communities' Councils of Australia). 2010. *Submission to the Review of the General Skilled Migration Points Test Discussion Paper.* Canberra: FECCA.

Ferreira, P. 2008. *Submission of the Canadian Ethnocultural Council to the Standing Committee of Finance Inquiry into Bill C-50.* Ottawa: Parliament of Canada, Standing Committee of Finance, 14 May 2008: 1535.

Fevre, R. 1989. 'Informal Practices, Flexible Firms and Private Labour Markets.' *Sociology* 23 (1): 90–109.

Fincher, R. 1997. 'Gender, Age, and Ethnicity in Immigration for an Australian Nation.' *Environment and Planning A* 29: 217–36.

Fincher, R., L. Foster, W. Giles, and V. Preston. 1994. 'Gender and Migration Policy.' In *Immigration and Refugee Policy: Australia and Canada Compared,* edited by H. Adelman, A. Borowski, M. Burstein and L. Foster, 149–84. Toronto/Buffalo: University of Toronto Press.

Finley, D. 2008. Statement of Minister for Immigration and Citizenship, Diane Finley before the Standing Committee on Finance. Ottawa: Parliament of Canada, Standing Committee on Finance, 28 April 2008.

Flabbi, L., and M. Tejada. 2012. Fields of Study Choices, Occupational Choices and Gender Differentials. *Background Paper for the OECD Gender Initiative.* Paris: OECD.

Flecker, K. 2011. The Positives and Pitfalls of Canada's Temporary Foreign Worker Program (TFWP). *Report from the Global Forum on Migration and Development (GFMD).* Geneva.

Flynn, G. 2011. 'Court Decisions: NIMBY Claims, and the Sitting of Unwanted Facilities: Policy Fames and the Impact of Judicialization in Locating a Landfill for Toronto's Solid Waste.' *Canadian Public Policy* XXXVII (3): 381–93.

Folbre, N. 2009. *Greed, Lust and Gender: A History of Economic Ideas.* Oxford: Oxford University Press.

—— 2012. 'The Political Economy of Human Capital.' *Review of Radical Political Economics* 44 (3): 281–92.

Freeman, G. 1986. 'Migration and the Political Economy of the Welfare State.' *Annals, AAPSS* XXIX (4).

——1995. 'Modes of Immigration Policies in Liberal Democratic States.' *International Migration Review* 29 (4): 881–902.

——1998. 'The Decline of Sovereignty? Politics and Immigration Restriction in Liberal States.' In *Challenge to the Nation-State,* edited by C. Joppke. Oxford: Oxford University Press.

—— 1999. 'The Quest for Skill.' In *Migration and Refugee Policies: An Overview,* edited by A. Bernstein and M. Weiner, 84–118. London: Pinter.

——2005. 'Political Science and Comparative Immigration Politics.' In *International Migration Research: Constructions, Omissions and the Promises of Inter-disciplinarity,* edited by M. Bommes and E. Morawska, 111–28. London: Ashgate.

——2006. 'National Models, Policy Types and the Politics of Immigration in Liberal Democracies.' *West European Politics* 29 (2): 227–47.

Freeman, G., and K. Betts. 1992. 'The Politics of Interests and Immigration Policymaking in Australia and the United States.' In *Nation of Immigrants: Australia, the United States, and International Migration,* edited by G. Freeman and J. Jupp, 72–88. New York: Oxford University Press.

Freeman, G. P., and D. K. Hill. 2006. 'Disaggregating Immigration Policy: The Politics of Skilled Labor Recruitment in the U.S.' In *The Human Face of Global Mobility: International Highly Skilled Migration in Europe, North America and the Asia-Pacific,* edited by M. P. Smith and A. Favell, 103–29. New Brunswick: Transaction Publishers.

Fudge, J., and F. MacPhail. 2009. 'The Temporary Foreign Worker Program in Canada: Low-skilled Workers as an Extreme Form of Flexible Labor.' *Comparative Labor Law and Policy Journal* 31 (5): 5–46.

Gabriel, C. 2005. 'A Question of Skills: Gender, Migration Policy and Global Economy.' In *Global Regulation: Managing Crisis after the Imperial Turn,* edited by L. Assassi, K. van der Pijl and D. Wigan, 162–76. London: Palgrave MacMillan.

—— 2008. 'A "Healthy" Trade? NAFTA, Labour Mobility and Canadian Nurses.' In *Governing International Labour Migration. Current Issues, Challenges and Dilemmas,* edited by C. Gabriel and H. Pellerin, 112–27. London: Routledge.

Gabriel, C., and H. Pellerin. 2008. *Governing International Labour Migration: Current Issues, Challenges and Dilemmas.* London: Routledge.

Gageler, S. 2010. 'Impact of Migration Law on the Development of Australian Administrative Law.' *Australian Journal of Administrative Law* 17: 92–105.

Gardiner, J. 2000. 'Gender and Family in the Formation of Human Capital.' In *Towards a Gendered Political Economy*, edited by J. Cook, J. Roberts and G. Waylen, 61–76. Sheffield: PERC.

Gest, J., A. Boucher, and S. Challen. 2014. 'Measuring and Comparing Migration, Asylum and Naturalisation Policies: The International Migration Policy and Law Analysis (IMPALA) Project.' *Global Policy* 5 (3): 261–74.

Goar, C. 2007. 'Compounding Immigration Mess.' *The Toronto Star*, 19 November 2007.

Goertz, G., and A. Mazur. 2008. 'Mapping Gender and Politics Concepts: Ten Guidelines.' In *Politics, Gender and Concepts: Theory and Methodology*, edited by G. Goertz and A. Mazur, 14–43. Cambridge: Cambridge University Press.

Gottfried, H. 2012. *Gender, Work, and Economy: Unpacking the Global Economy.* Cambridge: Polity.

Gornick, J. C., and M. K. Meyers. 2008a. 'Creating Gender Egalitarian Societies: An Agenda for Reform.' *Politics and Society* 36 (3): 313–49.

—— 2008b. *Gender Equality: Transforming Family Divisions of Labor.* London/New York: Verso.

Goutor, D., and C. Ramsaroop. 2009. 'No Thanksgiving for Migrant Workers.' *The Toronto Star*, 8 October 2010.

Government of Canada. 2009. *Canada Gazette Part 1* 143 (51): 3714–3809.

Government of Canada. 2010. *Government of Canada Response to the Report of the Standing Committee on Citizenship and Immigration: Temporary Foreign Workers and Non-Status Workers.* Ottawa: Parliament of Canada.

Graycar, R., and J. Morgan. 2002. *The Hidden Gender of Law.* Leichardt, Sydney: The Federation Press.

Green, A. G. 1976. *Immigration and Postwar Canadian Economy.* Toronto: Macmillan.

—— 2002. Presentation of the Chair of the Immigration Law Specialty Committee of the Law Society of Upper Canada on the Regulations to the Immigration Refugee Protection Act. Standing Committee of Citizenship and Immigration. Ottawa Parliament of Canada.

Green, A. G., and D. Green. 1999. 'The Economic Goals of Canada's Immigration Policy.' *Canadian Public Policy* 25: 425–51.

—— 2004. 'The Goals of Canada's Immigration Policy: A Historical Perspective.' *Canadian Journal of Urban Research* 13 (1): 102–39.

Green, F. 2011. 'What is Skill? An Inter-disciplinary Synthesis.' *LLAKES Research Paper.* London: Institute of Education.

Green, S. 2008. *Submission of the Canadian Bar Association to Bill C-50 before the Standing Committee on Citizenship and Immigration.* Ottawa: Parliament of Canada, Standing Committee on Citizenship and Immigration, 12 May 2008: 1105–15.

Grewal, R. 2011. 'Conservative Parm Gill Defeats Ruby Dhalla in Brampton-Springdale.' *The Star*, 3 May 2011. www.thestar.com/news/canada/2011/05/03/conservative_parm_gill_defeats_ruby_dhalla_in_bramptonspringdale.html, accessed 29 June 2015.

Grieco, E. M., and M. Boyd. 1998. *Women and Migration: Incorporating Gender into International Migration Theory*. Florida: Centre for the Study of Population, Florida State University.

Grønbjerg, K. 1993. *Understanding Nonprofit Funding: Managing Revenues in Social Services and Community Development Organizations*. San Francisco: Jossey-Bass.

Grugulis, I., and S. Vincent. 2009. 'Whose Skill is it Anyway? Soft Skills and Polarization.' *Work, Employment and Society* 23 (4): 597–615.

Grugulis, I., C. Warhurst, and E. Keep. 2004. 'What's Happening to "Skill"?' In *The Skills That Matter*, edited by C. Warhurst, E. Keep and I. Grugulis, 1–18. London: Palgrave.

Guiraudon, V. 1997. 'Policy Change Behind Gilded Doors: Explaining the Evolution of Aliens' Rights in Contemporary Western Europe.' Department of Government, Harvard University.

—— 1999. 'European Integration and Policy-Making: The Implications of Vertical Policy-Making.' European Community Studies Association, Pittsburgh, United States, 2–6 June 1999.

—— 2000. 'The Marshallian Triptych: The Role of Courts and Bureaucracy in Furthering Migrants' Social Rights.' In *Immigration and Welfare: Challenging the Borders of the Welfare State*, edited by M. Bommes and A. Geddes, 72–89. London: Routledge.

—— 2003. 'The Constitution of a European Immigration Policy Domain: A Political Sociology Approach.' *Journal of European Public Policy* 10 (2): 263–82.

Habermas, J. 1989. *The Structural Transformation of the Public Sphere: An Inquiry into a Category of Bourgeois Society*. Cambridge, MA: MIT Press.

Hakim, C. 2002. 'Lifestyle Preferences as Determinants of Women's Differentiated Labour Market Careers.' *Work and Occupations* 29: 428–59.

Hall, P., and D. Soskice. 2001. *Varieties of Capitalism: The Institutional Foundation of Comparative Advantage*. Oxford: Oxford University Press.

Halsaa, B. 1998. 'A Strategic Partnership for Women's Policies in Norway.' In *Women's Movements and Public Policy in Europe, Latin America, and the Caribbean*, edited by G. Lycklama a Nijeholt, V. Vargas and S. Wieringa, 167–189. New York: Garland Publishing.

Hand, G. 1992. Gerry Hand, Minister for Immigration, Local Government and Ethnic Affairs, Response to consultations over settlement services, Canberra, 25 February 1992, 7/92. Stored in the ANESBWA files 1985–2000, State Library of NSW, MLMSS 7883, Box 24/31.

Hannan, E. 2013. 'Aussies First: Union Push for More Visa Controls.' *The Australian*, 22 May 2013.

Hardcastle, L., A. Parkin, A. Simmons, and N. Suyama. 1994. 'The Making of Immigration and Refugee Policy: Politicians, Bureaucrats and Citizens.' In

Immigration and Refugee Policy: Australia and Canada Compared, edited by H. Adelman, A. Borowski, M. Burstein and L. Foster, 95–124. Toronto/ Buffalo: Toronto University Press.

Hathaway, J. C. 1994. 'Implementation of a Contexualised System of Family Class Immigration.' *Discussion Paper on the National Consultation on Family Class Immigration*. York University.

Haus, L. 2002. *Unions, Immigration and Internationalization: New Challenges and Changing Conditions in the United States and France*. New York: Palgrave Macmillan.

Hawkins, F. 1989. *Critical Years in Immigration: Australia and Canada Compared*. Ontario: McGill Queen's University Press.

Hawthorne, L. 1996. 'Reversing Past Stereotypes: Skilled NESB Women in Australia.' *Journal of Intercultural Studies* 17 (1–2): 42–52.

––––– 2001. 'The Globalisation of the Nursing Workforce: Barriers Confronting Overseas-Qualified Nurses in Australia.' *Nursing Inquiry* 8 (4): 213–29.

––––– 2005. ' "Picking Winners": The Recent Transformation of Australia's Skilled Migration Policy.' *International Migration Review* 39 (5): 663–96.

–––––2007. *Labour Market Outcomes for Migrant Professionals: Canada and Australian Compared*. Melbourne: University of Melbourne.

––––– 2008a. *The Impact of Economic Selection Policy on Labour Market Outcomes for Degree-Qualified Migrants in Canada and Australia*. Montreal: Institute for Research on Public Policy.

–––––2008b. 'The Race for Talent – Comparing Canada, US and Australia's Approach to Skilled Worker Migration.' Maytree Foundation/Institute for Research on Public Policy, University of Toronto, 26 September 2008.

––––– 2011. *Competing for Skills: Migration Policies and Trends in New Zealand and Australia*. Wellington, New Zealand: Australian Department of Immigration and Citizenship/Department of Labour.

––––– 2014. 'Indian Students and the Evolution of the Study-Migration Pathway in Australia.' *International Migration* 52 (2): 3–19.

Healy, G. 2008. 'Migration Not Helping Skills Shortage.' *The Australian*, 16 October 2008, 4.

Henz, U. 2006. 'Informal Caregiving at Working Age: Effects of Job Characteristics and Family Configuration.' *Journal of Marriage and Family* 67: 222–39.

Hernandez, C. R. 1988. 'The Coalition of Visible Minority Women.' In *Social Movements/ Social Change: The Politics and Practices of Organizing*, edited by F. Cunningham, S. Findlay, M. Kadar, A. Lennon and E. Silva, 157–68. Toronto: Socialist Studies.

Hiebert, D. 1999. 'Local Geographies of Labor Market Segmentation: Montreal, Toronto and Vancouver, 1991.' *Economic Geography* 75 (4): 339–69.

Hind, R. 2014. 'Darwin Region Migration Agreement Won't Hurt Local Workers: Michaelia Cash.' *ABC News*, 12 August 2014. www.abc.net.au/ news/2014-08-12/darwin-specific-migration-agreement/5664488, accessed 24 June 2015.

Hinz, B. 2009. *Many Hopes, One Dream: The Story of the Ethnic Communities' Council of Victoria*. Melbourne: Australian Scholarly Publishing.

—— 2010. 'Ethnic Associations, Networks and the Construction of Australian Multiculturalism.' Canadian Political Science Association Annual Conference, Concordia University, Montreal, 1–3 June 2010.

Hojnacki, M. 1998. 'Organized Interests' Advocacy Behavior in Alliances.' *Political Research Quarterly* 51: 437–59.

Hollifield, J. F. 2000. 'The Politics of International Migration.' In *Migration Theory – Talking Across Disciplines*, edited by C. B. Brettell and J. F. Hollifield, 137–86. London/New York: Routledge.

Hollifield, J. F., V. F. Hunt, and D. Tichenor. 2006. 'Immigrants, Markets, and the American State: The Political Economy of U.S. Immigration.' In *Dialogues on Migration Policy*, edited by M. Giugni and F. Passy, 91–107. Oxford: Lexington Books.

Holly, G. 2009. 'Shifting Political Opportunities and Strategies: The Case of Childcare Advocacy in 2004–2006.' In *The New Federal Policy Agenda and the Voluntary Sector*, edited by R. Laforest, 109–35. Kingston: Queen's University Press.

Howard, R. 1998. 'Minister Agrees with Critics: Robillard Seeks to Cool Immigrant Tempers over Language Proposal.' *The Globe and Mail*, 28 February 1998, A11.

Hubbard, L., and J. C. Tham. 2013. '457 Visa Scheme: Time for a Proper Debate.' *Guardian online*, 17 June 2013.

Hughes, C. 2012. 'Costly Benefits and Gendered Costs: Guatemalans' Experiences of Canada's "Low-Skill Pilot Project".' In *Legislated Inequality: Temporary Labour Migration in Canada*, edited by P. T. Lenard and C. Straehle, 139–57. Montreal: McGill Queen's University Press.

Hunt, V. 2002. 'The Multiple and Changing Goals of Immigration Reform: A Comparison of House and Senate Activity, 1947–1993.' In *Policy Dynamics*, edited by F. R. Baumgartner and B. Jones, 73–95. Chicago/London: University of Chicago Press.

Hurst, D. 2013. 'Employers Must Prove Local Skill Absent Before 457 Go-ahead.' *The Sydney Morning Herald*, 7 June 2013.

Hyndman, J. 1999. 'Gender and Canadian Immigration Policy.' *Canadian Woman Studies* 19 (3): 6–10.

Hynes, K., and M. Clarkberg. 2005. 'Women's Employment Patterns During Early Parenthood: A Group-Based Trajectory Analysis.' *Journal of Marriage and Family* 67: 222–39.

ILO (International Labour Organisation). 2012. *Global Employment Trends for Women*. Geneva: ILO.

ILRAG (Immigration Legislative Review Advisory Group). 1997. *Not Just Numbers: A Canadian Framework for Future Immigration*. Ottawa: Minister of Public Works and Government Services, Canada.

Inglis, C., A. Birch, and G. Sherington. 1994. 'An Overview of Australian and Canadian Migration Patterns and Policies.' In *Immigration and Refugee Policy: Australia and Canada Compared*, edited by H. Adelman, A. Borowski, M. Burstein and L. Foster, 3–30. Toronto/Buffalo: University of Toronto Press.

Intercede. 2000. *The Immigration and Refugee Protection Act Viewed Through Migrant Women's Eyes*. Edited by F. Villasin. Ottawa: Standing Committee on Citizenship and Immigration, Parliament of Canada.

Intercede. 2001. *Summary of Recommendations to Bill C-11, Intercede: For the Rights of Domestic Workers, Caregivers and Newcomers*. Ottawa: Standing Committee on Citizenship and Immigration, Parliament of Canada.

IOM (International Organization of Migration). 2013. *Crushed Hopes: Underemployment and Deskilling among Skilled Migrant Women*. Geneva: IOM.

Iredale, R. 2005. 'Gender, Immigration Policies and Accreditation: Valuing the Skills of Professional Women Migrants.' *Geoforum* 36: 155–66.

Ireland, P. 2004. *Becoming Europe: Immigration, Integration, and the Welfare State*. Pittsburgh, PA: University of Pittsburgh Press.

Jackson, V. C. 2009. 'Citizenships, Federalisms, and Gender.' In *Migrations and Mobilities: Citizenships, Borders, and Gender*, edited by S. Benhabib and J. Resnik, 439–85. New York/London: New York University Press.

Jakubowicz, A. 1981. 'State and Ethnicity: Multiculturalism as Ideology.' *Australian-New Zealand Journal of Sociology* 17 (3): 4–13.

Javed, N. and N. Keung. 2008. 'New Rules to Fast-Track Skilled Immigrants; 38 Job Categories Listed in Bid to Clear Backlog; Critics Say the Move Offers "No Solution".' *The Toronto Star*, 29 November 2008, A27.

Jenkins, D. 1990. 'The Tricky Task of Cutting Immigration.' *Sydney Morning Herald*, 14 May 1990, 17.

Jenson, J., and S. D. Phillips. 1996. 'Regime Shift: New Citizenship Practices in Canada.' *International Journal of Canadian Studies* 14: 111–35.

Jewson, N., and D. Mason. 1986. 'Modes of Discrimination in the Recruitment Process: Formalisation, Fairness and Efficiency.' *Sociology* 20 (1): 43–63.

Jimenez, M. 2004. 'Settlement of Lawsuit Applies Old, Softer Rules to Would-be Immigrants.' *The Globe and Mail*, 20 November 2004, A5.

John, P. 2006. 'Explaining Policy Change: The Impact of the Media, Public Opinion and Political Violence on Urban Budgets in England.' *Journal of European Public Policy* 13 (7): 1053–68.

John, P., and H. Margetts. 2003. 'Policy Punctuations in the UK: Fluctuations and Equilibria in Central Government Expenditure Since 1951.' *Public Administration Review* 81 (3): 411–32.

Joppke, C. 2005. *Selecting by Origin: Ethnic Migration in the Liberal State*. Cambridge, MA/London: Harvard University Press.

Joyce, M. S., and W. A. Schambra. 1996. 'A New Civic Life.' In *Empower the People: From State to Civil Society*, edited by M. Novak, 11–20. Washington, D.C.: AEI Press.

JSCM (Joint Standing Committee on Migration). 2007. *Temporary Visas, Permanent Benefits: Ensuring the Effectiveness, Fairness and Integrity of the Temporary Business Visa Program*. Canberra: The Parliament of the Commonwealth of Australia.

Jupp, J. 2002. 'Ethnicity and Immigration.' In *2001: The Centenary Election*, edited by J. Warhurst and M. Simms, 261–69. St Lucia, Queensland: University of Queensland Press.

Kahanec, M., and K. F. Zimmermann. 2010. 'High-Skilled Immigration Policy in Europe.' *IZA Discussion Paper*. Bonn: Forschungsinstitut zur Zukunft der Arbeit.

Kahn, J. R., J. García-Manglano, and S. M. Bianchi. 2014. 'The Motherhood Penalty at Midlife: Long-term Effects of Children on Women's Careers.' *Journal of Family and Marriage* 76: 56–72.

Kalleberg, A. L., B. F. Reskin, and K. Hudson. 2000. 'Bad Jobs in America: Standard and Nonstandard Employment Relations and Job Quality in the United States.' *American Sociological Review* 65 (2): 256–78.

Kantola, J., and J. Outshoorn. 2007. 'Changing State Feminism.' In *Changing State Feminism*, edited by J. Outshoorn and J. Kantola, 1–19. Houndsmill: Palgrave Macmillan.

Keep, E. 2013. 'Opening the "Black Box" – The Increasing Importance of a Public Policy Focus on What Happens in the Workplace.' In *Skills Development Scotland*, Scottish Funding Council.

Keep, E., and S. James. 2010. 'Recruitment and Selection – the Great Neglected Topic.' Cardiff/Oxford Centre on Skills, Knowledge and Organisational Performance.

Keung, N. 2011. 'Suits Threatened over Immigration Backlog.' *The Toronto Star*, 24 November 2011, A7.

—— 2012. 'Court Asked to Enforce Immigration Delay Deal; Ottawa Accused of Going Against Protocol Reached With Foreign Applicants.' *The Toronto Star*, 30 June 2012, A10.

Khan, S. 2007. Interview with Sunera Thobani: Anti-Racism and the Women's Movement. In *Upping the Anti: A Journal of Theory and Action*. http://uppingtheanti.org/journal/article/05-the-fight-for-feminism, accessed 29 June 2015.

Khoo, S. E., E. Ho, and C. Voigt-Graft. 2008. 'Gendered Migration in Oceania: Trends, Policies and Outcomes.' In *New Perspectives on Gender and Migration*, edited by N. Piper, 101–36. London: Routledge.

Kilkey, M., H. Lutz, and E. Palenga-Möllenbeck. 2010. 'Introduction: Domestic and Care Work at the Intersection of Welfare, Gender and Migration Regimes: European Experiences.' *Social Policy and Society* 9 (3): 379–94.

Kitty, S. 2014. 'Employment Trajectories and Later Employment Outcomes for Mothers in the British Household Panel Survey: An Analysis by Skill Level.' *Journal of Social Policy* 43 (1): 87–108.

Kobayashi, A. 2000. 'Advocacy from the Margins: The Role of Minority Ethnocultural Associations in Affecting Public Policy in Canada.' In *The Nonprofit Sector in Canada: Roles and Relationships*, edited by K. A. Banting, 229–61. Montreal: McGill Queen's University Press.

—— 2008. 'Ethnocultural and Political Mobilization, Multiculturalism and Human Rights in Canada.' In *Group Politics and Social Movements in Canada*, edited by M. Smith, 131–57. Peterborough: Broadview Press.

Kofman, E. 2000. 'The Invisibility of Female Skilled Migrants and Gender Relations in Studies of Skilled Migration in Europe.' *International Journal of Population Geography* 6 (1): 45–59.

—— 2003. 'Skilled International Female Migrants: Migratory Strategies and Settlement Experiences.' Report. *Canadian Faculty Research Program Grant*.

—— 2004. 'Gendered Global Migrations: Diversity and Stratification.' *International Feminist Journal of Politics* 6 (4): 642–64.

—— 2005. 'Gendered Migration: Towards Gender Sensitive Policies in the UK.' *Asylum and Migration Working Paper*, Institute for Public Policy Research, United Kingdom: 13–21, 32–45.

—— 2007. 'The Knowledge Economy, Gender and Stratified Migrations.' *Studies in Social Justice* 1 (2): 30–43.

—— 2013. 'Gender Labour Migrations in Europe and Emblematic Migratory Figures.' *Journal of Ethnic and Migration Studies* 39 (4): 579–600.

—— 2014. 'Towards a Gendered Evaluation of (Highly) Skilled Immigration Policies in Europe.' *International Migration* 52 (3): 116–28.

Kofman, E., S. Likes, A. D'Angelo, and N. Montagna. 2009. 'The Equality Implications of Being a Migrant in Britain.' Equality and Human Rights Commission Research Report.

Kofman, E., and V. Meetoo. 2008. 'Chapter 6: Family Migration.' In *World Migration 2008*, edited by International Organization for Migration (IOM), 151–72. Geneva: IOM.

Kofman, E., and P. Raghuram. 2004. 'Out of Asia: Skilling, Re-skilling and Deskilling of Female Migrants.' *Women's Studies International Forum* 27: 95–100.

Kofman, E. 2006. 'Gender and Global Labour Migration: Incorporating Skilled Workers.' *Antipode* 38 (2): 282–303.

—— 2009. 'Skilled Female Labour Migration.' *Bundeszentrale für politische Bildung* 13 (April).

—— 2012. 'Women, Migration and Care: Explorations of Diversity and Dynamism in the South.' *Social Politics* 19 (3): 408–32.

Kofman, E., P. Raghuram, and M. Merefield. 2005. 'Gendered Migrations: Towards Gender Sensitive Policies in the UK.' Working paper 6 of the 'Asylum and Migration' series.

Koser, K., and J. Salt. 1997. 'The Geography of Highly Skilled International Migration.' *International Journal of Population Geography* 3: 285–303.

Koslowski, R. 2014. 'Selective Migration Policy Models.' *International Migration* 52 (3): 26–39.

Kreimer, M., and H. Schiffbänker. 2005. 'Informal Family-based Care Work in the Austrian Care Arrangement.' In *Care and Social Integration in European Societies*, edited by B. Pfau-Effinger and B. Geissler, 172–94. Bristol: The Policy Press.

Ku, J. 2011. 'Ethnic Activism and Multicultural Politics in Immigrant Settlement in Toronto, Canada.' *Social Identities* 17 (2): 271–89.

Kukoc, K. 2011. 'Key Issues in Skilled Migration to Australia.' In *Australia–Canada Roundtable on Foreign Qualification Recognition*, 13 April 2011.

Lahav, G. 2004. *Immigration and Politics in the New Europe: Reinventing Borders*. Cambridge: Cambridge University Press.

LeMay, M. C. 1989. 'US Immigration Policy and Politics.' In *The Gatekeepers: Comparative Immigration Policy*, edited by M. C. LeMay, 1–22. New York: Praeger.

Lennon, R., D. Sprott, and M. Gatton. 1995. *About Migrant Women: A Statistical Profile*. Canberra: Bureau of Immigration and Population Research.

Lewis, J. 1992. 'Gender and the Development of Welfare Regimes.' *Journal of European Social Policy* 2 (3): 159–73.

——2012. 'Gender Equality and Work-Family Balance in a Cross-National Perspective.' In *Gendered Lives: Gender Inequalities in Production and Reproduction*, edited by J. Scott, S. Dex and A. C. Plagnol, 206–24. Cheltenham: Edward Elgar.

Lewis, J., D. Ben-Galim, and M. Campbell. 2007. 'Equality and Diversity: A New Approach to Gender Equality Policy in the UK.' *International Journal of Law in Context* 3 (1): 19–33.

Li, P. S. 2003. *Destination Canada: Immigration Debates and Issues*. Don Mills, Ontario: Oxford University Press.

Lijphart, A. 1999. *Patterns of Democracy: Government Forms and Performance in Thirty-Six Countries*. New Haven, CT: Yale University Press.

Lipset, S. 1990. *Continental Divide: The Values and Institutions of the United States and Canada*. New York/London: Routledge.

Lipsky, M. 1980. *Street Level Bureaucracy*. New York: Russell Sage Foundation.

Littler, C. 1982. *The Development of the Labour Process in Capitalist Societies*. London: Heinemann.

Liversage, A. 2009. 'Vital Conjunctures, Shifting Horizons: High-skilled Female Immigrants Looking for Work.' *Work, Employment and Society* 23 (1): 120–41.

Lohkamp-Himmighofen, M., and C. Dienel. 2000. 'Reconciliation Policies from a Comparative Perspective.' In *Gendered Policies in Europe: Reconciling Employment and Family Life*, edited by L. Hantrais, 49–67. London: Macmillan Press.

Loretto, W., and S. Vickerstaff. 2011. 'The Relationship between Gender and Age.' In *Managing an Age-Diverse Workforce*, edited by E. Parry and S. Tyson, 59–79. Basingstoke: Palgrave Macmillan.

Lowell, L. 2005. *Policies and Regulations for Managing Skilled International Migration for Work*. New York: United Nations, Mortality and Migration Section, Population Division/DESA.

Lowi, T. 1969. *The End of Liberalism: Ideology, Policy, and the Crisis of Public Authority*. New York: Norton.

MAC (Migration Advisory Committee). 2008. *Skilled, Shortage, Sensible: The Recommended Shortage Occupations Lists for the UK and Scotland*. London: MAC.

Macklin, A. 1992. 'Foreign Domestic Workers: Surrogate Housewife or Mail Order Servant?' *McGill Law Journal* 37 (3): 681–760.

——2002. 'Public Entrance/Private Member.' In *Privatization, Law, and the Challenge to Feminism*, edited by B. Cossman and J. Fudge, 218–64. Toronto: University of Toronto Press.

Maddison, S., and R. Denniss. 2005. 'Democratic Constraint and Embrace: Implications for Progressive Non-government Advocacy Organisations in Australia.' *Australian Journal of Political Science* 40 (3): 374–89.

Maher, S., J. Kelly, A. Burrell, and B. Guest. 2012. 'Now Labor Bungles the Class War: Rinehart Deal Infuriates Unions.' *The Australian*, 26 May 2012, 2.

Mahoney, C. 2008. *Brussels vs. the Beltway: Advocacy in the United States and the European Union*. Washington, D.C.: Georgetown University Press.

Mainland of Nova Scotia Building and Construction Trades Council. 2008. *Submission to the House of Commons Standing Committee on Citizenship and Immigration*,

Re: Temporary Foreign Workers and Undocumented Workers. Ottawa: Standing Committee on Citizenship and Immigration, Parliament of Canada.

Manheim, J. B., R. C. Rich, L. Willnat, and C. L. Brians. 2006. *Empirical Political Analysis: Research Methods in Political Science.* New York: Pearson: Longman.

Mares, P. 2011. 'Internationalisation and a Big Australia: Debates on Migration, Education and Population.' TAFE Directors Australia 2011 National Conference, Sydney.

———2013. '457s and Temporary Migration: The Bigger Picture.' *Inside Story,* 26 June 2013.

Marsden, S. 2010. 'Assessing the Regulation of Temporary Foreign Workers in Canada.' *Osgoode Hall Law Journal* 49: 39–70.

Martin, J. 1991. 'Multiculturalism and Feminism.' In *Intersexions,* edited by D. Bottomley, M. de Lepervanche and J. Martin. Sydney: Allen and Unwin.

Martin, P. L. 1980. *Guestworker Programs: Lessons from Europe,* 110–31. Washington, D.C.: Department of Labor.

Matthews, T. 1997. 'Interest Groups.' In *Politics in Australia,* edited by R. Smith, 269–90. Cambridge: Cambridge University Press.

Matthews, T., and J. Warhurst. 1993. 'Australia: Interest Groups in the Shadow of Strong Political Parties.' In *First World Interest Groups: A Comparative Perspective,* edited by C. S. Thomas, 81–95. Westport, CT: Greenwood Press.

Maurer, A., and R. Parkes. 2007. 'The Prospects for Policy-Change in EU Asylum Policy: Venue and Image at the European Level.' *European Journal of Migration and Law* 9 (2): 173–205.

Mazur, A. 2002. *Theorizing Feminist Public Policy.* Oxford: Oxford University Press.

Mazur, A., and G. Goertz. 2008. 'Introduction.' In *Politics, Gender and Concepts: Theory and Methodology,* edited by G. Goertz and A. Mazur, 1–13. Cambridge: Cambridge University Press.

MCA (Migration Council of Australia). 2013. *More Than Temporary: Australia's 457 Visa Program.* Canberra: MCA.

McAllister, I. 1993. 'Immigration, Bipartisanship and Public Opinion.' In *The Politics of Australian Immigration,* edited by J. Jupp and M. Kabala, 161–78. Canberra: AGPS.

McBride, S. 2000. 'Policy from What? Neoliberal and Human-capital Theoretical Foundations of Recent Canadian Labour-market Policy.' In *Restructuring and Resistance: Canadian Public Policy in an Age of Global Capitalism,* edited by M. Burke, C. Mowers and J. Shields, 159–77. Halifax: Fernwood.

McNamara, T., and E. Shohamy. 2008. 'Language Tests and Human Rights.' *International Journal of Applied Linguistics* 18 (1): 89–95.

McRoberts, K. 1993. 'Federal Structures and the Policy Process.' In *Governing Canada: Institutions and Public Policy,* edited by M. M. Atkinson, 149–78. Toronto: Harcourt Brace Jovanovich, Canada.

Menz, G. 2007. 'Employers, Trade Unions and Labor Migration Policies: Examining the Role of Non-State Actors.' European Unions Studies Association Tenth Biennial Conference, Montreal, Canada, 17 May 2007.

——— 2008. *The Political Economy of Managed Migration: Nonstate Actors, Europeanization, and the Politics of Designing Migration Policies.* Oxford: Oxford University Press.

—— 2010. 'Stopping, Shaping and Moulding Europe: Two-Level Games, Non-state Actors and the Europeanization of Migration Policies.' *Journal of Common Market Studies* 49 (2): 437–62.

Metro (Metro Toronto Chinese and Southeast Asian Legal Clinic). 2000. *Submission to Bill C-31*. Edited by A. Yao-Yao Go. Ottawa: Standing Committee on Citizenship and Immigration, Parliament of Canada.

Metro (Metro Toronto Chinese and Southeast Asian Legal Clinic). 2001. *Submission to the Standing Committee on Citizenship and Immigration, with Respect to Bill C-11*. Ottawa: Standing Committee on Citizenship and Immigration, Parliament of Canada.

Mezey, M. L. 1979. *Comparative Legislatures*. Durham, NC.: Duke University Press.

Millett, M. 1996. 'Migration Shake-up Hits Families.' *Sydney Morning Herald*, 4 July 1996, 1.

—— 1997. 'Migrant Cutback: Families to Suffer; Asian Communities Will Bear the Brunt as Ruddock Slashes Places Reserved for Parents from 6,000 to 1,000.' *Sydney Morning Herald*, 22 May 1997, 4.

Mincer, J., and H. Olec. 1982. 'Interrupted Work Careers: Depreciation and Restoration of Human Capital.' *Journal of Human Resources* 17: 3–24.

Mincer, J., and S. Polachek. 1974. 'Family Investments in Human Capital: Earnings of Women.' *Journal of Political Economy* 82 (2): 76–108.

Mojab, S. 1999. 'De-skilling Immigrant Women.' *Canadian Woman Studies* 19 (3): 123–8.

Moriarty, J. 2010. 'Competing with Myths: Migrant Labour in Social Care.' In *Who Needs Migrant Workers? Labour Shortages, Immigration, and Public Policy*, edited by M. Ruhs and B. Anderson. Oxford: Oxford University Press.

Mortensen, P. B. 2007. 'Stability and Change in Public Policy: A Longitudinal Study of Comparative Subsystem Dynamics.' *Policy Studies Journal* 35 (3): 373–94.

Moss, P., and C. Tilly. 1996. ' "Soft" Skills and Race: An Investigation of Black Men's Employment Problems.' *Work and Occupations* 23 (3): 252–76.

NAC (National Action Committee on the Status of Women). 2001. *Submission to Bill C-11*. Ottawa: Ottawa: Standing Committee on Citizenship and Immigration, Parliament of Canada.

NAC (National Action Committee on the Status of Women). 2002. *Submission to the Regulations to the Immigration and Refugee Protection Act*. Ottawa: Standing Committee on Citizenship and Immigration, Parliament of Canada.

Nakache, D., and S. D'Aoust. 2012. *Provincial/Territorial Nominee Programs: An Avenue to Permanent Residency for Low-Skilled Temporary Foreign Workers, Legislated Inequality: Temporary Labour Migration in Canada*. Montreal: McGill Queen's University Press.

Nakache, D., and P. J. Kinoshita. 2010. *The Canadian Temporary Foreign Worker Program: Do Short-Term Economic Needs Prevail over Human Rights Concerns?* Montreal: IPPR.

NAWL (National Association of Women and the Law). 1999. Gender Analysis of Immigration and Refugee Protection Legislation and Policy. Submitted to Citizenship and Immigration Canada. Ottawa, provided to author.

NAWL (National Association of Women and the Law). 2000. Brief on the proposed immigration and refugee act, Bill C-31. Ottawa, Standing Committee on Citizenship and Immigration, Parliament of Canada, filed in National Archives of Canada, Ottawa, RG14, BAN 2004-01584-5, Box 6, Wallet 7.

NAWL (National Association of Women and the Law). 2001. National Association of Women and the Law Brief on the Proposed Refugee and Immigration Protection Act (Bill C-11). Submitted to the Standing Committee on Citizenship and Immigration, Filed in the National Archives of Canada, Ottawa, RG14, BAN 2007-00060-1, Box 17, Wallet 3.

NAWL (National Association of Women and the Law). 2002. *Submission to the Regulations to the Immigration and Refugee Protection Act before the Standing Committee on Citizenship and Immigration.* Edited by C. Tie, S. Aiken and A. Cote. Ottawa: Standing Committee on Citizenship and Immigration, Parliament of Canada.

NCCC (National Congress of Chinese Canadians). 2002. *Submission to the Standing Committee on Citizenship and Immigration on the Regulations to the Immigration and Refugee Protection Act.* Ottawa: Standing Committee on Citizenship and Immigration, Parliament of Canada.

Ndiaye, N. 2006. 'Overview: Situation and Contributions of Migrant Women.' In *Female Migrants: Bridging the Gaps Throughout the Life Cycle, Selected Papers of the UNFPA-IOM Expert Group Meeting, 2–3 May 2006,* 15–22. New York.

Needham, K. 2011. 'Quick Fix for Skills Shortage.' *The Sydney Morning Herald,* 11 May 2011, 7.

Newman, M. A., and L. White. 2006. *Women, Politics and Public Policy: The Political Struggles of Canadian Women.* Don Mills, Ontario: Oxford University Press.

Nickson, D., and C. Warhurst. 2001. *Looking Good, Sounding Right.* London: Industrial Society.

Nishikawa, M. 2011. '(Re)defining Care Workers as Knowledge Workers.' *Gender, Work and Organisation* 18 (1): 113–36.

NOIVMWC (National Organisation of Immigrant and Visible Minority Women of Canada). 2002. *Submission to the Regulations to the Immigration and Refugee Protection Act.* Ottawa: Standing Committee on Citizenship and Immigration, Parliament of Canada.

Nova Scotia Federation of Labour. 2008. *Presentation to the House of Commons Standing Committee on Immigration.* Ottawa: Standing Committee on Citizenship and Immigration, Parliament of Canada.

O'Connor, J. S., A. Orloff, and S. Shaver. 1999. *States, Markets and Families: Gender, Liberalism and Social Policy in Australia, Canada, Great Britain and the United States.* Cambridge: Cambridge University Press.

O'Malley, N. 2006. 'Foreign Meat Workers Caught up in Visa Row.' *Sydney Morning Herald,* 14 December 2006.

O'Neil, D. A., M. M. Hopkins, and D. Bilimoria. 2008. 'Women's Careers at the Start of the 21st Century: Patterns and Paradoxes.' *Journal of Business Ethics* 80 (4): 727–43.

OCASI (Ontario Council of Agencies Serving Immigrants). 1999. *OCASI Annual Report 1999,* Ontario Council of Agencies Serving Immigrants, 1978–1999, Toronto, Canada. Available at www.ocasi.org, accessed 19 April 2010.

OCASI (Ontario Council of Agencies Serving Immigrants). 2006. *OCASI Annual Report 2006*, Ontario Council of Agencies Serving Immigrants, 1978–1999, Toronto, Canada. Available at www.ocasi.org, accessed 19 April 2010.

OCASI (Ontario Council of Agencies Serving Immigrants). 2009. OCASI Deputation on Changes to IRPA under Bill C-50. Toronto. www.ocasi.org/index.php?qid=967, accessed 16 April 2009.

OECD (Organisation of Economic Co-operation and Development). 1998. *SOPEMI 1997 Annual Report (Trends in International Migration)*. Paris: OECD.

OECD (Organisation of Economic Co-operation and Development). 1999. *SOPEMI 1998 Annual Report (Trends in International Migration)*. Paris: OECD.

OECD (Organisation of Economic Co-operation and Development). 2006. *SOPEMI 2005 Annual Report (Trends in International Migration)*. Paris: OECD.

OECD (Organisation of Economic Co-operation and Development). 2008. 'Part-time Employment as Percentage of Employment, Male and Female.' In *Labour Force Statistics 1987–2007*. Paris: OECD.

OECD (Organisation of Economic Co-operation and Development). 2011a. 'Gender Analysis and Regulatory Impact Analysis.' Document prepared by the DAC Network on Poverty Reduction (POVNET). Paris: OECD.

OECD (Organisation of Economic Co-operation and Development). 2011b. *International Migration Outlook 2011*. Paris: OECD.

OECD (Organisation of Economic Co-operation and Development). 2011c. Survey on Gender Analysis and Regulatory Impact Assessments. Survey conducted by the OECD on countries' regulatory management systems. Paris: OECD.

OECD (Organisation of Economic Co-operation and Development). 2012a. *Closing the Gap: Act Now*. Paris: OECD.

OECD (Organisation of Economic Co-operation and Development). 2012b. *International Migration Outlook 2012*. Paris: OECD.

OECD (Organisation of Economic Co-operation and Development). 2013. *International Migration Outlook 2013*. Paris: OECD.

Office of the Fairness Commissioner. 2012. *Citizenship and Immigration Canada – Proposed Regulations Amending the Immigration and Refugee Protection Regulations*. Toronto: Office of the Fairness Commissioner.

Olasky, M. N. 1992. *The Tragedy of American Compassion*. Washington, D.C.: Regnery Gateway.

Oliver, E. A. 2009. 'Promoting Women? Lessons Learned from a Study of Mobility and Fixed-Term Work in Early Career Researchers.' In *Gender and Migration in 21st Century Europe*, edited by H. Stalford, S. Currie and S. Velluti, 63–84. Farnham: Ashgate.

Onyx, J., B. Dalton, R. Melville, J. Casey, and R. Banks. 2008. 'Implications of Government Funding of Advocacy for Third-Sector Independence and Exploration of Alternative Advocacy Funding Models.' *Australian Journal of Social Issues* 43 (4): 638–48.

OSCE (Organisation for Security and Co-operation in Europe). 2009. *Guide on Gender-Sensitive Labour Migration Policies*. Vienna: Organisation for Security and Co-operation in Europe Secretariat.

Pal, L. 1993. *Interests of State: The Politics of Language, Multiculturalism, and Feminism in Canada.* Montreal: McGill Queen's University Press.

Pal, L., and R. K. Weaver. 2003. 'The Politics of Pain.' In *The Government Taketh Away: The Politics of Pain in the United States and Canada,* edited by L. Pal and R. K. Weaver. Washington, D.C.: Georgetown University Press.

Palmer, E., and J. Eveline. 2012. 'Sustaining Low Pay in Aged Care Work.' *Gender, Work and Organisation* 19 (3): 254–75.

Papademetriou, D. G. 2008. Selecting Economic Stream Immigrants through Points Systems. *Migration Information Source,* May 2007. Accessed 3 December 2008.

Papademetriou, D. G., W. Somerville, and H. Tanaka. 2008. *Hybrid Immigrant-Selection Systems: The Next Generation of Economic Migration Systems.* Washington, D.C.: Migration Policy Institute.

Parkdale Community Legal Centre. 2008. *Submission to the Standing Committee on Citizenship and Immigration with respect to undocumented workers and temporary foreign workers, immigration consultants, and proposed changes to IRPA under Bill C-50.* Toronto: Standing Committee on Citizenship and Immigration, Parliament of Canada.

Parliament of the Commonwealth of Australia, House of Representatives. 2013. *Votes and Proceedings over the Protecting Local Jobs (Regulating Enterprise Migration Agreements) Bill 2012.* Canberra: Parliament of the Commonwealth of Australia, House of Representatives.

Passaris, C. E. A. 1984. 'The Economic Determinants of Canada's Multicultural Immigration.' *International Migration Review* 22 (2): 90–100.

Payne, J. 2009. 'Emotional Labour and Skill: A Reappraisal.' *Gender, Work and Organisation* 16 (3): 348–67.

Peck, J. 1996. *Work Place: The Social Regulation of Labor Markets.* New York: Guilford.

Penner, E., K. Blidook, and S. Soroka. 2006. 'Legislative Priorities and Public Opinion: Representation of Partisan Agendas in the Canadian House of Commons.' *Journal of European Public Policy* 13 (7): 1006–20.

Perrenas, R. S. 2000. 'Migrant Filipina Domestic Workers and the International Division of Reproductive Labor.' *Gender and Society* 14 (4): 560–80.

Phelps, E. 1972. 'The Statistical Theory of Racism and Sexism.' *American Economic Review* 62 (4): 659–61.

Phillips, A., and B. Taylor. 1980. 'Sex and Skill: Notes towards a Feminist Economics.' *Feminist Review* 6: 79–88.

Phillips, J., and H. Spinks. 2012. *Skilled Migration: Temporary and Permanent Flows to Australia.* Canberra: Parliament of Australia, Social Policy Section.

Phillips, S. D. 1996. 'Discourse, Identity, and Voice: Feminist Contributions to Policy Studies.' In *Policy Studies in Canada: The State of the Art,* edited by L. Dobuzinskis, M. Howlett and D. Laycock, 242–4. Toronto: University of Toronto Press.

Phillips, S. D., R. Laforest, and A. Graham. 2010. 'From Shopping to Social Innovation: Getting Public Financing Right in Canada.' *Policy and Society* 29: 189–99.

Pierson, P. 2004. *Politics in Time: History, Institutions and Social Analysis.* Princeton/Oxford: Princeton University Press.

—— 2006. 'The New Politics of the Welfare State.' In *Comparative Politics: Critical Concepts in Political Science*, edited by H. J. Wiarda, 107–40. London/New York: Routledge.

Pillinger, J. 2006. *Introduction to the Situation and Experience of Women Migrant Workers in Ireland*. Dublin: Equality Authority.

—— 2007. *The Feminisation of Migration: Experiences and Opportunities in Ireland*. Dublin: Immigrant Council of Ireland.

PINAY. 2008. 'Warning! Domestic Work Can Be Dangerous to Your Status, Health, Safety and Wallet!' Report on the findings of a community-based survey on the work conditions of Montreal domestic workers. Laselle, Quebec: PINAY.

Piper, N. 2006. 'Gendering the Politics of Migration.' *International Migration Review* 40 (1): 133–64.

—— 2008. 'International Migration and Gendered Axes of Stratification – Introduction.' In *New Perspectives on Gender and Migration – Rights, Entitlements and Livelihoods*, edited by N. Piper, 1–18. London: Routledge.

Piper, N., and K. Yamanaka. 2008. 'Feminised Migration in East and Southeast Asia and the Securing of Livelihoods.' In *New Perspectives on Gender and Migration: Livelihoods, Rights and Entitlements*, edited by N. Piper, 159–88. London: Routledge.

Polachek, S. 1981. 'Occupational Self-Selection: A Human Capital Approach to Sex Differences.' *The Review of Economics and Statistics* 63 (1): 60–9.

Pralle, S. 2006a. 'The "Mouse that Roared": Agenda Setting in Canadian Pesticides Politics.' *Policy Studies Journal* 34 (2): 171–94.

——2006b. 'Timing and Sequence in Agenda Setting and Policy Change: A Comparative Study of Lawn Care Pesticide Politics in Canada and the US.' *Journal of European Politics* 13 (7): 987–1005.

—— 2007. *Branching Out, Digging In: Environmental Advocacy and Agenda Setting*. Washington, D.C.: Georgetown University Press.

—— 2010. 'Shopping Around: Environmental Organizations and the Search for Policy Venues.' In *Advocacy Organizations and Collective Action*, edited by A. Prakash and M. K. Gugerty, 177–291. New York: Cambridge University Press.

Pratt, G. 2004. *Working Feminism*. Edinburgh: Edinburgh University Press.

Presthus, R. V. 1973. *Elite Accommodation in Canadian Politics*. Toronto: Macmillan of Canada.

Princen, S. 2007. 'Agenda-setting in the European Union: A Theoretical Exploration and Agenda for Research.' *Journal of European Public Policy* 14 (1): 21–38.

Pross, A. P. 1993. 'The Mirror of the State: Canada's Interest Group System.' In *First World Interest Groups: A Comparative Perspective*, edited by C. S. Thomas, 67–79. Westport, CT: Greenwood Press.

Purcell, K., P. Elias, and N. Wilton. 2006. 'Looking through the Glass Ceiling: A Detailed Investigation of Factors that Contribute to Gendered Career Inequalities.' Warwick Institute for Employment Research, Warwick University.

Purkayastha, B. 2005. 'Skilled Migration and Cumulative Disadvantage: The Case of Highly Qualified Asian Indian Immigrant Women in the US.' *Geoforum* 36: 181–96.

PWCDC (Philippine Women Centre of British Columbia). 2001. *Submission to Bill C-11*. Ottawa: Standing Committee on Citizenship and Immigration, Parliament of Canada, Filed in the National Archives of Canada, Ottawa, RG14, BAN 2007-00060-1, Box 17, Wallet 3.

Quash, E. 2009. *Submission before the Standing Committee on Citizenship and Immigration Investigation into the Live-in Caregiver Program*. Ottawa: Standing Committee on Citizenship and Immigration, 14 May 2009: 0920.

Rafaeli, A., and R. I. Sutton. 1987. 'The Expression of Emotion as Part of the Work Role.' *Academy of Management Review* 12 (1): 23–37.

Raghuram, P. 2008. 'Migrant Women in Male-Dominated Sectors of the Labour Market: A Research Agenda.' *Population, Space and Place* 14: 43–57.

Rankin, J. 1994. 'Immigration Cuts Slammed, Reform Party's Claims Dismissed by Protesters.' *Toronto Star*, 6 November 1994, A12.

Ray, R. 1988a. *Ministerial Statement Made to the Senate*. Canberra: Senate, 8 December 1988, 3753.

—— 1988b. Minister for Immigration, Local Government and Ethnic Affairs, Robert Ray. *Migration Legislation Amendment Bill 1989*, Senate Hansard. Canberra: Parliament of Australia, 30 May 1989.

Rees, T. 2005. 'Reflections on the Uneven Development of Gender Mainstreaming in Europe.' *International Feminist Journal of Politics* 7(4): 555–74.

Reitz, J. 2012. 'The Distinctiveness of Canadian Immigration Experience.' *Patterns of Prejudice* 46 (5): 518–38.

Rhodes, R. A. W., J. Wanna, and J. Weller. 2009. *Comparing Westminster*. Oxford: Oxford University Press.

Richards, D. 1996. 'Elite Interviewing: Approaches and Pitfalls.' *Politics* 16 (3): 199–204.

Richardson, J., and L. Lester. 2004. *A Comparison of Australian and Canadian Immigration Policies and Labour Market Outcomes*. Adelaide: The National Institute of Labour Studies, Flinders University.

Richardson, S., S. Stack, L. Lester, J. Healy, D. Ilsley, and J. Horrocks. 2004. *The Changing Labour Force Experience of New Migrants: Inter-Wave Comparisons for Cohort 1 and 2 of the LSIA*. Adelaide: National Institute of Labour Studies, Flinders University.

Riker, W. H. 1993. 'Federalism.' In *A Companion to Contemporary Political Philosophy*, edited by G. Goodin and P. Pettit, 508–14. Oxford: Blackwell.

Roach, N. 1995. *Committee of Inquiry into the Temporary Entry of Business People and Highly Skilled Specialists*. Canberra: Australian Govt. Pub. Service.

Rubenstein, C. 1993. 'Immigration and the Liberal Party in Australia.' In *The Politics of Australian Immigration*, edited by J. Jupp and M. Kabala, 144–60. Canberra: Australian Government Publishing.

Ruddick, E., and M. Burstein. 1993. 'New Directions for the Management of the Canadian Immigration Program.' *People and Place* 1 (4): 24–9.

Ruddock, P. 1996a. 'Migration Program Revamped to Benefit Australia.' Media release.

—— 1996b. Questions without Notice, Migration, Skills Category. Canberra: House of Representatives, 11 December 1996, 8251.

————— 1997. Letter from Minister for Immigration and Multicultural Affairs, Philip Ruddock to Sevgi Kilic, Chair of the Association of Non-English Background Women of Australia, Canberra to Sydney, dated 19 May 1997, provided to author by former member of ANESBWA.

————— 1998. 'Government to Maintain Balanced Migration (Non-humanitarian) Program.' Media Centre, Media release. Press statement 36/98.

————— 1999. '1999–2000 Migration (Non-humanitarian) Program.' Media Centre, Media release. Press statement 62/99.

————— 2002. 'Minister Announces 2002–03 Migration (Non-humanitarian) Program.' Media Centre, Media release. Press statement MPS 30/200.

Ruhs, M. 2011. *Openness, Skills and Rights: An Empirical Analysis of Labour Immigration Programs in 46 High and Middle Income Countries.* Oxford: COMPAS.

————— 2013. *The Price of Rights: Regulating International Labor Migration.* Princeton: Princeton University Press.

Ruhs, M., and B. Anderson. 2010. 'Migrant Workers: Who Needs Them? A Framework for the Analysis of Staff Shortages, Immigration, and Public Policy.' In *Who Needs Migrant Workers? Labour Shortages, Immigration and Public Policy*, 1–47. Oxford: Oxford University Press.

Sabelis, I., and E. Schilling. 2013. 'Editorial: Frayed Careers: Exploring Rhythms of Working Lives.' *Gender, Work & Organization* 20: 127–32.

Sarick, L. 1994. 'Marchi's Immigration Shift Criticized: Minister's New Targets May Hurt Family Reunification, Conference Told.' *The Globe and Mail*, 14 September 1994, A2.

Sawer, M. 1990. *Sisters in Suits: Women and Public Policy in Australia.* Sydney: Allen and Unwin.

————— 1991. 'Why Has the Australian Women's Movement Had More Impact on Government in Australia than Elsewhere?' In *Australia Compared*, edited by F. C. Castles, 258–278. Sydney: Allen and Unwin.

————— 1996. *Femocrats and Ecorats: Women's Political Machinery in Australia, Canada and New Zealand.* Geneva: United Nations Research Institute for Social Development.

————— 2002. 'Governing for the Mainstream: Implications for Community Representation.' *Australian Journal of Public Administration* 61 (1): 39–49.

————— 2006. 'From Women's Interests to Special Interests: Reframing Equality Claims.' In *The Politics of Women's Interests: New Comparative Perspectives*, edited by L. Chappell and D. K. Hill, 111–29. New York: Routledge.

————— 2008. 'Framing Feminists: Market Populism and Its Impact on Public Policy in Australia and Canada.' In *Gendering the Nation-State: Canadian and Comparative Perspectives*, edited by Y. Abu-Laban, 120–38. Vancouver: UBC Press.

————— 2010. *FaHCSIA Gender Assessment Project.* Canberra: FaHCSIA.

————— 2012. 'A Voice for the Voiceless, Coopted Constituencies or Unaccountable Rent-seekers? Advocacy Organisations and Democratic Representation in Australia and Canada.' Bell Chair in Canadian Parliamentary Democracy Lecture, 27 September 2013. Ottawa: Carleton University.

Sawer, M., and J. Vickers. 2001. 'Women's Constitutional Activism in Australia and Canada.' *Canadian Journal of Women and the Law* 13 (1): 1–36.

Schaafsma, J., and A. Sweetman. 2001. 'Immigrant Earnings: Age at Immigration Matters.' *Canadian Journal of Economics* 34 (4): 1066–99.

Schlozman, K. L., and J. T. Tierney. 1986. *Organised Interests and American Democracy*. New York: Harper and Row.

Schmitz, C. 2013. 'Immigration Backlog Battle Is Not Over Yet, Galati Vows.' *The Lawyers Weekly*, 3 May 2013.

Schneider, K. 2013. 'Canada Immigration Minister Jason Kenney Calls for Tighter Rules, Higher Standards for Foreign Workers.' *Calgary Sun*, 20 April 2013.

Seccombe, M. 1988. '12,000 Added to Migrant Numbers.' *The Sydney Morning Herald*, 7 April 1988, 3.

Shachar, A. 2006. 'The Race for Talent: Highly Skilled Migrants and Competitive Immigration Regimes.' *New York University Law Review* 81: 148–206.

Sharma, N. 2006. *Home Economics: Nationalism and the Making of 'Migrant Workers' in Canada*. Toronto: Toronto University Press.

Sharman, C. 1999. 'The Representation of Small Parties and Independents in the Senate.' *Australian Journal of Political Science* 34 (3): 353–61.

Simeon, R. 1972. *Federal-Provincial Diplomacy: The Making of Recent Policy in Canada*. Toronto: University of Toronto Press.

Simmons, A. B., and K. Keohane. 1992. 'Canadian Immigration Policy: State Strategies and the Quest for Legitimacy.' *Canadian Review of Sociology and Anthropology* 29 (4): 421–52.

Sirianni, C., and C. Negrey. 2000. 'Working Time as Gendered Time.' *Feminist Economics* 6 (1): 59–76.

Sloan, J. 2012. 'EMAs Essential for Resource Project Viability.' *The Australian*, 28 May 2012, 6.

Smith, M. 2005. 'Institutionalism in the Study of Canadian Politics: The English-Canadian Tradition.' In *New Institutionalism: Theory and Analysis*, edited by A. Lecours, 101–27. Toronto: University of Toronto Press.

——— 2009. 'Analysis Note: Gender Equality on the Labour Market: Challenges in the EU after 2010.' In *EGGE – European Network of Experts on Employment and Gender Equality Issues*. Fondazione Giacomo Brodolini.

Smith, R. A. 1984. 'Advocacy, Interpretation and Influence in the U.S. Congress.' *American Political Science Review* 78: 44–63.

Sossin, L. 2008. 'Access to Administrative Justice and Other Worries.' In *Administrative Law in Context*, edited by C. M. Flood and L. Sossin, 391–409. Toronto: Emond Montgomery Publications.

Sparrow, A. (2008). 'Points-based Immigration System Comes into Effect.' *The Guardian*, 29 February 2008.

Spencer, S., S. Martin, I. L. Bourgeault, and E. O'Shea. 2010. 'The Role of Migrant Care Workers in Ageing Societies: Report on Research Findings in the United Kingdom, Ireland, Canada and the United States.' *IOM Migration Research Series*. Geneva: International Organization for Migration.

Squires, J. 2007. *The New Politics of Gender Equality*. Houndsmill, Basingstoke: Palgrave Macmillan.

Standing Committee on Citizenship and Immigration. 1995. Report: Economic Impact of Recent Immigration, First report of the Sub-Committee on Diminishing Returns, Eighth Report of the Standing Committee on Citizenship and Immigration, November 1995, Issue No. 51, 2 November 1995.

Standing Committee on Citizenship and Immigration. 2002. *Building a Nation: The Regulations under the Immigration and Refugee Protection Act*. Ottawa: Standing Committee on Citizenship and Immigration.

Standing Committee on Citizenship and Immigration. 2009a. *Migrant Workers and Ghost Consultants: Report of the Standing Committee on Citizenship and Immigration*. 40th Parliament, 2nd Session. Ottawa: Parliament of Canada.

Standing Committee on Citizenship and Immigration. 2009b. *Temporary Foreign Workers and Non-Status Workers: Report of the Standing Committee on Citizenship and Immigration*. 40th Parliament, 2nd Session. Ottawa: Parliament of Canada.

Standing Committee on Citizenship and Immigration. 2012. *Cutting the Queue: Reducing Canada's Immigration Backlogs and Wait Times*. Ottawa: Parliament of Canada.

Steiber, N., and B. Haas. 2012. 'Advances in Explaining Women's Employment Patterns.' *Socio-Economic Review* 10 (2): 343–67.

Steinberg, R. J. 1990. 'Social Construction of Skill: Gender, Power, and Comparable Worth.' *Work and Occupations* 17 (4): 449–82.

Steinberg, R. J., and D. M. Figart. 1999. 'Emotional Labor since the Managed Heart.' *Annals of the American Journal of Political and Social Science* 561 (1): 8–26.

Stetson, D. 2001. *Abortion Politics, Women's Movements, and the Democratic State: A Comparative Study of State Feminism*. New York: Oxford University Press.

Stetson, D., and A. Mazur. 1995. *Comparative State Feminism*. Thousand Oaks, CA: Sage.

Studlar, D. T. 2007. 'Ideas, Institutions, and Diffusion: What Explains Tobacco Control Policy in Australia, Canada, and New Zealand.' *Commonwealth and Comparative Politics* 45 (2): 164–84.

Sturdy, A., D. Knights, and H. Willmott. 1992. *Skill and Consent: Contemporary Studies in the Labour Process*. London/New York: Routledge.

SWC (Status of Women Canada). 2000. Descriptive list of approved grants and contributions provided through the Women's Program, Status of Women Canada, 1 April 1999 to 31 March 2000. Ottawa: SWC.

Swers, M. 2002. *The Difference Women Make: The Policy Impact of Women in Congress*. Chicago: University of Chicago Press.

Sweetman, A., and C. Warman. 2010. 'A New Source of Immigration: The Canadian Experience Class.' *Policy Options* (July–August): 58–61.

Swirski, B. 2011. Adva Center Information on Equality and Social Justice in Israel, Gender Mainstreaming Calls for Gender Breakdowns: Case Study. *Israeli Ministry of Industry, Trade and Labour*.

Symons, E. K. 2006. 'Welcome Up to a Point.' *The Australian*, 3 June 2006, 27.

Tancred, P. 1995. 'Women's Work: A Challenge to the Sociology of Work.' *Gender, Work and Organisation* 2 (1): 11–17.

Tansey, O. 2007. 'Process Tracing and Elite Interviewing: A Case for Non-probability Sampling.' *Political Science & Politics* 40: 765–72.

Tarrow, S. 1994. *Power in Movement: Social Movements, Collective Action and Politics.* Cambridge: Cambridge University Press.

Tattersall, A. 2010. *Power in Coalition: Strategies in Strong Unions and Social Change.* Ithaca, NY: Cornell University Press.

Taylor, L. 2012. 'Some Facts on Roy Hill Deal, but Lots of Secrecy.' *Sydney Morning Herald*, 30 May 2012. www.smh.com.au/federal-politics/political-opinion/some-facts-on-roy-hill-deal-but-lots-of-secrecy-20120529-1zhfp.html, accessed 29 June 2015.

Teghtsoonian, K. 2005. 'Gendering Policy Analysis in the Government of British Columbia: Strategies, Possibilities and Constraints.' *Studies in Political Economy* 61: 105–27.

Teitelbaum, M. S., and J. Winter. 1998. *A Question of Numbers: High Migration, Low Fertility and the Politics of National Identity.* New York: Hill & Wang.

Tham, J. C. 2012. '457 Reasons for Reform.' *The Age*, 29 May 2012.

Tham, J. C., and I. Campbell. 2011. *Temporary Migrant Labour in Australia: The 457 Visa Scheme and Challenges for Labour Regulation.* Melbourne: Centre for Employment and Labour Relations Law, University of Melbourne.

Thelen, K. 2002. 'The Political Economy of Business and Labor in the Developed Democracies.' In *The State of the Discipline*, edited by H. I. Milner and I. Katznelson, 371–97. New York: W. W. Norton.

Thobani, S. 2007. *Exalted Subjects: Studies in the Making of Race and Nation in Canada.* Toronto: University of Toronto Press.

Thomas, C. S. 2006. 'Understanding and Comparing Interest Groups in Western Democracies.' In *Comparative Politics: Critical Concepts in Political Science*, edited by H. J. Wiarda, 143–66. New York/London: Routledge.

Thomas, P. 2009. 'Parliamentary Scrutiny of Government Performance in Australia.' *Australian Journal of Public Administration* 68 (3): 373–98.

Thompson, A. 2002. 'MPs Plan to Revolt over Entry Proposals.' *Toronto Star*, 29 January 2002, 17.

——— (2001). 'We Need the Brightest, Best.' *Toronto Star*, 20 December 2001: A01.

Thompson, F., and W. T. Stanbury. 1979. 'The Political Economy of Interest Groups in the Legislative Process in Canada.' Occasional Paper No. 9. Montreal: Institute for Research on Public Policy.

Thorvaldsdóttir, T., and T. Einarsdóttir. 2006. 'Equality Discourses at Crossroads. Gender Equality vs. Diversity.' 6th European Gender Research Conference. Gender and Citizenship in Multicultural Context. University of Lodz, Poland, 31 August–3 September 2006.

Tichenor, D. 2002. *Dividing Lines: The Politics of Immigration Control in America.* Princeton: Princeton University Press.

Timmermans, A. 2001. 'Arenas as Institutional Sites for Policymaking: Patterns and Effects in Comparative Perspective.' *Journal of Comparative Policy Analysis* 3: 311–37.

Timmermans, A., and P. Scholten. 2006. 'The Political Flow of Wisdom: Science Institutions as Policy Venues in The Netherlands.' *Journal of European Public Policy* 13 (7): 1104–18.

Tocqueville, A., de. [1835] 1945. *Democracy in America*. New York: A. A. Knopf.

Togman, J. 2002. *The Ramparts of Nations: Institutions and Immigration Policies in France and the United States*. Westport, CT: Praeger.

Tong, R. 1989. *Feminist Thought: A Comprehensive Introduction*. Boulder, CT: Westview Press.

Triadafilopoulos, T. 2013. *Wanted and Welcome? Policies for Highly Skilled Immigrants in Comparative Perspective, Immigrants and Minorities: Politics and Policy*. Berlin: Springer Verlag.

Trister, B. 2002. *Submission of the Chair, Immigration Law and Policy Taskforce, Canadian Chamber of Commerce. Standing Committee of Citizenship and Immigration*. Ottawa: Parliament of Canada.

Truss, C., E. Conway, A. d'Amato, G. Kelly, K. Monks, E. Hannon, and P. C. Flood. 2012. 'Knowledge Work: Gender-blind or Gender-biased?' *Work, Employment and Society* 26 (5): 735–54.

Tsebelis, G. 2000. 'Veto Players and Institutional Analysis.' *Governance: An International Journal of Policy and Administration* 14 (4): 441–74.

TWAG (Temporary Workers Advocacy Group). 2009. *Final Outcomes: TWAG Meeting*. Provided to author by Karl Flecker, CLC.

UCC (Ukrainian Canadian Congress). 2002. *Submission on the Regulations to the Immigration Refugee Protection Act*. Standing Committee on Citizenship and Immigration, Parliament of Canada, Ottawa, Filed in the National Archives of Canada, Ottawa, RG14, BAN 2007-000060-1, FA14, Box 18, Wallet 5.

UDI (Utlendingsdirektoratet). 2013. 'Norwegian Directorate of Immigration Statistics.' www.udi.no/Norwegian-Directorate-of-Immigration/Oversiktsider/statistics/, accessed 13 August 2013.

UNDESA (United Nations Department of Economic and Social Affairs). 2010. *The World's Women 2010: Trends and Statistics*. New York: UNDESA.

UNDESA (United Nations Department of Economic and Social Affairs). 2012. *World Population Prospects: The 2012 Revision*. New York: UNDESA.

United Kingdom Border Agency. 2011. *Tier 2 Shortage List – Government-approved Version*. London: UKBA.

United Kingdom Border Agency. 2013. *Tier 2 (General) English Language*. London: UKBA.

United Kingdom Home Office. 2002. *Secure Borders, Safe Havens, Integration with Diversity in Modern Britain*. London: Home Office.United Nations. 1994. *The Migration of Women: Methodological Issues in the Measurement and Analysis of Internal and International Migration*. San Domingo, Dominican Republic: International Research and Training Institute for the Advancement of Women.

United Kingdom Home Office. 2002. *Further Actions and Initiatives to Implement the Beijing Declaration and Platform for Action*. New York: UN.

United States Senate. 2013. *The Border Security, Economic Opportunity, and Immigration Modernization Act*. Washington, D.C.: United States Senate.

Van Rijn, N. 2003. 'Court Rejects Change in Entry Rules.' *Toronto Star*, 22 February 2003, A04.

Vanderklippe, N. 2011. 'Gearing Up for a New Labour Crunch.' *The Globe and Mail*, 22 May 2011.

Vargas, V., and S. Wieringa. 1998. 'The Triangles of Empowerment: Processes and Actors in the Making of Public Policy.' In *Women's Movements and Public Policy in Europe, Latin America, and the Caribbean*, edited by G. Lycklama a Nijeholt, V. Vargas and S. Wieringa, 3–23. New York: Garland.

Vasta, E. 1992. 'Immigrant Women and the Politics of Resistance.' The Politics of Speaking Out, Immigrant Women Ten Years On conference, Granville, NSW.

Velasco, P. 2009. *Submission before the Standing Committee on Citizenship and Immigration Investigation into the Live-in Caregiver Program*. Ottawa: Standing Committee on Citizenship and Immigration. 12 May 2009: 0905.

Vromen, A. 2005. 'Political Strategies of the Australian Third Sector.' *Third Sector Review* 11 (2): 95–115.

VSW (Vancouver Status of Women). 2001. *Submission to the Standing Committee on Citizenship and Immigration on Bill C-11*. Ottawa: Standing Committee on Citizenship and Immigration, Parliament of Canada.

Walby, S. 2011. 'Is the Knowledge Society Gendered?' *Gender, Work and Organisation* 18 (11): 1–29.

Walker, J. 2008. '457 Nurse Sacked for Arriving Pregnant.' *The Australian*, 29 November 2008. www.theaustralian.com.au/news/nation/nurse-sacked-for-arriving-pregnant/story-e6frg6nf-1111118174341, accessed 29 June 2015.

Walker, W. 1999. 'Canada Puts Off Entry-law Shake-up.' *Toronto Star*, 6 January 1999.

Watts, J. 2002. *Immigrant Policy and the Challenge of Globalisation: Unions and Employers in Unlikely Alliance*. Ithaca, NY: Cornell University Press.

WCDWA (West Coast Domestic Workers Association). 2001. *Equality for Domestic Workers under Canada's Immigration System. Submission to the Standing Committee on Citizenship and Immigration to Bill C-11*. Ottawa: Standing Committee on Citizenship and Immigration, Parliament of Canada.

WCDWA (West Coast Domestic Workers Association). 2002. *Submission to the Regulations to the Immigration and Refugee Protection Act*. Ottawa: Standing Committee on Citizenship and Immigration, Parliament of Canada.

WCDWA (West Coast Domestic Workers Association). 2010. 'Funders.' Available at www.wcdwa.ca, accessed 20 April 2010.

Weaver, R., and B. Rockman. 1991. 'Assessing the Effects of Institutions.' In *Do Institutions Matter? Government Capabilities in the United States and Abroad*, edited by R. Weaver and B. Rockman, 1–41. Washington, D.C.: The Brookings Institution.

Weinberger, C. J. 2011. 'In Search of the Glass Ceiling: Gender and Earnings Growth among US College Graduates in the 1990s.' *Industrial and Labor Relations Review* 64 (5): 949–80.

Wilkins, V. M. 2007. 'Exploring the Causal Story: Gender, Active Representation, and Bureaucratic Priorities.' *Journal of Public Administration Research and Theory* 17 (1): 77–94.

Williams, L. S., J. Murphy, and C. Brooks. 1997. *Initial Labour Market Experiences of Immigrants*. Canberra: Joint Commonwealth/State/Territory Population, Immigration and Multicultural Research Program.

Wilson, J. Q. 1980. *The Politics of Regulation*. New York: Basic Books.

Wood, R. 2006. 'The Dynamics of Incrementalism: Subsystems, Politics and Public Lands.' *Policy Studies Journal* 34 (2): 1–16.

Wright, C. 2012. 'Immigration Policy and Market Institutions in Liberal Market Economies.' *Industrial Relations Journal* 43 (2): 110–36.

Wright, C. F. 2014. 'How Do States Implement Liberal Immigration Policies? Control Signals and Skilled Immigration Reform in Australia.' *Governance* 27 (3): 397–421.

Young, L. 1999. 'Minor Parties and the Legislative Process in the Australian Senate: A Study of the 1993 Budget.' *Australian Journal of Political Science* 34 (1): 7–27.

Zlotnik, H. 1995. 'Migration and the Family: The Female Perspective.' *Asian and Pacific Migration Journal* 4 (2–3): 253ff.

Index